DINING WITH MADMEN

THOMAS FAHY

DINING WITH MADMEN

FAT, FOOD, AND THE ENVIRONMENT IN 1980s HORROR

University Press of Mississippi / Jackson

The University Press of Mississippi is the scholarly publishing agency of
the Mississippi Institutions of Higher Learning: Alcorn State University,
Delta State University, Jackson State University, Mississippi State University,
Mississippi University for Women, Mississippi Valley State University,
University of Mississippi, and University of Southern Mississippi.

www.upress.state.ms.us

The University Press of Mississippi is a
member of the Association of University Presses.

Copyright © 2019 by University Press of Mississippi
All rights reserved

First printing 2019

∞

Library of Congress Cataloging-in-Publication Data

Names: Fahy, Thomas Richard, author.
Title: Dining with madmen: fat, food, and the environment in 1980s horror /
Thomas Fahy.
Description: Jackson: University Press of Mississippi, [2019] | Includes
bibliographical references and index. |
Identifiers: LCCN 2018038889 (print) | LCCN 2018043655 (ebook) | ISBN
9781496821553 (epub single) | ISBN 9781496821560 (epub institutional) |
ISBN 9781496821577 (pdf single) | ISBN 9781496821584 (pdf institutional)
| ISBN 9781496821539 (cloth) | ISBN 9781496821546 (pbk.)
Subjects: LCSH: Horror films—United States—History and criticism. | Food in
motion pictures. | Motion pictures—Social aspects.
Classification: LCC PN1995.9.H6 (ebook) | LCC PN1995.9.H6 F25 2019 (print) |
DDC 791.43/6164—dc23
LC record available at https://lccn.loc.gov/2018038889

British Library Cataloging-in-Publication Data available

In memory of Elaine Markson (1930–2018)

CONTENTS

Acknowledgments ix

INTRODUCTION
Dining with Madmen 3

CHAPTER ONE
Disturbing Appetites: Fat, Fitness, and Fine Dining 15
   Thinner
   Geek Love
   The Silence of the Lambs
   American Psycho

CHAPTER TWO
A Sharp, Sweet Tooth: Junk Food, Addiction, and Vampires 87
   The Lost Boys
   Near Dark
   Once Bitten
   My Best Friend Is a Vampire
   A Return to Salem's Lot
   Fright Night and *Fright Night Part 2*
   The Queen of the Damned
   The Hunger

CHAPTER THREE
Eat Your Heart Out: Zombies, Overpopulation, and the Environment 139
   Night of the Living Dead
   Dawn of the Dead
   Day of the Dead
   The Return of the Living Dead and *The Return of the Living Dead Part II*

Toxic Zombies
Surf II
Redneck Zombies
Book of the Dead
Motel Hell

CONCLUSION
"Enough Is Never Enough": Junk Food, Dieting, and Environmental Harm in *The Stuff* 187
   The Stuff

Notes 199

Works Cited. 213

Filmography 227

Index 231

ACKNOWLEDGMENTS

I want to begin by thanking my editor, Katie Keene, and the University Press of Mississippi for their enthusiastic support and partnership on this project.

I benefited greatly from the insightful feedback of several friends, especially Kati Fargo Ahern, Kirstin Ringelberg, and Daniel Kurtzman, and from suggestions by the readers and editors at the *Journal of Popular Culture* (Wiley-Blackwell) and *Food and Foodways* (Taylor and Francis). Kristen Roedel also provided invaluable assistance with the manuscript at the eleventh hour. I introduced some of these ideas to a class of talented, dynamic graduate students. Their engagement and ideas helped make this a better book. I am also grateful to Long Island University and to my inspirational colleagues in the departments of English and History.

No book would be possible without the love and support of my family on both coasts. I particularly want to give my heartfelt thanks to Tatyana Tsinberg, who lived with this project for a long time despite her general aversion to horror, and Nicolai Fahy, who brings me boundless joy with his love of reading, stuffed animals, and Michael Jackson's music—which makes him an honorary child of the 1980s.

Finally, I dedicate this book to the memory of my wonderful agent and friend, Elaine Markson. She found a home for my first horror novel and always supported me and my work. She guided me through the madness of the publishing industry with class, kindness, and wit. I will be forever grateful.

DINING WITH MADMEN

INTRODUCTION

Dining with Madmen

Nightmares on Elm Street

In *A Nightmare on Elm Street 4: The Dream Master* (1988), Alice (Lisa Wilcox) works double shifts at the Crave Inn to keep herself from sleeping. This 1950s-style diner serves all manner of junk food that can literally keep one awake at night. As any teenager in a Freddy Krueger film will tell you, sugar and caffeine provide the first line of defense against a supernatural predator that kills people in their dreams. The diner's name not only alludes to filmmaker Wes Craven, who created Krueger's character in 1984, but it also plays on the word "craving" to underscore the addictive quality of such foods. The Elm Street teenagers regularly consume unhealthy snacks from chips to cheeseburgers, and they guzzle soda pop by the gallon.

One of Alice's dreams places her in a movie theater where she sips on an extra-large Pepsi and eats popcorn. As soon as a black-and-white image of the Crave Inn appears onscreen, it becomes a type of vacuum that sucks her into the film, suggesting both her powerlessness to escape Freddy (Robert Englund) and her inability to resist junk food. Once inside, Alice encounters Freddy on a bar stool in his signature red-and-green-striped sweater. "If the food doesn't kill you," he quips, "the service will." A waitress (an older version of herself) then delivers a pizza with meatballs showing the screaming faces of his victims. Though these toppings prove too tempting for Freddy to resist (he eats one in front of her), his insatiable hunger for killing mirrors the characters' self-destructive appetites. All of the teens in these films crave something that Freddy exploits to torment and destroy them. The processed foods at the diner may appear more benign than a monster with knives for fingers, but they can prove deadly as well. While Freddy isn't going to wait

Freddy Krueger (Robert Englund) looks forward to some pizza in Wes Craven's *Nightmare on Elm Street 4* (1988). © New Line Cinema/Warner Brothers.

around for heart disease and high cholesterol, these details suggest that such cravings will be our undoing.

While penning *A Nightmare on Elm Street*, Wes Craven could never have imagined the immense popularity of Freddy Krueger. His character inspired several sequels, popular songs, video games, Halloween costumes, and a television series by the end of the decade alone. In one example of this cultural appeal, the music video for "Are You Ready for Freddy?" (1988) features the Fat Boys rapping nervously inside the Elm Street house.[1] The singers' tightly fitted sweaters set up a stark contrast between their heavyset build and Freddy's narrow body. In the closing moments, they flee the house and trample a bystander carrying groceries—pausing long enough to take one of his doughnuts. This moment certainly plays into the video's self-referential humor about body weight that one would expect from a band calling itself the Fat Boys. At the same time, these jokes reflect the widespread vilification of fatness in the 1980s. The fat body was something to mock. It signaled laziness and a lack of self-control. As such, this act of eating doughnuts—instead of fruit—implies that fatness can be attributed to choice. Yet addiction emerges as the real culprit here. The singers' cravings trump the risk of spending more time in front of Freddy's house. Sugar literally threatens their lives.

While none of the Elm Street films makes an explicit link between junk food and fatness, the franchise does explore anxieties about body weight. *A Nightmare on Elm Street 5: The Dream Child* (1989) addresses this issue through Greta's (Erika Anderson's) bulimia. After falling asleep during a dinner party in which her mother's guests discuss the "perfect body for modeling," Greta dreams of confronting them about the pressures on women to be thin. She even proposes gorging herself to the point of sickness and returning for seconds. On cue, Freddy appears in the guise of a waiter. He shoves food into her mouth, cuts open her stomach, and proclaims gleefully that "you are what you eat!" Of course, Greta has not been eating at all—she is too afraid of gaining weight for that. Instead, her starvation reflects a cultural ethos that privileges thinness and equates the fat-free body with desirability. In a country suffuse with junk food, "you are what you eat" was a terrifying prospect in the 1980s, and Americans invested a great deal in exercise and diet fads to prove otherwise. Whether force-feeding someone or using a barbell to break the arms of an obsessed bodybuilder, Freddy ruthlessly mocks a society that demands thinness while supersizing meals. He revels in a marketplace that facilitates overindulgence only to sell diet foods and exercise tapes. And he finds the self-destructive behaviors encouraged by these contradictions to be fertile ground for the horrific.

All of this consumption had environmental consequences as well. The eighties witnessed devastating heat waves, a shortage of landfills, and enough damage to the ozone layer to exacerbate fears about global warming. Like the rest of America, the Elm Street teens contributed to these problems. Not only did they eat too much junk food, but they also spent too much money on cars, clothes, exercise equipment, video games, and other material goods that taxed natural resources. In a fitting choice, the opening dream in *A Nightmare on Elm Street 2: Freddy's Revenge* (1985) features Krueger driving a suburban school bus into the desert. This barren landscape, characterized by lightning storms without rain, becomes increasingly apocalyptic. The juxtaposition of these teens with an environmental wasteland casts suburban consumerism as the culprit. Whether through the development of tract housing, the car culture enabling it, or the goods filling these houses, suburbia posed a serious ecological threat in the 1980s. Such an interpretation aligns with actor Robert Englund's reading of his character. In a 1988 interview, he explained that "Freddy is pollution. Freddy is evil. Freddy is what's wrong with the world [. . .] racism, pollution, child molestation, child abuse, alcohol, drugs" (Fo 72). Freddy, in other words, represents the harm we do to ourselves, each other, and the planet.

1980s Horror and American Culture

Most film critics consider 1980s horror, like Freddy Krueger himself, to be the bastard son of a hundred maniacs. It's a decade that lacked originality and good taste, producing countless sequels and B-movies such as *Splatter University* (1984), *Cannibal Hookers* (1987), *Cheerleader Camp* (originally titled *Bloody Pom Poms*; 1988), and *Las Vegas Bloodbath* (1989). It abandoned the gritty, countercultural sensibility of the previous decade, with films such as *The Texas Chainsaw Massacre* (1974) and *Halloween* (1978), for serial killers wielding knives and campy one-liners with equal ferocity. It privileged special effects over characterization, serving up a host of interchangeable victims that made audiences root for the likes of Freddy, Jason, Michael, and even a doll named Chucky. And its shift from remote, rural settings to a suburban landscape teeming with consumer products revealed a shameless attempt to capitalize on the teenage market. Coca-Cola even acquired Columbia Pictures in 1982 to secure more advertising in film, television, and cable (Prince 51). From this vantage point, it is not surprising that critics like Robin Wood find "little to salvage" in 1980s horror (169).

These characteristics, however, need to be understood and evaluated in the context of eighties culture—beginning with its predilection for sequels. Nineteen eighty-nine marked a banner year for sequels, featuring the fifth installments of *Halloween, A Nightmare on Elm Street*, and *The Howling* as well as *Amityville 4: The Evil Escapes* and *Friday the 13th Part VIII: Jason Takes Manhattan*. Even technology, through the development of the videotape and videocassette recorder (VCR), fueled repetition: "Yearly sales of VCRs jumped from 802,000 in 1980 to 11–12 million per year during the second half of the decade," and over 200 million prerecorded videocassettes were sold in 1989 alone (Prince 94). One could now record films on television, rewatch tapes at will, and copy videos for others. This proliferation of tapes and sequels embodied the orgiastic celebration of consumerism in the Reagan era. Watching another installment of *Friday the 13th* or perusing the crammed shelves at Blockbuster, which first opened in 1985, promised more of a good thing in a culture that believed enough was never enough.

Special effects played an important role in many of these films as well. Vivid onscreen transformations—like those experienced by David (David Naughton) in *An American Werewolf in London* (1981) and Seth (Jeff Goldblum) in *The Fly* (1986)—marveled and horrified audiences. At the same time, this imagery played into the country's growing obsession with the body. The exercise craze, fad diets, and plastic surgery gave testament to America's self-punishing desire to rip away the old skin for something new. In many ways, eighties horror presented the killer's violence as a metaphor for what many people were doing to themselves to be thin and "beautiful." All manner of tools—knives, axes, cleavers, drills, arrows, spears, chainsaws, ice picks—were used to shred the body in these films, and many Americans appeared hell-bent on doing the same. Not surprisingly, some filmmakers considered the gym a perfect setting for this self-destructive obsession. One trailer for *Killer Workout* (1987) weaves images of weightlifting and aerobics with a description of failed dieting: "You've tried Atkins, South Beach, and even the Cookie Diet. This October, lose those extra pounds with *Killer Workout.*" The film itself features enough dance routines to rival a music video, and the killer eliminates clients with everything from a barbell to an enlarged safety pin.² Likewise, high-tech weight training equipment and tanning beds become the weapons of choice for a vengeful spirit in *Death Spa* (1989). These gruesome murders, which tacitly encourage pale skin and lapsed gym memberships, also warn against the relentless push for bodily change.

This emphasis on bodies may explain another aspect of 1980s horror that is typically lambasted by critics—the limited characterization of its victims. In *Shock Value*, Jason Zinoman criticizes the "flood of unnecessary sequels" for elevating the status of the monster at the expense of developing his victims into sympathetic figures: "Just as the killers seemed increasingly ordinary in mainstream horror, the victims in the most popular horror movies became completely interchangeable, forgettable blank slates. This shifted the audience identification radically. People rooted for the killers and saw their victims as irrelevant casualties" (216). Yet one could argue that eighties audiences identified with both killers and indistinguishable victims. Dieting to look more like Christie Brinkley and working out to achieve the muscle tone of Sylvester Stallone made physical appearance the marker for personal value. It suggested that everyone should look the same, and in a sense, it made millions of Americans feel like Victim Number Three. No novel critiqued this dynamic more savagely than Bret Easton Ellis's masterpiece *American Psycho* (1991). Protagonist Patrick Bateman views women as hardbodies and himself (as well as other men) in terms of ripped abdominals, body fat, fashion sense, and an encyclopedic knowledge of skincare products. Everything in eighties yuppie culture, according to Ellis, de-individualized people, and he reinforces this message by making all of the characters indistinguishable from one another. As the novel suggests, this context makes it easy for people to identify with being nothing more than a body.

Lastly, horror films tended to migrate to the suburbs in this decade, and Carter Soles attributes this geographical shift to teen culture: "For as teenagers (rather than whole families) became the sole focus of late 1970s and 1980s slashers, the sites of their encounters with killers migrated to suburban neighborhoods, summer camps, sorority houses, and the like" ("Sympathy" 247–48). Just as Soles argues that the 1970s cannibalistic hillbilly enabled (sub)urban viewers "to project their fears of environmental collapse" (235), the violation of suburban spaces in 1980s horror speaks to similar concerns about the environmental costs of these communities. Whether through the destruction of marshes, swamps, forests, or rivers, suburbia devoured more than a million acres of land annually in the 1980s. *Poltergeist* (1982), for example, critiques these excesses when the Freelings learn that Cuesta Verde was built on an old cemetery. Zombies, too, found themselves at home in the suburbs. The use of an unfinished housing development in *The Return of the Living Dead Part II* challenges audiences to see beyond the veneer of tract housing, manicured lawns, and white picket fences to consider the environmental consequences of so much construction.

Unlike Robin Wood's assertion that eighties horror essentially reinforces the dominant ideology, my reading of this period argues the opposite. All of the critical focus on slasher films,[3] which has made figures like Freddy Krueger shorthand for the decade's horror, tends to overshadow the genre's diversity and its nuanced engagement with cultural issues. As Kendall R. Phillips has argued, horror films tend to project the nation's collective anxieties on the screen, and in doing so, they engage in "the broader politics of their day" (8). The preoccupation with fat bias, processed foods, and environmental harm in 1980s horror offers a powerful example of this. A great deal of these works explores concerns central to American life, and they do so in ways that remain provocative and socially relevant today. Placed in the context of eighties America, they demonstrate a richness and versatility often overlooked by critics, and they warn that real horror can be found in what we eat as well as what we do to ourselves and the planet.

Dining with Madmen: An Overview

Dining with Madmen: Fat, Food, and the Environment in 1980s Horror explores America's preoccupation with body weight, processed foods, and pollution through the lens of horror. Conspicuous consumption may have communicated personal and financial success in the eighties, but only if it did not become visible on the body. American society had come to view fatness as a horrifying transformation. It exposed the potential consequences of junk food from bundled meals at McDonald's to sixty-four-ounce sodas. It gave lie to the promises of workout and diet culture. And it represented the country's worst consumer impulses, inviting questions about the personal and environmental consequences of excess. While changing into a vampire or a zombie often represented widespread fears about addiction and overeating, it also played into concerns about pollution. Ozone depletion, acid rain, and toxic waste already demonstrated the irrevocable harm being done to the planet. The horror genre responded by presenting this damage as an urgent problem, and, through the sudden violence of killers, vampires, and zombies, it depicted the consequences of inaction as terrifying.

Chapter 1, "Disturbing Appetites: Fat, Fitness, and Fine Dining," uses the critical lens of Fat Studies to examine the way 1980s horror critiqued the country's self-destructive preoccupation with exercise and dieting. Scholars Jana Evans Braziel and Kathleen LeBesco have noted the link between fat prejudice and other forms of discrimination throughout the twentieth century. In *Bodies Out of Bounds: Fatness and Transgression*, they argue that heightened sensitivity toward humor about race, gender, and disability has yet to change social attitudes about fatness. Fat remains "a four-letter word [. . .] because it is a subject-marking experience over which we are perceived to have some degree of control (unlike gender or race [. . .])" (2). Fat Studies scholars have mapped out the impact of these biases in social, economic, and psychological terms. In addition to public harassment and humiliation, fat people have experienced discrimination in the workplace, in medical offices, in the marketplace, and in the educational system. A 1979 study showed weight to be a determining factor in hiring and other employment decisions; in a work setting, for instance, overweight people were viewed "as significantly less desirable employees who, compared with others, were less competent, less productive, not industrious, disorganized, indecisive, and less successful" (Larken and Pines 315–16). Likewise, by the early 1990s, Daniel Hamermesh and Jeff Biddle found that people considered ugly earned 5 to 10 percent less than coworkers considered beautiful.[4]

Fat prejudice has profound psychological consequences as well. In her essay "Fat Studies: An Invitation to Revolution," Marilyn Wann argues that "every person who lives in a fat-hating culture inevitably absorbs anti-fat beliefs, assumptions, and stereotypes" (xi). The culture of chronic dieting in America has only intensified this problem. It tends to make individuals feel ashamed for not keeping off the weight and as such contributes to depression and various eating disorders. As April Michelle Herndon has persuasively argued, it even sends the message to children that they "can and should change their bodies in order to appear 'normal' or 'healthy' to ease people's anxieties about [today's] childhood obesity epidemic" (138–39). For Wann, Herndon, and others, these issues demand social and political activism for and among fat people.

Though the Fat Studies movement traces its origins to the Civil Rights Act of 1964, the foundation of the National Association to Advance Fat Acceptance (NAAFA) in 1969 and its establishment of a Declaration of Health Rights for

Fat People signaled the first collective effort to combat myths about fatness through public education, scholarly research, and advocacy.[5] Such efforts condemned the cult of thinness in America as harmful physically and psychologically. Much like the term *queer* during the gay rights movement, these activists sought to reclaim "fat" from its pejorative associations. Perhaps the most significant development occurred in the 1980s with the Health at Every Size (HAES) approach to weight. Throughout this decade, various studies such as Kim Chernin's *The Obsession: Reflections on the Tyranny of Slenderness* (1981) and William Bennett's *The Dieter's Dilemma* (1982) fueled a HAES movement that emphasized healthy living for people of all sizes, instead of focusing on weight loss. This approach sought to reduce the stigmatization of fat people and to foster a greater acceptance of bodily difference. As Abigail C. Saguy explains in *What's Wrong with Fat*, "this movement argues that we would do better as a society to invest public resources in raising consciousness about the negative social implications of weight-based stigma and discrimination, rather than engage in a futile and unethical attempt to eliminate fat people" (14). Despite these efforts, the vilification of fat bodies became a dominant ideology in 1980s America. Celebrities sold millions of workout videos, making exercise a national obsession, and fad diets and weight-loss products became a multibillion-dollar industry.

Some of the most notable characters in contemporary horror shared these obsessions. Patrick Bateman from *American Psycho* wants nothing more than to work out and make restaurant reservations. Buffalo Bill kills heavyset women to make a skin suit in *The Silence of the Lambs* (1988). Katharine Dunn's frozen food heiress and sideshow performers in *Geek Love* (1989) offer a condemnation of fat shame. And Stephen King's *Thinner* (1984) presents junk food addiction and diet culture as two sides of the same coin. These provocative works explore the tension between consumption and deprivation, fat and thin. They do so, in part, to suggest that the pursuit of thinness can be just as dangerous as the unhealthy eating and living habits responsible for significant weight gain. They situate horror in a marketplace that capitalizes on being both the problem and the solution, encouraging one to eat more and to buy diet books. Consumerism, in other words, becomes the vehicle for both excess and restraint. In this way, bodily extremes interrogate the dangers of this culture and challenge readers to rethink their relationship with food, dieting, and body size.

The second chapter, "A Sharp, Sweet Tooth: Junk Food, Addiction, and Vampires," examines the eating practices in vampire fiction from the vantage point of Food Studies. This interdisciplinary field, with strong roots in anthropology, history, and sociology,[6] explores the way eating choices communicate individual and cultural preferences. It interrogates the various forces that shape production, distribution, and disposal. And as Carole Counihan and Penny Van Esterik note, it supports the efforts of food activists to end world hunger and to bring about universal access to nutritious and adequate food" (10). This emphasis on activism is echoed by Mustafa Koç, Jennifer Sumner, and Tony Winson in *Critical Perspectives in Food Studies*, which considers the field both an academic discipline and "a means to change society" (xii).

The 1980s proved to be a watershed decade for Food Studies, and several important works helped establish it as a distinct field. Sydney M. Mintz's *Sweetness and Power: The Place of Sugar in Modern History* (1985), for instance, examines sugar production and consumption from its domestication in New Guinea around 8000 BC to twentieth-century British life. With a particular emphasis on its connection to Western colonialism, which began in earnest after Columbus's second voyage to the New World in 1493, Mintz maps sugar's gradual shift from aristocratic delicacy to everyday treat.[7] In another example, historian Warren Belasco's *Appetite for Change: How the Counterculture Took on the Food Industry* (1989) explores the ways sixties radicalism forged an organic paradigm that changed the country's perception of eating. Ironically, its success in presenting farmers as "trustees of the soil" and food as "an edible dynamic" opened the door for corporate America to coopt the health-food movement (75). Equally important scholarship continued in the 1990s, and sociologist George Ritzer offers one notable example of these efforts. His study, *The McDonaldization of Society* (1993), explores the application of assembly-line techniques in fast-food production to other aspects of consumer society. From toy stores to IKEA and child care to higher education, standardizing production, making it as predictable and calculable as possible, not only homogenizes culture, but it also tends to dehumanize workers, forcing them to "deny their humanity and act like robots" (36). All of these efforts contributed to the formation of Food Studies as an academic field.

Any examination of food and foodways begins, as Warren Belasco has noted, with understanding "what, how, and why we eat" (*Food* 2). Answering these questions, however, continues to be a complex and conflicted process—one which psychologist Paul Rozin labeled "the omnivore's dilemma" in 1976.[8] Omnivores (from the Latin term meaning "all devouring") eat both plants and animals for nutrients, but among humans, choosing what to eat has always been shaped by both a desire for novelty and a fear of eating the wrong thing. The development of food practices has certainly "[lessened] the anxiety surrounding what to eat [. . . by] offering a tried and tested guarantee of safety" (Crowther 8). Yet this presumed safety has come into question with the rise of processed foods since the second half of the twentieth century.

As Michael Pollan argues, "The cornucopia of the American supermarket has thrown us back on a bewildering food landscape where we once again have to worry that some of those tasty-looking morsels might kill us" (4–5). Overwhelmed with choice, manipulated by marketing experts, and ever fearful of the "hidden" dangers in processed foods, what we eat and what it says about who we are have once again become critically important questions.

These questions preoccupy 1980s vampires as well. Next to blood, fast food and junk food make up the most common meals in these works. Whether munching on chips, devouring a Big Mac, or slurping down soda, humans use these foods to satisfy hunger, assuage anxiety, provide a needed jolt of caffeine, and pass the time between sunset and sunrise. Vampires tend to function in one of three ways in these works. They can serve as metaphors for the food industry, preying on young and old with products designed to foster overconsumption and addiction. They can symbolize the country's addiction to processed foods and the excesses of consumerism more broadly. And finally, they can even emerge as ironic images for healthy eating as they seek a natural, more organic diet than their junk-food-addicted victims. They consume only what they need to survive, and this utilitarian approach to food helps them maintain thin, youthful, vigorous bodies—the aspirational goal of 1980s exercise and weight-loss culture. In each case, these creatures indict an industry that profited from turning consumers into junkies, craving foods that promised heart disease, high cholesterol, and obesity. Nevertheless, the humans and half-vampires in these works can still choose where and what to eat, just as they have the choice to drink a vampire's blood or to invite one inside. As such, the half-vampires in *The Lost Boys* (1987), *Near Dark* (1987), *Once Bitten* (1985), and *Fright Night Part 2* (1988) can restore their humanity by making the right choices. The vampires in Anne Rice's and Whitley Strieber's novels—much like the protagonist in *My Best Friend Is a Vampire* (1987)—can determine whether to feed on humans or animals. By extension, 1980s audiences still had the power to save themselves from the clutches of sugary, processed, and fast foods before it was too late.

Through the lens of ecocriticism, chapter 3, "Eat Your Heart Out: Zombies, Overpopulation, and the Environment," considers the way zombie fiction tapped into apocalyptic fears about overpopulation and pollution. As many scholars have noted, the modern environmental movement began with the publication of Rachel Carson's *Silent Spring* (1962). Her study on the impact of synthetic pesticides galvanized readers and influenced public policy, leading to a ban on DDT in American agriculture and to the formation of the US Environmental Protection Agency. In the opening chapter, Carson offers an apocalyptic vision of one bucolic town seized by a mysterious plague. The land cannot yield crops. Flocks of cattle, chicken, and sheep die without explanation. And a new, communicable disease begins killing children. This devastation, however, is man-made, for it resides in the choice to use insecticides. She goes on to compare these poisons to nuclear waste. It "comes to earth in rain or drifts down as fallout, lodges in soil, enters into the grass or corn or wheat grown there, and in time takes up its abode in the bones of a human being" (6). For Ralph H. Lutts, the effectiveness of Carson's book can be attributed to this very association between pesticides and atomic weapons: "the generation that promoted Earth Day 1970 grew up in the shadow of nuclear destruction. [. . .], [and she wrote] one of the first and most eloquent of books bridging the gap between the environmental movement and this new fearful vision of Armageddon" (223). Such imagery not only stressed the urgency of the problem, but it also challenged Americans to make a different set of choices.

Carson's work inspired what many describe as the first wave of ecocriticism—the efforts of cultural and literary critics to examine the relationship between the humanities and the natural world. While some consider Ralph Waldo Emerson's *Nature* (1836) its foundational text, Lawrence Buell views Leo Marx's *The Machine in the Garden* (1964) and Raymond Williams's *The Country and the City* (1973) as the starting point (*Future*, 13). Their examination of technology, industrialization, and political power demanded a reconsideration of the pastoral ideal in nineteenth-century literature. Environmental scholarship continued throughout the 1970s, and by the end of the decade, William Rueckert coined the term *ecocriticism* to describe this approach for making "connections between literature and the sun, between teaching literature and the health of the biosphere" (75). Within the next fifteen years, the interdisciplinary efforts of these early ecocritics codified into a recognized field. In her introduction to *The Ecocriticism Reader* (1996), Cheryll Glotfelty highlights the edited collection *Teaching Environmental Literature* (1985) and the founding of *The American Nature Writing Newsletter* (1989) as the two most important efforts in the eighties (xvii). The following decade saw the establishment of the Association for the Study of Literature and the Environment (ASLE) in 1992 and the publication of books such as Lawrence Buell's *The Environmental Imagination: Thoreau, Nature Writing, and the Formation of American Culture*. The cumulative effect of this work helped establish ecocriticism as a discipline and as an important partner for ecological science.

Unlike the first wave's preoccupation with nature writing and the wilderness as imagined by nineteenth-century writers, the second wave has developed a "'social ecocriticism' that takes urban and degraded landscapes just as seriously as 'natural' landscapes" (Buell, *Future* 22). This twenty-first century scholarship tends to be more concerned with contemporary environmental issues, demanding hands-on engagement with ecojustice as opposed to the theoretical approach of the first wave. Through critics such as Ursula K. Heise, Anna Lowerhaupt Tsing, and Rob Nixon, the second wave incorporates a wider geographical focus, moving outward from spaces like Walden Pond to consider the well-being of the entire planet. It also views environmental justice, particularly the way ethnicity and class impact one's exposure to pollution, as critical to its social and political project.

Much zombie fiction in the 1980s presents the apocalypse as a direct consequence of irresponsible environmental practices. Both George A. Romero's trilogy and *The Return of the Living Dead* series, for example, use shopping malls, defunct mines, and suburbia to depict the American marketplace as swallowing up natural resources at an unsustainable rate. Zombies crowd each of these settings, ultimately overwhelming survivors, and these indefatigable eaters represent a country—a planet—with too many mouths to feed. Furthermore, the harm caused by toxic waste, which functions as a central trope in *The Return of the Living Dead* (1985), *Toxic Zombies* (1980), *Surf II* (1984), and *Redneck Zombies* (1987), highlights concerns about the human and environmental impact of chemicals and other poisons. Nature strikes back in these works, using various tools such as acid rain, ozone depletion (as in Stephen King's "Home Delivery"), and radiation to reanimate the dead. Nature not only punishes people by making human flesh an endangered resource for the undead, but in *Day of the Dead* and Stephen Boyett's "Like Pavlov's Dogs," it also puts survivors in the position of being too afraid to go outside. This denied access to natural beauty serves as a warning about the potential costs of America's reckless disregard for the environment—the loss of nature itself.

Whether through Hannibal Lecter's cannibalism, a vampire's thirst for blood, or an overwhelming number of insatiable zombies, 1980s horror uses out-of-control hunger to capture deep-seated concerns about the physical and material consequences of unchecked consumption. Its presentation of American appetites resonated powerfully for audiences preoccupied with body size, food choices, and pollution. And its use of bodily change, alongside the bloodlust of killers and the desolate landscapes of apocalyptic fiction, demanded a recognition of the potentially horrifying consequences of the marketplace on nature, society, and the self.

CHAPTER ONE

Disturbing Appetites: Fat, Fitness, and Fine Dining

Perhaps it is not surprising that 1980s horror features extreme bodies and appetites as sources of terror. While American culture encouraged the public to view spending more, owning more, and eating more as markers of personal success, it also valorized self-restraint and denial. In the same year McDonald's launched supersized meals in 1972, for instance, *Dr. Atkins' Diet Revolution* made publishing history with hardcover sales topping $1.1 million (Seid 4). Such conflicting messages only intensified in the following decade. Weight Watchers, aerobics, televised exercise shows, and low-calorie soft drinks competed with fast food, 7-Eleven, and all-you-can-eat buffets. Amid these contradictions, the fat body emerged as an image for what not to be. It defied cultural norms that valorized the thin body. It justified discrimination. And it was treated with disgust and disparagement.

Fat ridicule in horror comedies offers one example of this trend. In Fred Dekker's *The Monster Squad* (1987), Fat Kid (Brent Chalem) blames his weight and junk-food addiction on "a glandular problem." He even considers taking a bite of garlic pizza before using it as a weapon against Dracula. A similar character, Chubby (Mark Holton), appears in both *Teen Wolf* (1985) and *Teen Wolf Too* (1987). Like his name suggests, he gets defined entirely by his weight. Chubby's eating habits, such as hiding food in his locker and swallowing an entire bowl of Jell-O, provide an ongoing opportunity for mockery.[1] Similarly, Richard Donner's *The Goonies* (1985), based on a story by Steven Spielberg that fuses action, fantasy, gangster, and horror conventions, includes Chunk (Jeff Cohen), a boy who devours Miracle Whip, Baby Ruth candy bars, pizza, Twinkies, milk shakes, and ice cream. His body serves as a source of humor among his friends who often force him to do the "Truffle Shuffle" (lifting up

Chunk (Jeff Cohen) does the "Truffle Shuffle" in Richard Donner's *The Goonies* (1985). © Warner Brothers.

his shirt and jiggling his stomach). While these types of films typically attribute fatness to poor dietary choices, they downplay weight-based derision by presenting these characters as heroic members of a tightknit group. Fat Kid and Chunk, for instance, act valiantly to fight danger, and Chubby can score a basket or win a boxing match when his team needs it most. Nevertheless, fatness defines and limits these boys. It shapes the way others perceive them, and it guarantees ridicule long after the final credits roll.

Despite such problematic depictions of the fat body, Fat Studies has been reluctant to examine horror. Casey McKittrick, in *Hitchcock's Appetites: The Corpulent Plots of Desire and Dread*, attributes this hesitancy to the field's traditional focus on social sciences (as opposed to the humanities), on women, and on discrimination. For scholar Niall Richardson, the problem stems from the way horror can often excuse fat-phobia, and he specifically critiques Brett Leonard's *Feed* (2006) for making excessive fat "the most terrifying visual element of the text" (45). Yet as McKittrick and Richardson demonstrate, Fat Studies offers an invaluable framework for interpreting bodily extremes in horror—whether appreciating the genre's efforts to combat fat bias or pointing out its shortcomings. In the case of the 1980s, some of the most provocative works of horror fiction, including Stephen King's *Thinner* (1984), Katherine Dunn's *Geek Love* (1989), Thomas Harris's *The Silence of the Lambs*

(1988), and Bret Easton Ellis's *American Psycho* (1991), engage in fat activism by exploring the tension between consumption and deprivation, fat and thin.

Beginning with an overview of the exercise craze, diet foods, and weight-loss programs, this chapter considers the way horror responded to these practices. Philosopher Noël Carroll acknowledges that horror "may typically only command a limited following, [. . . but it can garner] mass attention when its iconography and structures are deployed in such a way that they articulate the widespread anxiety of times of stress" (214). Contemporary horror spoke to profound fears about fatness throughout the decade. From Buffalo Bill's obsession with heavyset women in *The Silence of the Lambs* to Billy's emaciated body in *Thinner*, these works suggest that the pursuit of thinness can be just as dangerous as the unhealthy habits responsible for significant weight gain. They situate horror in a marketplace that capitalizes on being both the problem and the solution, encouraging one to supersize meals and buy diet books. In this way, 1980s horror uses bodily extremes to interrogate the dangers of consumer culture and to challenge readers to rethink their relationship with food, dieting, and body size.

Weighing In: Fitness, Diet Culture, and Food

In 1963 British-born Olivia Newton-John made her singing debut on Australian television at the age of fifteen, and the release of her first single three years later launched an award-winning musical career that would span decades and sell over 100 million records. While she had earned three Grammys by 1974, it was her onscreen romance with John Travolta in *Grease* (1978) that catapulted Newton-John to stardom in the United States. Two years later she found herself alongside legendary Gene Kelly, but no amount of ballroom dancing (or roller skating!) could rescue *Xanadu* from critical and box-office failure. Its soundtrack, however, sold over 2 million copies with two chart-topping songs by Newton-John. When she released the title song from *Physical* in 1981, it reached number-one on the *Billboard* charts for ten weeks and remained a hit song throughout most of 1982.[2] The music video, which helped secure the song's success, features Newton-John as a beleaguered fitness instructor of fat white men. With the empathy of a drill sergeant, she marches around the gym, ratcheting up the speed of treadmills and exercise bikes much to the chagrin of her sweaty, clumsy clients. She grabs, shoves, chokes, and even straddles these men while urging them to work harder. Their milk-white bodies nearly burst out of the tiny shirts and gym shorts designed to accentuate their fatness. Large bellies—often shown in close-up—jiggle and roll. A

Olivia Newton-John and her fat clients in "Physical" (1981). MCA Records/Photofest. © MCA Records

grimace accompanies each aerobic step, and long before the end of the routine, each man falls to the floor from exhaustion. Newton-John rolls her eyes with exasperation and resigns herself to a shower. Yet when she returns in a perky tennis outfit, most of her clients have transformed into lean, well-oiled, well-shaved specimens of masculinity, flexing their muscles and wearing thongs. She inspects their biceps and flat stomachs—as if to choose her next lover—but the men begin to pair off together, holding hands and wrapping their arms around each other. It would seem that fit men prefer other fit men.[3]

This sadistic workout and its portrayal of heavyset men are in keeping with derisive attitudes about fatness that intensified throughout the decade. Donning the type of outfit that both Jane Fonda would cultivate for her 1980s workout videos and Alex Owens (Jennifer Beals) would wear for her audition in *Flashdance* (1983), Newton-John implores a would-be lover to stop talking and to revert to animalistic, physical impulses. Part of the song's refrain—about hearing the body talk—is simply a call to action. Nevertheless, the video's setting clearly suggests that being sexually desired means the cultivation of a lean, muscular body. Its tongue-and-cheek humor reinforces this message. Most of the "jokes" come at the expense of large bodies, particularly because of the men's vaudeville-like antics as they flounder through aerobics routines and use Nautilus equipment like rodeo cowboys on an angry bull. In the context of "Physical," fatness needs to be controlled. It needs to be transformed into something desirable through intense effort, self-discipline, and masochistic levels of exercise. Otherwise, one will be reduced to some of the commonplace stereotypes about fat people at the time: as lazy, sloppy, greedy, stupid, and lacking self-restraint. Only by shedding pounds will these men escape this fate. Only by reclaiming the thin bodies hidden beneath the excess weight will they be able to "get physical."

As a thirty-three-year-old pop singer with a youthful appearance, Olivia Newton-John could still write music that resonated with American teens in 1981. She may have been ten years older than Madonna, who released her first single in 1982 and her first album a year later, but Newton-John's aerobics outfit in "Physical" played into a burgeoning trend, while downplaying the sexually explicit lyrics of the song. At the time she had no desire to release a workout video, publish a predominantly vegetarian cookbook (as she would in 2012), or produce her own wine (as she would in 2015).[4] Jane Fonda, however, saw an opportunity to channel her activism through physical fitness. Her outrage over the impact of *Playboy* culture on women throughout the world inspired her to view fitness as a means for liberation. As she explains in *Jane Fonda's Workout Book* (1981), "your goal is not to get pencil thin or to look like someone else. Your goal should be to take your body and make it as healthy, strong, flexible, and well-proportioned as you can—[. . . to be] comfortable and confident about your physical self" (64). The forty-four-year-old Fonda may have been the perfect celebrity to launch a fitness movement. In addition to her own struggles with dieting, eating disorders, and drug addiction,[5] her image as a wife, mother, and progressive, countercultural activist made her a trustworthy voice for women who wanted to take control of their own bodies.

For Fonda, however, aerobics was also a means for rejecting the cultural devaluation of aging. She cautioned against fats, sugars, meats, and processed foods, in part, because such foods—along with a lack of exercise—exacerbated the aging process. Next to fatness, nothing could be worse in America than getting old. In many ways, her view of aerobics as a fountain of youth inadvertently promoted some of the same attitudes she had been railing against. As Eric Oliver explains in *Fat Politics: The Real Story behind America's Obesity Epidemic*, "Although women cannot reverse their age, they can affect something that is highly correlated with youth: body weight. This means that women will begin to assess themselves relative to their own thinness" (92). The more thin bodies get equated with youth, in other words, the more pressure women feel to control their weight. Scholars Joseph Maguire and Louise Mansfiend come to a similar conclusion in their analysis of 1980s aerobics: "Aerobics class reflects and reinforces the dominant desire to be thin and is an exercise practice that harnesses a great degree of oppression for the women who participate" (111). Ultimately, the sculpted female body—whether promoted through Fonda's videotapes or the images produced by Madison Avenue—tended to fuel an unhealthy desire among women to remain thin, beautiful, and young.

Of course, Fonda did not invent aerobics nor did she produce its first video. Based on the work of exercise physiologist Dr. Kenneth Cooper in his book *Aerobics* (1968), both Judi Sheppard Misset and Jacki Sorensen invented the type of aerobics Fonda would catapult into a national obsession. Most experts considered exercise a valuable supplement to dieting at the time, but it was not viewed as essential for weight loss and bodily transformation until the late 1970s. According to Roberta Pollack Seid, "only 21 percent of American adults exercised regularly" in 1961, yet twenty years later, "the percentage had leapt to 60" (8). Furthermore, "between 1981 and 1985 an estimated 25 million Americans had joined the latest activity, aerobic dance classes, which proved to be primarily a female form of burning fat and building muscles" (236). These remarkable numbers were fueled, in part, by *Jane Fonda's Workout Book* and her subsequent videos, including *Jane Fonda's Workout* (1982), *Pregnancy, Birth and Recovery* (1983), *Workout Challenge* (1984), *Prime Time Workout* (1984), *New Workout* (1985), *Low-Impact Aerobic Workout* (1986), *Sportsaid* (1987), and *Workout with Weights* (1987). Elizabeth Kagan and Margaret Morse reported at the time that "Twenty-nine percent of aerobics participants in 1986 used aerobics videos, and, overall, 15 million tapes [had] been sold since the first one went on the market, 3.5 million of them by Jane Fonda" (164–65). A wide range of celebrities such as Raquel Welch, Richard Simmons, Marie Osmond, Bruce Jenner, Martina Navratilova, Lou Ferrigno, and Arnold Schwarzenegger joined Fonda in flooding the market with fitness programs. Exercising soon became a national ethos. The demand for home workout equipment grew 150 percent between 1978 and 1983. The clothing industry saw a 60 percent increase in sales of exercise outfits between 1981 and 1982, and women purchased 30.2 million leotards in 1983 (Seid 8).

Unlike any prior period in American history, the 1980s viewed the toned, fat-free body as its goal. Only through the pain of strenuous exercise could one achieve it: "You must be committed to working hard, sweating hard, and getting sore," Fonda writes. "No sweatless quickies" (55). Failure to do so guaranteed some degree of social marginalization and ridicule. It meant the possibility of being viewed as one of the fat, uncoordinated clients in "Physical." Aerobics and bodybuilding—alongside images in popular culture such

Cover for *Jane Fonda's Low-Impact Workout* (1986). Karl Lorimar Video/Photofest. © Karl Lorimar Video.

as Newton-John's video—sent a clear message about appearance as the measure for personal worth. The taut body, as well as the exercise regimen to achieve it, reflected admirable personal characteristics such as determination, dedication, and self-control. As Susan Bordo argues in *Unbearable Weight: Feminism, Western Culture, and the Body*, "the firm, developed body [became] a symbol of correct *attitude*; it [meant] that one 'cares' about oneself and how one appears to others, suggesting willpower, energy, control over infantile impulse, the ability to 'shape your life'" (199). These symbolic meanings fueled a growing hostility toward fatness and buttressed a national weight-loss imperative that viewed fat as a problem to be overcome. Unlike shifting attitudes toward alcohol and drug addiction, which became more widely accepted as problems of physiological dependency, fatness was a failure of will and a sign of moral weakness.

At the same time, 1980s workout culture thrived alongside diet products that reinforced similar messages about the body. Twenty-one years after Weight Watchers opened for business in 1963, it had 13 million participants with nearly 500,000 people attending weekly classes, and another 825,000 people subscribing to its magazine (Seid 6; Schwartz 241). Diet soft drinks had been growing in sales since the 1960s, and after the FDA approved the artificial sweetener aspartame in 1981, they cornered 20 percent of the overall soda market by 1984. In the same year, the company that developed NutraSweet earned $585 million in revenue. Over-the-counter drugs for weight control boomed as well. Laxatives, diuretics, and vitamin and mineral supplements climbed in sales throughout the decade. "Starch blockers" earned $150 million in 1982, and the products Appedrine, Prolamine, Control, and Dexatrim became a billion-dollar industry in 1985 (Schwartz 245).

As many scholars have noted, one remarkable feature about this diet culture has been its utter failure to achieve results. Americans got heavier in the second half of the century, not thinner. In 1958 Doctor Alan Stunkard determined that most people seeking "obesity treatment" would either not lose weight or simply regain any losses, and a 1992 NIT Technology Assessment Conference on Voluntary Methods of Weight Loss and Control "affirmed Stunkard's earlier findings that 90–95% of participants in all weight loss programs failed to attain and sustain weight loss beyond two to five years" (Lyons 77). By 1985 approximately 90 percent of Americans considered themselves overweight—a statistic that coincided with the fact that 313 diet books were in print and that 4 million people watched the *Richard Simmons Show* every week (Seid 3–4). Ironically, the designation of "overweight" in the early part of the decade required a BMI of 27.8 for men and 27.3 for women. Not until 1988 did the National Institutes of Health (NIH) change this standard, advising the medical community to label a BMI of 25 as "overweight" and a BMI of 30 as "obese." With this shift, 37 million Americans suddenly became overweight.[6]

This recommendation, however, was not based on any scientific evidence, and the NIH's claims that a BMI higher than 25 led to "significantly higher mortality" were not supported by the data in its own report (Oliver 22). Economic interests—particularly those of pharmaceutical corporations and scientific professionals—shaped these findings, not legitimate concerns for public health.[7] Nevertheless, as this 1985 survey indicates, the NIH was merely catching up with public sentiment. Most Americans already viewed themselves as too fat, making these new BMI standards a mere confirmation of their worst fears, not a revelation. The diet industry quickly capitalized on these findings by promising a solution to the obesity problem, but it failed to do so on every possible level. It did not help most people lose or keep off

New Yorkers try to escape both the Stay Puft Marshmallow Man and their addiction to sugar in Ivan Reitman's *Ghostbusters* (1984). Columbia Pictures/Photofest. © Columbia Pictures.

weight. Instead, it encouraged a climate of perpetual dieting. It fostered intolerance and hostility by vilifying bodily differences. And it led to public health policies that cast fatness as a profound social problem responsible for skyrocketing health-care costs, a lack of patriotism, and even global warming.[8]

As suggested by this brief overview of exercise and diet practices, a profound fear of fat remained at the center of American life in the 1980s. It demanded an obsessive pursuit of the thin body and captured a fundamental contradiction in American culture: the simultaneous desire for excess and self-control. Ivan Reitman's *Ghostbusters* (1984) offers a playful example of this dichotomy. The specter of fatness haunts most characters in the film, for failing to watch one's weight can mean spending an eternity like the fat green ghost that shovels food into its mouth, guzzles wine, and takes refuge in hot dog stands. Its eating habits—an image for the excesses of consumerism—stand in humorous contrast with the health consciousness of Louis (Rick Moranas), who "always [has] plenty of low sodium mineral water and other nutritious foods in the house," and Dana's (Sigourney Weaver's) aerobic workouts. However, she buys a bag of Stay Puft Marshmallows along with eggs and lettuce at the grocery store. She also fills her refrigerator with

Coca-Cola, processed bologna, and other items that make Dr. Peter Venkman (Bill Murray) proclaim, "Oh my God, look at all that junk food!" As these details indicate, her own vacillation between indulgence and restraint mirrors the country's. Even the Ghostbusters get celebrated for having a "super diet" by one newspaper despite consuming mostly Cheez-Its, Chinese fast food, sodas, and Twinkies. It seems fitting that they battle the Stay Puft Marshmallow Man in the closing moments of the film. This gigantic creature embodies the monolithic presence of sugar in America and the types of foods people tried desperately to flee but couldn't escape in the 1980s.

Consumer culture trapped people between having too much (supersizing meals, eating processed foods, and buying in bulk from wholesale outlets like Price Club and Costco) and investing in thinness. It encouraged excess through the acquisition of goods and services, inviting the public to revel in the abundance found at every supermarket, Tower Records, electronics store, and car dealership. Americans could have whatever they wanted whenever they wanted it. Yet as the fat body became an image for appetites out of control, exercise, dieting, and seemingly healthy foods provided the tools for curbing that body and, by extension, the nation's tendency toward overindulgence. One now needed to hire personal trainers, buy workout videos, join a gym, get surgery, purchase "natural" foods, and invest in diet programs to be thin—to keep one's desires in check. The contradictory impulses of eating and dieting became a central feature of American life.

Thinner

"A Bag of Doritos with Some Clam Dip on the Side": Billy Halleck, Bottomless Appetites, and Extreme Bodies in Thinner

Fat bodies appear throughout Stephen King's early fiction. From the large men (and boys) in *It* and *The Tommyknockers* to "crazy overweight ex-nurse" Annie in *Misery*, these characters often function as metaphors for monstrous appetites. King meditates on the potential horror of fatness in *Danse Macabre*, his nonfiction examination of horror in art and culture: "Take fat. How fat does a person have to be before he or she passes over the line and into a perversion of the human form severe enough to be called a monstrosity?" (47). Some of this interest can be attributed to personal experience. King witnessed a fat man getting trapped in a revolving door in the late 1970s, and a doctor once prescribed a workout regimen to King for losing weight. In *On Writing: A Memoir of the Craft*, the author also recalls a job at a laundry service in

Some of Billy's (Robert John Burke's) snack food in Tom Holland's *Thinner* (1996). Paramount Pictures/Photofest. © Paramount Pictures.

which he had to clean filthy, maggot-infested table linens from Maine seafood restaurants: "The maggots were bad; the smell of decomposing clams and lobster-meat was even worse. *Why are people such slobs?* I would wonder, loading feverish linens from Testa's of Bar Harbor into the machines. *Why are people such fucking slobs?*" (68). The term *slob* may not be synonymous with "fat" in King's fiction, but this type of insult often gets hurled at his heavyset characters. Likewise, the potential horrors of one's eating habits—like fatness itself—tend to represent the dangers of addiction and excess more broadly. As Bernadette Bosky has noted, fat bodies in King's early fiction get associated with immoral indulgence and uncontrolled appetites: "fat is always a sign of failure: social failure, psychological failure, and even moral failure. Especially, men described as 'fat' (rather than as 'big') tend to be cruel and abusive or lazy, weak, and self-indulgent" (138). Yet King's preoccupation with this issue assumes an even greater significance when placed in the context of anti-fat bias in the 1980s.

Toward the end of King's 1984 novel *Thinner* (published under the pseudonym of Richard Bachman⁹), Billy Halleck discovers the severed hand of Richie "The Hammer" Ginelli in his stolen car and a keychain with "a picture of Olivia Newton-John in a sweatband" dangling from the ignition (297). A few moments later (with the Newton-John keychain watching his every move), Billy pulls into a McDonald's drive-through to order "three Big Macs, two large orders of french fries, and a coffee milkshake" (298). Certainly, this keychain tempers the horror of Ginelli's death. The singer's outfit from her "Physical" video embodies contemporary workout culture, and it serves as a playful reminder that Billy's lack of exercise, along with his unhealthy eating habits, has contributed to his weight gain. The phrase "getting physical" is also a euphemism for fighting, which encapsulates Ginelli's role in the novel. He has single-handedly waged war on the gypsies to force Taduz Lemke, the clan's patriarch, to end the curse that is transforming Billy from fat to deathly thin. Yet the widespread vilification of fatness in the 1980s helps explain the way Olivia Newton-John's keychain reinforces some of King's most searing indictments of contemporary America—namely, its self-destructive preoccupation with eating, dieting, and the bodily extremes of fatness and thinness.

At first glance, Billy appears to embody a contemporary fantasy about food—losing weight while eating as much as you want. Billy, a lawyer who has done some legal work for the mob, has a successful suburban life and the waistline to prove it. At thirty-six years old, he weighs 246 pounds, and the stains on his suit serve as an ongoing testament to his love for fast food and every type of junk food on the market. When he accidentally kills a gypsy woman with his car, two friends (a cop and a judge) help him sidestep any legal responsibility for the incident, so the gypsy's husband places a curse on Billy as a means for justice. Billy begins losing weight no matter what he eats, and he soon realizes that he will die unless the curse is lifted. In a clever parody of contemporary weight-loss culture, King explores the dangers of excess through Halleck's move from fat to thin.

Food is the central obsession of Billy's life: "He liked his beer, all right, that was a given, but even more than that, he liked to eat" (23). He notes the smell of breakfast wafting upstairs in the mornings, and he takes a certain pride in his hefty dinners: "Halleck had put away his usual lumberjack's meal—three hamburgers (with buns and fixin's), four ears of corn (with butter), half a pint of french fries, and two helpings of peach cobbler with hard sauce" (140). At the same time, he consumes large quantities of food quickly and thoughtlessly: "He had lain waste to the scrambled eggs and of the bacon there was no sign" (9); he then ate the extra bacon "almost without being aware he was doing so" (13). His continual snacking functions in a similar way. It occurs out of habit, not need. Inside his car, he "scarfs" (38) hamburgers and other snacks such as "two packages of Twinkies" and airline peanuts, "stale, but edible [. . .], tasting them no more than he had tasted the Twinkies" (18–19). Eating has become a mindless obsession for Billy, divorced from the pleasures of taste. He even admits to preferring "a bag of Doritos with some clam dip" over dinner at a fine restaurant in New York City. While Hannibal Lecter wouldn't be caught dead with a bag of Doritos, Billy can't surrender his addiction to junk food despite his efforts to communicate an upper-middle-class identity in other ways. In fact, none of the meals in *Thinner* are savored or enjoyed. Eating merely functions as a tool for passing the time, coping with anxiety, or lashing out at an oppressive diet culture.

Only when Billy gets thinner does he begin to notice similar appetites around him: "Everyone seemed overweight and everyone—even the skateboard kids—seemed to be eating something: a slice of pizza here, a Chipwich there, a bag of Doritos, a bag of popcorn, a cone of cotton candy. He saw a fat man in an untucked white shirt, baggy green Bermudas, and thong sandals gobbling a foot-long hot dog [. . . with] two more dogs between his pudgy fingers" (166). The people at these seaside towns form a tableau of consumption for Billy. Eating, it appears, is what Americans do, and its excesses, as illustrated by the man with the hot dogs, suggest an insatiable appetite for pleasure. These towns not only provide endless opportunities for eating, but they also offer almost every type of indulgence—from "dirty book emporiums" to bars with "raucous rock music." Billy notices one man who, while kissing a woman, cups one of her buttocks with one hand and a can of Budweiser with the other (167). Even erotic desire gets accompanied by something to consume. For King, American life is characterized by a perpetual longing for more—more food, more alcohol, more music, more entertainment, more sex, and more stuff. Scholar Michael Collings has argued that the use of brand-name foods in the novel reflects King's exploration of contemporary fears about obesity, "the dangers of it, [. . . and the inability] to do anything about it" (126). Yet these specific brands also highlight the role of corporations in instilling this never-ending desire. The capitalistic marketplace, which made hamburgers, chips, ice cream, and beer ubiquitous in the eighties, fueled a dangerous addiction to harmful foods.

At the same time, a consumer culture that promotes restraint as well as excess traps Billy further, and this bind enables King to expose the adverse effects of the weight-loss industry. For starters, physical fitness regimes have proven short lived for Billy: "In the basement a set of weights sat brooding in a corner, gathering cobwebs and rust. They seemed to reproach him every time he went down" (23). Just as women sought out aerobics classes to sculpt their bodies into some version of Olivia Newton-John and Jane Fonda, men were being sold the muscularity of Arnold Schwarzenegger and Sylvester Stallone. Billy does not transform his body through bench presses, but weight loss alone inspires his daughter to liken him to a 1980s action star: "You're starting to look like Sylvester Stallone, Daddy" (39). Nothing could be further from the truth, however. Billy's entire body—including muscle mass—has begun to wither away, leaving him little in common with the protagonists of *First Blood* (1982) and *Conan the Barbarian* (1982).

It is worth noting that Stallone's and Schwarzenegger's bodies surprised moviegoers at the time. Their bulging biceps and massive chests, which no shirt seemed able to contain, represented a masculine physique that virtually disappeared after the failures of Vietnam and President Carter's ineffectual handling of the Iran hostage crisis. These muscular bodies came to represent a renewed vision of America's political, economic, and military power—a vision both Ronald Reagan and Hollywood cultivated throughout the decade. As Susan Jeffords demonstrates in her analysis of *First Blood*, the film's call for reclaiming the masculine body required "rejecting the corpulent body altogether. [. . .] The true success of *First Blood*, both symbolically and as a marketing tool, is to have created the desire in citizens/audiences to see more bodies like Rambo's, an achievement to which the blockbuster films of the 1980s can attest" (32, 34). Indeed, these action films made the physique of Stallone and Schwarzenegger an aspirational ideal for most men.

Schwarzenegger's body in particular offered an extreme model for male fitness, and long before obesity played a central role in his policies as governor of California (2003–2011),[10] he advocated for physical fitness as central to crafting a desired—and desirable—body. In addition to earning the title of Mr. Universe in 1967, he won the Mr. Olympia competition six times between 1970 and 1975, and his unprecedented success made him the centerpiece of the 1977 documentary *Pumping Iron*. These accomplishments created opportunities for Schwarzenegger in Hollywood, and while training for his role in *Conan the Barbarian*, he entered—and won—the Mr. Universe competition one last time in 1980. Like Jane Fonda, he also participated in contemporary exercise culture by releasing both the album *Arnold Schwarzenegger's Total Body Workout* (1983), which offers exercise advice over the backdrop of popular songs such as Journey's "Don't Stop Believin',"[11] and workout videos.

The opening of *Shape Up with Arnold* (1982), for instance, features close-ups of flexing biceps and shiny weightlifting equipment before introducing Schwarzenegger himself. Here he pauses from his workout, turns to the

Arnold Schwarzenegger at the release of his debut album, *Arnold Schwarzenegger's Total Body Workout* (1983). Columbia Records/Photofest. © Columbia Records.

camera, and promises an effective regimen for both men and women: "It doesn't matter what your goals are. If you're a woman and you want to reduce inches around your thighs or flatten your stomach or increase a little bit on your bust line. Or if you're a man and want to get stronger, more muscular, you can do all of it with weight training." He sprinkles similar commentary throughout the video, and it becomes clear that men need muscles while women need toned thinness: "For women with some special problem areas like their legs and hips [. . .], the next two exercises will get rid of those saddlebags that so many women get." Although both men and women felt the need to alter their bodies, they experienced these pressures in very different terms. Schwarzenegger's narrative offers just one example of this workout ideology, which compelled women to equate size reduction with attractiveness and convinced men to achieve muscular strength as a means for communicating power and authority.[12]

Not surprisingly, King explores some of these gendered messages through the role of sexual desire in *Thinner*. Billy's rusty barbells signal a failed attempt to achieve this bodily ideal but with few consequences. Billy is neither ridiculed openly for his weight nor perceived as unattractive. Not only does his daughter compare him to Stallone, but his wife, Heidi, also maintains a voracious sexual attraction to him. During a weekend getaway early in the novel, they have sex six times in three days (21), and he even claims to do it simply for her sake on occasion: *"This one is for her"* (106). Most significantly, the car accident that kills the gypsy woman happens while his wife is giving him a hand job. (In the 1996 film adaptation of *Thinner*, Heidi performs fellatio during the incident, and this act functions as another example of pleasureless consumption. Billy's mindless addiction to eating parallels her erotic desire—both for her husband and possibly for Dr. Houston.) Likewise, Billy's excessive weight, which stems from his consumption of unhealthy, processed foods, does not cause impotence. Nothing about his body, in other words, compromises his masculinity.

Of course, it is tempting to imagine a version of *Thinner* with Heidi as the overweight lawyer cursed by gypsies. She might notice a stack of dusty Jane Fonda videos in the basement or reference a Weight Watchers point chart on the refrigerator. One of Billy's passing comments, however, reveals how radically different this version would be. Just before King introduces the Newton-John keychain, Billy tells his wife not to quit smoking: "When you quit smoking, you get fat" (296). On one level, his hypocrisy reflects the draconian body standards imposed on women. On another level, it indicates that any story about Heidi's fatness would focus entirely on her body. Billy would not be sexually attracted to her nor would he be forgiving about lapsed diets or missed aerobics classes. Heidi, by contrast, stays quiet about his failed dieting to help him preserve his dignity, and her intense fears about Billy's inexplicable weight loss compel him to see a doctor. She even weeps uncontrollably at the idea that he might be ill: "[losing weight] can mean [a person] is sick. It's one of the seven warning signs of cancer" (32). Yet Billy's comment about smoking suggests that he would rather have his wife suffer from cancer than fatness. Her thinning body would not be a cause for medical concern. It would be a cause for celebration. And the "thinner" curse would merely reflect the cultural mandate for women to be thin, not a gypsy incantation.

To return to the novel, the depiction of Billy's failed fitness routines parallels King's condemnation of the diet industry. Billy has spent much of his married life as a yo-yo dieter, and these efforts are a byproduct of 1980s culture. He recognizes that his daughter's ideas about "masculine beauty" have been shaped by a "lifetime of network TV" (47), for example, and with similar standards in mind, he tries various weight-loss programs without success: "A hot dog or two in the early afternoon to supplement the yogurt lunch, or maybe a hastily gobbled hamburger or two on a Saturday afternoon" (22–23). In fact, diets inspire Billy's worst food-related impulses such as eating convenience store sandwiches that resemble "toasted skin grafts." Ultimately, Billy remains trapped in the double-bind of buying both addictive, processed food and the tools to lose weight. Instead of inspiring positive changes, dieting has encouraged deception, guilt, and desperation.

The oppressiveness of diet culture comes across most powerfully through the image of Billy's scale. Numerous chapter titles state nothing more than the protagonist's weight in pounds (e.g., 246, 217, 172, 137, 127), and this emphasis on quantifying the body reflects the way weight-loss imperatives reduce people to numbers. It encourages a degree of scrutiny that promotes a harmful self-image. The act of weighing makes one hyperaware of even the smallest fluctuation in size. In fact, the Hallecks are so attuned to their weight that Heidi immediately dismisses Billy's claim about the scale reading "light": "It doesn't weigh light, and it never has. [. . .] Someone who's overweight *likes* an inaccurate scale. It makes the actual facts easier to dismiss" (35). By commenting on "overweight" people in general, Heidi recognizes the widespread psychological impact of fat scrutiny. Deception becomes a tool for maintaining self-respect, and in a cultural context that equates thinness with moral and social value, the scale can easily inspire self-loathing. Billy's description of his morning ritual, which includes disrobing, emptying the bladder, and trying to have a bowel movement, suggests as much. He repeatedly denigrates his body (most often in the bedroom and bathroom), comparing his stomach to that of a pregnant woman's and describing it as the "House that Budweiser Built" (22). Not surprisingly, he refers to the scale as a "confessional" (39), and with mock religious language, he views its use as a "genuflection. [. . .] *In the name of cholesterol and saturated fats we pray. Amen*" (39). In America, the cult of weight loss had replaced religion, and the numbers on a scale could either grant absolution for the day or condemn one to eating less and working out more.

Historically, the evolution of the American scale from public to private use and its association with carnivals further reinforce King's critique of contemporary weight-loss culture. In the early nineteenth century, most state fairs featured industrial scales not to weigh crops or heavy machinery but to give entire families a chance to weigh-in at the same time. These enormous scales dwarfed the participants, and this visual contrast signaled the kind of playfulness one could expect to find on the fairgrounds. Sideshow managers frequently paired skeleton men with fat ladies and giants with dwarfs. These juxtapositions put bodily extremes on display in a way that invited audiences to think about thinness and fatness in domestic life—whether someone else's or their own.[13] As weighing technology evolved, particularly with the introduction of ballbearings, the Fairbanks Scale Company developed a product for people under three hundred pounds. It retained the shape of a commercial platform scale, but it "was portable enough for hotels, clubs, racecourses and athletic facilities. It was meant as well for doctors' offices and insurance examiners, whose forms had begun to insist on exact weights" (Schwartz 165). These devices, ranging in cost from seventy to one hundred dollars, were too expensive for most people, and even many insurance examiners could not afford them. Instead they relied on the proliferation of penny scales, which could be found at pharmacies and grocery stores throughout the United States by 1900. One could simply walk a prospective client to the nearest penny scale to complete his or her application for life insurance. From the late 1880s onward, these scales also featured weight and height charts, and as an added bonus, most told fortunes, issuing cards that revealed something about the future. The introduction of "Guess Your Weight" scales in 1904, however, signaled a heightened consciousness about body size in the country. As Hillel Schwartz argues, they "reflected a growing belief that you should know your exact weight" (166), and their popularity soared in the 1920s and 1930s. In 1927 alone, 40,000 penny scales recorded 500,000,000 weights. Public interest was certainly spurred by the release of Continental Scale Works' "Health-O-Meter" in 1919—the first American bathroom scale. With this, weighing quickly moved from a public to a private affair.

King presents Billy as a product of this history, and he uses its connection with carnivals to depict America's obsession with thinness as a perverse spectacle—an extreme (and unhealthy) response to fatness. As evident by his daily weighing ritual and the precise numbers used for chapter titles, Billy has internalized the social expectations of knowing one's exact weight at all times and of scrutinizing the body with ruthless frequency.[14] The recurring connection with sideshows also enables King to set up his own P. T. Barnum-like contrast between fat and thin. After Billy observes the bulging bodies at Old Orchard Beach—the man gobbling hot dogs with "pudgy fingers" and the woman with a "prodigal" gut and "grotesquely fat poodle dog" (167)—he hears a huckster yelling: "Guess your weight! [. . .] If I miss by more than five pounds, you win the dollaya choice!" (168). While this game-playing harkens back to the scale's early role at fairgrounds, a public weighing in the 1980s had far different implications. Most Americans found little entertainment value in body size at the time. As noted earlier, nearly 90 percent of the country considered themselves fat by 1985, and amid the diet and fitness crazes of the decade, the scale functioned more as a recrimination than an amusement.

Billy's own thinness becomes a spectacle as well. He even refers to himself as the "Incredible Shrinking Man" (6) and a "Human Skeleton" (115), reluctantly admitting that "above the waist he really *was* turning into a carny freak" (160). In fact, all of the cursed men acquire physical conditions typically exploited by nineteenth-century sideshows. Judge Rossington develops a disease that turns his skin into scales, fashioning him into a type of Alligator Man (90, 105), and Officer Hopley becomes afflicted with disfiguring acne (125). These punishments make sense from a gypsy whose ethnicity, poverty, and itinerant life have rendered him and his family outcasts. The curse forces these men to experience a similar marginalization by transforming their bodies into something freakish. This link between thinness and freakishness reinforces King's condemnation of the fitness craze and its celebration of the emaciated body. Thinness could be just as much of a spectacle as fatness (or acne and scaly skin) in a culture that idealized certain body types and made no room for bodily diversity.

In addition to heightened weight consciousness, the scale also fueled anti-fat prejudice, and King captures this dynamic, in part, through Billy's use of language. The privacy of the bathroom scale may have intensified self-scrutiny, but it also encouraged people to turn that critical gaze outward—to judge others in equally unrealistic terms. Billy's experiences as a fat man have created a heightened sensitivity about the perception of others. Early in the text, he goes to great lengths to avoid the term *fat*, describing himself as getting "a little less beefy" and admitting that he has gotten "a *lot* heavier" in his sixteen years of marriage (12, 26). In an argument with his wife, he accuses her of wanting to call him "a great big hog. Say it right out if you want, Heidi. What the hell I can take it" (31). His avoidance of "fat"—like his reluctance to echo "thinner," the gypsy's word for invoking the curse—suggests that Billy cannot take it. His experiences with self-hatred and his fear of ridicule have made "fat" a forbidden epithet in the Halleck house.

However, as Billy gets thinner, he begins using this term and other pejorative language for fatness, such as "pudgy," "grotesquely fat," and "jiggling." In fact, his view of body fat becomes increasingly mean-spirited as he loses more and more weight. The "fat [. . .] jiggling women" on the boardwalk wore "obscenely small bikinis [. . . that] were under the same terrible pressures as a submarine cruising far below the rated depth. If any of the iridescent miracle fabric gave way, fat would fly" (189). Of course, Billy has heard such sentiments throughout his life. His physician, for instance, tosses around terms such as "fatty" (57), and Billy's savior, Ginelli, uses equally degrading language: "And this fat guy comes walking in. I mean, he goes a good two-fifty and his ass looks like two dogs fightin' under a blanket" (219). This description captures the social condemnation of fatness at the time and provides Billy with insight into the way his own heaviness has been perceived by others. Nevertheless, his experiences as a fat man have not made him more compassionate or understanding. The shedding of pounds has gone hand-in-hand with a loss of empathy on his part. Since he blames Heidi for the car accident, he becomes increasingly enraged by the fact that she is not being punished, and he decides to kill her by passing along the curse. He also promises to watch his weight while waiting for her to eat the cursed strawberry pie: *"I'm never going to get fat the way I was again"* (315). Once again, King inverts the contemporary associations with fatness (negative) and thinness (positive) here. Billy's commitment to thinness is not healthy and ennobling. It requires a ruthlessness on his part. It encourages a value system that celebrates the lean, muscular body at the expense of others. It promotes punishing degrees of self-restraint, and it encourages acts of anger and callousness. His journey has clearly taught him nothing about body size, forgiveness, and personal responsibility.

In a deft touch, King makes pie, the epitome of sugary treats, the vehicle for Billy's salvation as long as he willingly passes the curse onto someone else. As Lemke, the gypsy, explains, "Nothing is your fault . . . there are reasons . . . you have friends. [. . .] Why not eat your own pie, white man from town? You die, but you die strong" (291). Novelist Jack Kerouac helped solidify pie's place as the all-American dessert in post–World War II America through his hungry, endlessly wandering hipsters in *On the Road*. While pie for Kerouac represents a consumer culture that even the Beats couldn't escape, King uses it to capture the double-bind facing the country at the time—desiring more while trying to restrain the self. Pie has contributed to the very weight gain that has caused such anguish for Billy. His addiction to junk foods developed alongside a deep-seated guilt for eating them, and the combination has devastating consequences. In the closing moments of the text, he commits himself to watching his weight immediately *after* he binges on McDonald's fast food. The oppositional forces of dieting and excess eating have too strong a hold on his psyche. When his plan to kill Heidi backfires (once he discovers that his daughter has eaten part of the pie as well), he decides to take a slice for himself. Like Billy throughout most of his life, his wife and daughter cannot resist this late-night snack, but his newfound callousness makes him realize too late that they are just like him. They, too, are driven by impulses that can be unhealthy and destructive. For King, Billy's change from fatness to thinness, in other words, reflects the worse impulses of American culture. These extremes not only celebrate unrealistic ideals and denigrate those who fail to meet it, but they also get internalized by those participating in it. They encourage a dichotomous view of the world—fat/thin, white/nonwhite, love/hate, innocence/guilt—that promotes intolerance, and Billy's transformation from loving husband to potential murderer offers one example of this danger.

Disturbing Appetites

The Fattest Man in the World and Thinner

In 1983, while King was still working on *Thinner*, Jon Brower Minnoch, the heaviest man in medical history, died. He weighed 294 pounds at the age of twelve, and he continued to get heavier throughout his life. At twenty-two, he weighed 392 pounds and would put on an additional 308 pounds within three years.[15] Minnoch tried to live a fairly conventional life despite the challenges of his condition. He married a woman who weighed a little more than 100 pounds, and they had two children together. When Minnoch was hospitalized in 1978 for cardiac and respiratory failure, however, the difficulty of treating him received national news coverage. A dozen firemen needed a modified stretcher to get him out of his house. The University of Washington Medical Center in Seattle latched two beds together to support him, and thirteen attendants were required to roll him over. Though his health and poor mobility made the use of a scale impossible, the doctors on hand estimated his weight at over 1,400 pounds, and they attributed much of it to a massive edema, the accumulation of excess fluid as a result of disease. His doctors eventually discharged Minnoch with orders to restrict his diet to 1,200 calories per day, and within sixteen months, he lost an astounding 924 pounds. He soon began getting heavier again, however, and by October 1981, his doctors listed him at 952 pounds. He weighed 798 pounds at the time of his death two years later.

For most people, Jon Brower Minnoch was a nightmarish vision of excess. Of course, no one feared waking up in a 1,400-pound body as a result of overeating, but in the context of 1980s America, fatness of any kind had been utterly demonized. Nurses, physicians, nutritionists, physical trainers, dietitians, and even celebrities scrutinized every ounce of body fat. No effort or expense was too great for getting thinner. In the health and body craze of the decade, fatness became intolerable. It fueled self-hatred and inspired desperation, most notably through eating disorders. Despite Jon Brower Minnoch's extreme weight gains and losses, King did not imagine Billy Halleck in these terms. The author did not want a protagonist with genetic and medical reasons for his body size. Instead, he wanted Billy to have some agency over his fatness. At the time of Billy's marriage, he remembers himself as quite fit: "On their honeymoon, he had been slim and trim, only a kid, still in good shape from summers spent on a logging crew" (26). His weight gain, therefore, can be attributed to bad eating habits, a lack of exercise (as a white-collar lawyer without rigorous summer activity), and an addiction to processed foods high in sugar, fats, and cholesterol. When he begins thinning involuntarily, his body becomes a parody of the ideals promoted by the fitness industry and diet companies at the time. Not surprisingly, Billy resents Heidi's initial concerns about his thinning body: "But losing weight is a good thing" (31), he protests. Everything in American culture communicated that message. Yet for King, the radical extremes of Billy's body represented a society torn between indulgence and self-control. The investment in thinning was proving as equally unhealthy as excess. In effect, middle-class Americans were cursing themselves in pursuit of a physical goal that promoted intolerance and injustice. Much like the werewolf movies Billy watched as a child, his changing body becomes a metaphor for some of the horrifying transformations happening in the country at the time.

Geek Love

"I Want to Be Like You Are!": Beauty, Bodies, and the Terrors of Conformity in Katherine Dunn's Geek Love

Stanley (Stanislaus) Berent—better known as Sealo the Seal Boy—died in 1980. Born with hands that grew directly from the sockets of his shoulders, Berent suffered from a congenital condition commonly referred to as phocomelia (meaning "seal-like limbs"). He sold newspapers as a young boy on the streets of Pittsburgh until a sideshow scout offered him a job. For the rest of his life, he performed with freak shows and carnivals throughout the country. He also became a featured act in Coney Island until his retirement in 1976. Phocomelia has most commonly been attributed to thalidomide, a drug produced in Germany in the 1950s to alleviate morning sickness for pregnant women. By the time scientists discovered the link between thalidomide and severe birth defects, however, at least 10,000 cases of phocomelia had been reported. Only 50 percent of those infants survived into adulthood.[16] Although born long before its development, Berent was still actively performing at the height of the drug's controversy and its eventual ban in 1961.[17] For many audiences, his condition served as a reminder for the potential horrors of both modern medicine and the deviant body.

Berent, like any freak performer, recognized that sideshows sent reassuring messages about the value of conformity and social acceptance. Being able to stare at a freak made many people feel better about themselves and their own place in society. At the same time, Berent took tremendous pride in his professional career and in his act, which typically involved sawing a piece of wood in half and shaving. In 1972 he filed a lawsuit challenging an arcane

The Fattest Family Exhibit at the Rutland Fair in 1941. "A Sideshow at the Rutland Fair, Rutland, Vermont (1941)." Library of Congress, Prints and Photographs Division. Reproduction Number: LC-DIG-fsa-8a36672.

Florida law that banned the exhibition of people with disabilities. He never considered himself exploited by the sideshow, just the opposite. As he once told a colleague, "Save me from what? If I wanted to I could have lit cigars from five-dollar bills" (Hartzman 212). The court ruled in his favor, overturning the law in the name of giving everyone an opportunity to earn a living.

Berent's career—particularly his physical condition, association with thalidomide, and pride at being a freak show performer—resonates with several aspects of Katherine Dunn's cult masterpiece *Geek Love* (1989). Despite claims that she did not research freak shows or give much thought to the issue of disability while writing the book, Dunn started the manuscript shortly after Berent's death. Her character Arturo Binewski also shares some notable similarities with this sideshow icon. Arty is born with flippers for hands and feet, and his physical condition—like that of his siblings—is a direct result of his parents' experiments with "illicit and prescription drugs, insecticides, and eventually radioisotopes" (7). When business for the Binewski Carnival Fabulon begins to decline, Al Binewski and his wife, Chrystal Lil, seek out drugs like thalidomide in order to breed their own freak show. Their experiments result in Arty, the Aqua Boy, piano-playing Siamese twins, an albino hunchback dwarf, a normal-looking boy with telekinetic powers, and "Al's failures," four stillborn children that eventually get displayed in jars of formaldehyde.

Al's rationale, to give his children a way "to earn a living just by being themselves" (7), aligns with his philosophy about freakishness—that nothing could be more valuable and beautiful than "oddity" (9).

Geek Love, which became a National Book Award finalist in 1989 and sold over 450,000 copies in the United States by 2017,[18] weaves together two narratives about bodily transformation. One involves the Binewski family history with an emphasis on Arty, whose narcissism and hatred for society inspire the creation of a cult that promises transcendence through surgery. The second narrative, told in the "Notes for Now" chapters, focuses on the life of his sister, Oly, long after a massive fire has destroyed the carnival, the cult, and most of her family. Oly secretly watches over her blind, senile mother and her daughter, Miranda, whom she gave up for adoption as a baby. Miranda has a "thin, curling tail" (17) and part-time job at a strip club featuring women with extraordinary bodies. After a stranger offers Miranda money to have her tail surgically removed, Oly plots to kill this so-called benefactor, Mary Lick. Oly discovers that Miss Lick, in addition to being the heiress of a multimillion-dollar frozen food company, pays women to disfigure themselves. She views these surgeries as "freeing" women from objectification, enabling them to achieve success for something other than their bodies.

This provocative, disturbing, and beautifully crafted novel has inspired many critical reactions, and some disability scholars have viewed the text unfavorably. In an interview with the *Los Angeles Times* in 1989, for instance, Paul Longmore describes Dunn's unsavory characters as part of a broader tendency to view disability in symbolic terms. Such depictions "are not helpful at all to disabled people, and it also reflects that we're not really regarded as fully human."[19] *Geek Love* has weathered such critiques, though, and for three decades, it has received a considerable amount of praise for its insights into American culture. Most of this scholarship tends to focus on three issues: disability, class, and women's reproductive rights. David T. Mitchell and Sharon L. Snyder, for example, argue that Oly "serves Dunn's theorizing of a psyche that longs for a seamless integration into humanity in the midst of an experience of irreducible difference" (151), and Michael Hardin explores the way the book deconstructs hierarchies that foster intolerance about the extraordinary body. Other scholars have viewed Dunn's challenge to these social norms in terms of patriarchal power and class mobility.[20] For Emily Russell, the novel's examination of the body engages with national debates over laws preventing or terminating the pregnancies of disabled women.[21] Likewise, Rachel Adams examines the politics of blaming mothers "for creating abnormality" (197). Anchoring her study in the history of freak shows, she maps out the way this entertainment tapped into popular anxieties about procreation, arguing that

Dunn ultimately "affirms the necessity of women's sexual and reproductive freedom" (202).

In the context of 1980s America, Dunn's depiction of freak shows also condemns the harmful bodily standards that emerged from a medical community and weight-loss industry that benefited from the vilification of fatness. She dismantles the typical dynamics of this entertainment by crafting a family with no desire to participate in mainstream culture. Instead, they view the uniqueness of their bodies as enviable, and in this way the novel challenges readers to consider the "terror of [. . .] ordinariness" (223) and conformity. Through Arty's cult (which encourages members to surgically alter their appearance) and Miss Lick's efforts to deform women, Dunn offers a horrifying corollary to the social pressures many people—particularly women—felt to change their bodies.

Staging Fat Bodies: Freak Shows and Fatness

First appearing in museums and then as part of carnivals and world's fairs, hundreds of freak shows traveled throughout the United States between the 1840s and 1940s. For the price of admission (which usually ranged from ten cents to a dollar), one could stare at the fattest woman in the world, alligator men, dog-faced boys, tattooed princesses, midgets, the severely disabled, nonwhites, and anyone whose body could be presented as strange and unusual. The freak represented what the audience was not—the Other, someone excluded from mainstream society for being different. On one level, freak shows placed conformity at the center of middle-class values, equating the deviant body with extreme individualism. On another level, as Rosemarie Garland Thomson has argued, audiences were often drawn to the way these performers "embodied freedom's elusive and threatening promise of not being like everybody else" (69). To some extent, this paradox between individuality and conformity was mitigated by the freak, whose body made physical difference the clear basis for exclusion. Not surprisingly, a freak show's success hinged on its ability to maintain the distance between viewer and freak, to simultaneously challenge and reinforce binaries about the body—whether in terms of gender (male and female), race (white and nonwhite), disability (able and disabled), or size (fat and thin, tall and short).

Fatness became a featured part of these shows after P. T. Barnum purchased the American Museum in 1841. Under his management, the museum became one of the premiere attractions in the country. He took advantage of its location in Lower Manhattan—just across the street from New York's first luxury hotel, Astor House—to market these entertainments as fashionable and respectable. A consummate showman and entrepreneur, Barnum recognized the potential profitability of freak exhibits, advertising them through newspapers, photographs, "true life" pamphlets, transparencies, and brightly colored banners. He believed, as he explains in his autobiography, that "everything depended on getting people to think, and talk, and become curious and excited over and about the 'rare spectacles'" (76). As such, he "engaged in queer curiosities, and even monstrosities, simply to add to the notoriety of the Museum" (142). These efforts included diversifying the range of live performers to feature giants, dwarfs, fat people, and other individuals with extraordinary bodies. One of Barnum's first weight-based exhibits featured Vantile Mack.[22] Mack's biography boasts that he weighed 113 pounds at the age of three, but it also notes that he never ate too much: "Instead, therefore, of being fed to excess, he is simply provided with wholesome and nourishing diet, and whilst certainly permitted to indulge his appetite to his satisfaction, he is also restrained from doing so to his injury."[23] This description makes his condition genetic (as opposed to dietary), but it also reinforces fat bias by suggesting the need to monitor Mack's eating habits. Someone with his body simply cannot be trusted around food. As with most fat exhibits, clothing also helped accentuate Mack's size, and he was required to wear loose clothes for publicity photographs.[24] All of these details helped construct fatness as a spectacle for Barnum's audiences.

In addition to clothing and sensationalized biographical accounts, these performances often relied on juxtaposition to exaggerate the body. Staged marriages between fat ladies and skeleton men were common, and they proved an effective marketing tool. During the filming of Tod Browning's *Freaks* (1932), for example, skeleton man Peter Robinson (who weighed 58 pounds) met his future wife, sideshow performer Baby Bunny Smith. By the time Ringling Brothers hosted their wedding at Madison Square Garden, she weighed 467 pounds. The publicity for this event included photographs of the couple trying to embrace during their honeymoon breakfast. Other pictures showed Bunny offering Peter a bite to eat. As Robert Bodgan notes, these presentations were designed to parody "domestic tranquility. [. . . In those breakfast photographs], she is feeding him, stereotypically trying to do what any good wife was expected to do—fatten him up" (210).

Within *Geek Love*, these exhibits comment on the debilitating impact of fat shame in contemporary America. Oly recalls "an endless migrating herd of fat folks and giants. [. . .] Mama often said that fat folks went out of style because every tenth ass on the street now was wider than the one in the tent. Folks could see it free on any block" (278). Yet Oly observes that one of Arty's acolytes, Alma, "couldn't have made a penny as a pro. She didn't weigh as much as a single leg of 'Eleven Hundred Pound Jocko!' or 'Pedrita the Plump!' but she wasn't healthy. Jocko and Pedrita were the proudest people who'd ever worked for the show, according to Papa. Alma Witherspoon had the pride of a squashed possum" (181). The language of healthiness and pride highlights the way 1980s America encouraged self-destructive modes for weight loss instead of advocating healthy living. Only the freak show—a space largely accepting of bodily diversity—provides a context for Jocko and Pedrita to thrive. Only freak shows and subsequently the porn industry enable their other fat performer to view herself as erotic. Outside of the carnival, people like Alma feel demoralized because body fat marginalizes them. Arty, for example, has no problem referring to midwestern girls as "cows" and "rhinos"—even though he has sexual liaisons with them. When Siamese twins, Elly and Iphy, begin prostituting themselves for money, they agree not to do so "with anybody fat or old" (205). And Oly's daughter, Miranda, considers fatness a spectacle: "She has lured the fat man from the corner newsstand up to her room several times to model for her" (15). All of these moments reflect contemporary views of fatness as less than human, asexual, and worthy of ridicule.

These degrading physical standards operated in tandem with risky medical procedures for weight loss. In a savage parody of surgical intervention, Dunn presents Arty's cult as promising true enlightenment through the reduction of body size. In 1986, nearly 100,000 liposuctions were performed in the United States, and 11 people died from this procedure between 1982 and 1988 (Sullivan 61–62).[25] By the end of the decade, 1 out of every 225 Americans elected to have cosmetic surgery. Arty exploits this social context to manipulate his followers: "'You feel ugly, don't you, sweetheart?' [. . .] They all gasped, and she wasn't the only one nodding. 'You've tried everything, haven't you?' [. . .] 'Everything' murmured in the bones of the people. 'Pills, shots, hypnosis, diets, exercise. Everything. Because you want to be beautiful?' [. . .] They all sighed with tender sympathy for themselves" (177, 178). Arty's crowds have participated fully in diet culture. The nodding, sighing audience is not merely responding to bleachers that have been wired to vibrate with Arty's words. They are also reacting to daily reminders of their own bodily failures: "Can you be happy with the movies and the ads and the clothes in the stores and the doctors and the eyes as you walk down the street all telling you there is something *wrong* with you? No. You can't. You cannot be *happy*. Because, you poor darling baby, you *believe* them" (178). Including the medical community in these broader forces of surveillance and judgment establishes an important target for Dunn's critique.

For instance, Alma Witherspoon, the cult's first member, has a genetic predisposition for fatness that never gets considered by doctors—despite the fact that she carries around a picture of her heavyset mother. Instead, she has been "told" by Hollywood, Madison Avenue, clothing stores, fashion models, and her general practitioner to pursue thinness. Arty's reference to doctors can also allude to surgeons that offer a "quick fix" for weight loss. Such options send a message that there is no excuse for fatness. Trapped by popular culture, social pressure, and medical technology, Alma feels the need to change her body somehow, and Arty's words inspire her to claim: "I want to be like *you* are!" American culture had encouraged his audience to model themselves on others. It had convinced them that transforming the body provided the only path to happiness. And this ideology makes it possible for Arty to establish a cult with surgical modification as a goal.

Though Arty proclaims to help his followers escape fat stigma, he merely reconstitutes the same biases and "solutions." First, he establishes a new bodily ideal (his own) and then provides a diet and surgical plan for achieving it. An astute observer of the zeitgeist, Arty recognizes the inherent contradiction at the heart of food and diet practices—namely, economic forces that encourage both eating addictive foods and losing weight at the same time: "You don't want to stop eating! You love to eat! You don't want to be thin! [. . .] All you really want to know is that you're *all right!*" (178). He claims to offer a type of social acceptance that permits indulgence, but within the cult, Arty's followers end up hearing similar messages about the body. Alma, for instance, must follow "Dr. P's Vegetarian Nutri-Prescription for months," which has helped her lose weight naturally: "Her skin had some tone and she'd dropped a few chins [. . .] More of her face was visible" (183). Arty establishes "a special kitchen truck and mess tent to serve three wholesome meals per day to each and every one of his followers" (193), and he advises the cooks "to make sure a vegetarian menu was available for those who wanted it" (275). By removing their access to addictive foods (they can't afford the junk on the midway), Arty makes himself their sole addiction. Newspaper reports of burglarized grocery stores also reveal many of Arty's followers to be starving: "It seems they were hungry. A lot of them didn't have any money left after turning everything over to Arty. Trailing around after him they had no way to earn any" (193). Cult life has trapped them in a punishing social system with nothing but Arty and the desire for bodily change. Their hunger thus becomes a metaphor for the exploitation of both Arty's cult and the cult of thinness in America.

In the context of the eighties, the next likely step for Alma—and the other heavyset cult members—would have been surgery. She had attempted every other method of weight loss, but as the text reveals, she could not afford a medical procedure: Alma arrived at the carnival "flat broke." The cost of cosmetic surgery at the time ranged from $1,000 to $7,500,[26] and Arty's "services" mirror such expenses when he begins requiring the "Admitted" to pay a dowry of roughly $5,000 (227)—or, as Arty explains privately, "to fork over everything they had in the world" (185). For this fee, the Admitted have the privilege of caring for those with amputated limbs, attending Arty's shows, and getting "the surgical amputations performed by the Arturan medical staff" (227). Like countless Americans, these cult members sacrificed their money and bodies to achieve a certain physical standard. Alma's character provides the most detailed example of this process. After recovering from the amputation of her toes, she "[begs] for the privilege of having her feet and legs nipped away as well" (182). Soon she begins "testifying" about the benefits of Arturism. By this point, "she was down to the nubs [. . .]. Her legs were gone from the hip and her arms ended at the elbow. She looked better" (183). Oly not only considers Alma's appearance improved, but she also notes a change in her self-image. Alma becomes "chipper" and content, finally "'feeling good' about herself" (183), but she fails to recognize the way her body continues to define her—in this case as an embodiment of the cult's goal. For Dunn, these extreme amputations mock the radical methods people willingly embraced to mimic contemporary beauty ideals. Although the cult promised a refuge from the "horror of normalcy" and the pressure "to be unique" (223), these amputations—like cosmetic surgeries—robbed members of their individuality. They strived to be nothing more than copies.

Through Mary Lick's character, Dunn extends her indictment of the weight-loss industry to include diet foods that profit from fat shame. Miss Lick, who inherits sole control over Lick Enterprises after her father's death, oversees the manufacturing of their main product: "Lickety Split dinners—portable food for airlines and for institutions, from rest homes to schools, jails to asylums. Nineteen full menus with special Kiddie, Diabetic, Kosher, and NMR (No Mastication Required) lines. Everything from three to six courses in plastic trays with an indentation for each item" (149). Much like Stouffer's Lean Cuisine, which was introduced in 1981 and helped make frozen dinners a $1.4 billion industry in 1984,[27] Miss Lick's frozen meals get marketed as low-calorie, healthy choices. Consumers might feel good about eating only "nine hundred calories," but mass producing these foods to cost-cutting institutions requires cheap, low-quality ingredients. As historian Warren Belasco notes, "Virtually all frozen dinners" at the time contained additives and chemicals to enhance flavor and mouthfeel, and "the typical Lean Cuisine dinner had almost 1,200 mg sodium per serving" (*Appetite* 227). In similar fashion, Lickety Split dinners are made by "old but reliable machinery that poops out 3 ounces of gravy, 1.8 ounces of niblet corn, 3 ounces of turkey breast, 3.2 ounces of apple cobbler, each in its proper compartment of the plastic trays" (155).

The defecation imagery emphasizes the truth about what consumers get in terms of both quality and implied health benefits. As the proportions indicate, little nutritional value can be found in this dinner. It contains more sugar (apple cobbler) than any other item, slathers the protein in gravy (i.e., with more fat), leaves out vegetables, and includes kernels of corn, a grain associated with processed foods.

Interestingly, these precooked meals make up Miss Lick's primary source of nutrition. She prefers the Thanksgiving option with "turkey, dressing, pumpkin custard, whipped spuds, [and] gravy," describing her freezer as filled with "twenty-six Thanksgivings" (155). Dunn's choice of calorie-controlled Thanksgiving dinners highlights the contradictory food messages at the heart of American society. Thanksgiving became a celebration of both gastronomic and economic excess after Franklin Delano Roosevelt moved it to the penultimate Thursday of November in 1939.[28] This date gave merchants more time to sell goods before Christmas, and it helped solidify the holiday's association with national myths about American plentitude. The precisely controlled portions of Lick's frozen dinners, however, suggest otherwise. Despite countless pressures to overindulge during the holidays, many Americans felt the need to consume less. Miss Lick's meals may not be marketed to individuals (yet), but they become emblematic of the way corporations used diet foods to create the illusion of retrained indulgence. One can have it all—the tastes of Thanksgiving without the guilt—as long as it comes in a box with tiny compartments!

Miss Lick's preoccupation with weight—along with her daily scrutiny of calories—offers another condemnation of diet culture. Despite routine exercise, Miss Lick's massive, fleshy figure implies that her weight has nothing to do with eating. It is a biological issue. Yet in a culture equating beauty with thinness, she has learned to despise her "goddamn mountain" (327) of a body with its "massive jaw," "big solid belly," and "chubby toes" (327, 334). She spends a lifetime in pursuit of thinness, and she laments that her Thanksgiving meals have not helped achieve this goal: "That's all I eat. Nine hundred calories each. So why am I so big?" (155). Miss Lick not only buys into an ideology that denigrates her body type, but she also falls victim to the ploys used by processed food companies to manipulate consumers. Calorie counting, for instance, was a common tactic to deflect attention from the fat, cholesterol, and sodium levels of a product. Miss Lick ought to know better, but she has pinned her hopes for bodily transformation on portion-controlled, frozen meals. Ironically, these Thanksgivings, despite their traditional association with bountiful harvests, leave Miss Lick hungry and dissatisfied. This dissatisfaction comes partly from the food's quality and small portions, and partly from what it represents—the absence of community. Just as Lick Enterprises specializes in providing meals for people in places without family such as jails, rest homes, and asylums, Miss Lick's Thanksgivings have no connection with home-cooked meals. They are mass-produced items to be eaten alone. Not surprisingly, she compensates for this physiological and psychological lack by snacking. Even this indulgence reflects her full indoctrination into diet culture, which demands the constant policing of one's appetites. She only allows herself one thumb of whiskey at a time, for instance, and she fusses over each kernel of her yeast-dusted popcorn. Trapped in a perpetual cycle of trying to lose weight, she cannot reconcile the reality of her own experience (as a biologically large woman) with the promises of the processed foods she manufactures.

Much like Alma Witherspoon, Miss Lick's last resort for bodily change comes in the form of surgery, but she uses the alteration of *other* women's bodies to reject mainstream beauty standards. Convinced that women can achieve greater intellectual and professional success without being beautiful, Miss Lick pays young women to have their bodies disfigured. She draws inspiration from both Arturism and the experiences of a high school classmate with severe burns. This young girl "realized, you see, that she couldn't rely on being cute and catching a man—that the life she'd expected was out of reach. [. . .] She made another life—all brain stuff. [. . .] She's a chemical engineer. [. . .] She's told me time and again that the fire was the best thing that could have happened to her" (158). In effect, Miss Lick becomes the fire in the lives of desperate women.

"Poor as shit" Carina, for example, has a prostitute mother, and without some type of intervention, she seems destined for a similar fate. Enter Mary Lick. Her surgeon uses chemical acid on the young woman's face, leaving "deep purple gutters of scar" tissue, "twisted lips," and "distorted" nostrils. Only "her eyes and something in the barely discernable bone beneath the raddled flesh" (160) give any indication of her former appearance. In exchange, Carina receives money, tutors, schooling, and a preliminary job. She eventually graduates from college and becomes a professional translator with fluency in five languages. Miss Lick mostly considers Carina a success and a validation of her theories about physical beauty. As Oly explains, "Miss Lick's purpose is to liberate women who are liable to be exploited by male hungers. [. . .] If all these pretty women could shed the traits that made men want them (their prettiness) then they would no longer depend on their own exploitability but would use their talents and intelligences to become powerful" (162). A starring role in one of Lick's flicks (each surgery gets filmed and watched repeatedly by her), however, requires both mutilating the body and removing the most visible sign of one's individuality—the face. Ultimately, these surgeries present a distorted reflection of America's obsession with the body. Similar to the way Arty reduces each cult member to a weak imitation of himself, Lick's girls remain completely defined by appearance.

In addition to mutilating women's faces, Miss Lick uses body weight as another method for defying sexual objectification. In some cases, she reduces the size of women through double mastectomies, explaining to one girl that "those forty-fours of yours are a matched pair of concrete boots and you either ditch them or stay on here loading bread trucks and wait for the janitor to get so anxious to bury his face in your fat sacks that he offers to marry you" (163). Miss Lick avoids the word "breasts" here and insists on imagery associated with heaviness. They are burdensome "fat sacks" or "concrete boots" that anchor women to an endless working-class, heterosexual existence.[29] While "fatness" associated with female sexuality needs to be removed, Miss Lick helps other women gain weight. She refers to some of her potential projects as "skinny mice [who] have got nothing. All they can do is latch on to some man or die" (334). Their skinniness represents one of the defining characteristics of sexual attractiveness in Western culture, so Miss Lick transforms three of them into large, nearly immobile masses of flesh: "All three so fat they could barely move" (162). Miss Lick does not prescribe a course of addictive, processed foods to help these women gain weight, though. She instead instructs her doctor to administer thyroid treatments. With the mindset of a surgeon, Miss Lick demands irrevocable change from these women. The commodification of beauty is predicated on the fantasy of perpetual transformation. With the "right" products, foods, weight-loss programs, workout routines, or surgeries, one can become beautiful by getting thin or appearing younger at any time. Miss Lick ensures allegiance to her philosophy, in part, by removing this possibility. Permanence is antithetical to consumerism, and by taking away the possibility of future bodily change, she hopes to remove the influence of the marketplace.[30]

So What Is a Woman to Do? Feminism, Disfigured Bodies, and Geek Love

In the 1991 article "Women and the Knife: Cosmetic Surgery and the Colonization of Women's Bodies," Kathryn Pauly Morgan expresses profound dismay over the rise of elective cosmetic surgery in the 1980s: "Not only is elective cosmetic surgery moving out of the domain of the sleazy, the suspicious, the secretively deviant, or the pathologically narcissistic, it is becoming the norm," she argues. "This shift is leading to a predictable inversion of the domains of the deviant and the pathological, so that women who contemplate not using cosmetic surgery will increasingly be stigmatized and seen as deviant" (28). Although liposuction and breast augmentation were the most common cosmetic surgeries in 1990, Morgan notes the rising number of facelifts, nips, tucks, and rhinoplasties (nose jobs) as well.[31] These procedures highlight the way science and technology played an increasingly important role in crafting the perfect body.

At the same time, Morgan's concern over the stigmatization of nonsurgically altered bodies points to a larger problem with the willingness among women to conform to male expectations of femininity. Why would women willingly subject themselves to such drastic measures, to such pain and discomfort? Morgan begins to answer this question by challenging the term *elective* surgery; instead, she argues that "the pressure to achieve perfection through technology" (39) undermines the element of true choice or freedom. This pressure, she concludes, acts as a type of coercion. While natural beauty tended to give women access to social mobility and power denied to women viewed as "ugly," feminine beauty in the eighties was "becoming technologically achievable, a commodity for which each and every woman [could], in principle, sacrifice if she [were] to survive and succeed in the world, particularly in industrialized Western countries" (40). As a result, this pressure can offer one explanation for a woman's willingness to be carved, stitched, and stapled in the name of beauty—"that her access to other forms of power and empowerment are or appear to be so limited that cosmetic surgery is the primary domain in which she can experience some semblance of self-determination" (42).

So what is a woman to do? For Morgan, it is not simply enough to recognize surgery as another form of victimization. Aligning herself with activists that view the body as a "sight for feminist action through transformation, appropriation, parody, and protest" (44), Morgan challenges healthy women to utilize the very same surgical tools to reject oppressive beauty standards and the technology to achieve them. Specifically, she calls on women to engage in a radical form of revolt: disfigurement. Ugliness, she argues, "has always held its own fascination, its own particular kind of splendor" (45), and if women willingly used surgery to become "ugly," they could dismantle these modern beauty politics. She then suggests a similar project could be undertaken with the bias against aging. Women could begin dying their hair gray/white, using wrinkle-inducing creams, having wrinkles carved into the skin, and surgically altering their breasts—having them pulled down as opposed to lifted. She concludes:

> If we cringe from contemplating this alternative, this may, in fact, testify (so to speak) to the hold that the beauty imperative has on our imagination and our bodies. If we recoil from this lived alteration of the contours of our bodies and regard it as "mutilation," then so, too, ought we to shirk from contemplation of the cosmetic surgeons who de-skin and alter the contours of women's bodies so that we become more and more like athletic or emaciated (depending on what's in vogue) mannequins with large breasts in the shop windows of modern patriarchal culture. In what sense are these not equivalent mutilations? (46)

At quick glance, Katherine Dunn's character Miss Lick literally engages in Morgan's call to action. She facilitates the surgical transformation of women's bodies to reject conventional notions of beauty. For Miss Lick, sculpting an "ugly," asexual body provides a path to intellectual and socioeconomic freedom. It is the only way to protect oneself from sexual objectification: "Miss Lick has great faith in the truth of this theory. She herself is an example of what can be accomplished by one unencumbered by natural beauty" (162). As such, she scars faces, distorts body shape, provides double mastectomies, removes all hair, sews up vaginas, and would "seal up [one girl's] asshole" if she could (338). Though it is quite possible Morgan read *Geek Love* before writing her article, she would no doubt find Miss Lick's actions horrifying. Miss Lick never claims to use "force or coercion [. . . just] money" (162), but this choice is illusory. She targets women whose poverty makes them vulnerable to the kind of economic forces Miss Lick represents.

Cosmetic surgery offers a similar illusion of control. It promises a relatively fast method for change, emphasizing the final "product" as opposed to the painful recovery. For Miss Lick's women, they must not only become "ugly," but they also must relinquish their sexuality. Her version of female liberation demands complete desexualization through the removal of breasts and clitorises, for example. Ultimately, she reduces them to mannequins, not for the "shop windows of modern patriarchal culture," as Morgan states, but for her own voyeuristic pleasure. Like the cult members that get dismembered to appear like Arty, Miss Lick transforms these women into versions of herself—conventionally unattractive, large, and asexual. Throughout *Geek Love*, Dunn offers a nightmarish vision of what Morgan proposes, making the audience "cringe" and "recoil" in horror at the idea of surgical mutilation. In doing so, Dunn engages in a similar feminist project. She confronts audiences with the most extreme possibilities of "elective" surgery to challenge the tacit acceptance of these methods for achieving beauty. And she presents the widespread vilification of bodily diversity—whether through disability or fatness—as promoting intolerance and encouraging self-hatred.

Dr. Lecter (Anthony Hopkins) being promised three hots and a cot in Jonathan Demme's *The Silence of the Lambs* (1991). Orion Pictures/Photofest. © Orion Pictures.

The Silence of the Lambs

"How . . . Does . . . It Feel . . . to Be . . . So Beautiful?":
Fatness, Dieting, and Fine Dining in The Silence of the Lambs

Real estate in Fayette County, Pennsylvania, does not tend to attract national news, but in the summer of 2015, most major media outlets ran a story about a 1910 Victorian house that went on the market. There was nothing particularly special about its bedrooms, wrap-around veranda, swimming pool, or 1.76-acre lot. Even the initial asking price of $300,000 struck most journalists as reasonable. This house, however, happened to be the residence of serial killer Jame "Buffalo Bill" Gumb in the 1991 film *The Silence of the Lambs*. Director Jonathan Demme used the foyer and dining room for the scene in which FBI trainee Clarice Starling (Jodie Foster) realizes that Gumb (Ted Levine) is responsible for the killings. Although the property does not have a labyrinthian dungeon (all of those sequences were filmed on a soundstage), the listing on Realtor.com highlighted the basement as one of its desirable features: "The pit . . . now there is the question . . . is there really a pit in the basement, or is it all just movie magic? Just put on the lotion, and come see this home and find out!!!!"[32] Inviting people to lather up for an Open House might not have been the best marketing strategy, though. This allusion to Gumb's terrifying refrain ("It rubs the lotion on its skin or else it gets the hose again") certainly undermines the advertisement's efforts to present the house as "a near perfect expression of comfort" and "a statement of taste and prosperity." Gumb's lair serves as such a vivid expression of depravity that most prospective buyers would have trouble imagining otherwise. At the same time, the claims of refinement and taste mirror the language typically used to describe Hannibal Lecter, who masks savagery with the trappings of high-class culture and civility. Either way, you have the perfect home for a serial killer.

Trying to capitalize on the property's small place in cinema history is not surprising, but I suspect an unintended irony in the realtor's suggestion that one might use it as a "horror-themed bed and breakfast."[33] After all, Gumb nearly starves his "guests" in order to facilitate the process of flaying them. (So much for a morning meal!) Nevertheless, food—as it relates to dieting and haute cuisine—plays a pivotal role in *The Silence of the Lambs* and its preoccupation with change. Both Thomas Harris's 1988 novel and Ted Tally's screenplay tell the story of Clarice Starling's efforts in the federal manhunt for "Buffalo Bill," a serial killer who abducts, starves, and then murders heavy-set women to harvest their skins. In order to catch Buffalo Bill, Jack Crawford (Scott Glenn), the director of the FBI's Behavioral Sciences division, sends Starling to interview forensic psychiatrist and cannibalistic serial killer Hannibal Lecter (Anthony Hopkins). Crawford hopes her attractiveness and youthful inexperience will coax Lecter into sharing his insights on the case. Although this information helps Starling find Buffalo Bill before he claims his seventh victim,[34] Lecter barters his acumen for a temporary transfer that enables him to escape.

As this brief overview suggests, nearly every character yearns for some type of change: Gumb longs to be a woman; Clarice fights to become a full-fledged federal agent; Lecter hungers for literal as well as gastronomic freedom; and Crawford wants to capture Buffalo Bill while still ministering to his dying wife. Even the female victims sought transformation. They all desired a physique that American culture equated with beauty and sexual desirability. The preoccupation in *The Silence of the Lambs* with bodies—particularly having the "wrong" body or a body that betrays its owner—reflects contemporary anxieties about fatness, food, and dieting. In the context of the 1980s, the savagery of Buffalo Bill, who literally reduces the size of his victims, and Lecter's appetite for haute (cannibalistic) cuisine satirize the horrifying extremes of dieting and consumption at the time. Just as some people ate too little to lose weight, others ate too much of the wrong thing. All of these behaviors stemmed from a culture that equated self-worth with appearance and placed a ruthless bodily scrutiny at the center of modern life. When considered through this lens, *The Silence of the Lambs* tells a story about the horrors of dieting and the self-hatred it promulgated.

Dreaming of Butterflies: The Fantasy of Bodily Change

The iconic poster for the film adaptation of *The Silence of the Lambs* offers a close-up of Clarice Starling's face that replaces her mouth with a death's-head moth. This image along with the word "silence" highlights some of the gender politics of the work, particularly its portrait of women as objectified by patriarchal forces such as law enforcement and predatory men. This message gets further reinforced by the use of Salvador Dali and Philippe Halsman's *In Voluptas Mors* (1951) on the thorax of the moth. In the original photograph, Dali stands next to several women whose naked bodies have been posed to resemble a skull, but only the women appear on the poster. Artistically, Dali's absence makes sense since these women are intended to replicate the skull-shaped pattern on the insect. Yet his absence functions thematically as well, for Dali has been replaced by another artist here. In the film, Buffalo Bill asserts creative power over the women he uses for his own artistic design—with one important distinction. His desire to fashion art—namely, a dress of women's skin—will require the literal death of his subjects. As such, death is not voluptuous in *The Silence of the Lambs*. It is, instead, a perverse means for this killer/artist to become voluptuous himself.[35]

The moth's thorax and Clarice's eyes form an inverted triangle on the poster that invites closer scrutiny of her features. First, the skull offers an eerie miniature of Clarice's face without skin, suggesting the mortal risks involved in her quest to capture Buffalo Bill. Indeed, the manhunt will culminate in a gunfight that could render her another dead body in Gumb's tapestry of crimes. The golden-brown wings also match the color of Clarice's eyes—a startling substitution for Jodie Foster's blue irises. This color implies a deeper connection between her and the killer. Specifically, Clarice's insights into Buffalo Bill will require the disclosure of deeply personal truths to gain Dr. Lecter's help, allowing him and the audience to gaze deeply into her eyes. The tightly cropped face, which alludes to Demme's close-up shots throughout the film, captures this intimacy as well.[36] Psychological revelation comes at a cost in *The Silence of the Lambs*, and as Clarice knows, any exposure to Hannibal Lecter can be dangerous. The poster's depiction of her face further alludes to some of the dangers associated with looking for Gumb and letting Lecter look at her. Each side has been rendered differently. While the right side is drawn with precision, showing the bone structure beneath her eyebrow, cheek, and chin, the left side fades into porcelain-like whiteness. It is skin

Jonathan Demme insisted on using Salvador Dali and Philippe Halsman's *In Voluptas Mors* for the film's poster. *The Silence of the Lambs* (1991). Orion Pictures/Photofest. © Orion Pictures.

detached from the bone. This detail captures both Gumb's obsession with women's flesh and Lecter's ability to see beyond the masks that people wear to hide their darkest secrets. In these ways, the poster invites the viewer to consider the subject's duality. Clarice has two sides—the person whom she reveals to Lecter and the persona she projects for access to the boy's club of law enforcement.[37]

Lastly, the placement of the moth at the center of the poster reflects the centrality of this image for Thomas Harris's exploration of the body. These insects function as metaphors both for the changes Gumb's victims desire through weight loss and for the gender transformation he seeks through a woman's suit. Like Gumb, all of his victims yearned for butterfly-like metamorphosis into sexual desirability, and thinness served as a clear marker for this in American culture. Gumb merely enacts a literal version of the widespread demonization of fatness by punishing "fat" or "big" women for failing to become thin. When Clarice first interrogates him about Fredrica Bimmel in the film, for instance, he responds, "Oh wait . . . was she a great big fat person?" Even the memory of her body remains a source of ridicule. Gumb's ultimate solution to this problem—like his solution to gender confusion—is a perversely simple one: to put their fat skin on his thin body to make a more desirable version of them and of himself. Yvonne Tasker has observed that "Bill's starvation of his victims perhaps represents an attempt to shape them into his preferred version of femininity" (*Silence* 83). In the context of fat bias and exercise culture in the 1980s, however, the starved, thin body does not merely represent "his" version of femininity. It stems from a culture that demanded thinness of women and equated the thin body with beauty and desirability.

Throughout *The Silence of the Lambs*, the transformations from fat to thin and from male to female consistently get linked with moths and butterflies. The pupae placed in the throats of two victims not only provide Starling with an essential clue for tracking Gumb, but they also give Lecter an opportunity to explain their symbolic importance: "The significance of the chrysalis is change. Worm into butterfly, or moth. Billy thinks he wants to change. He's making himself a girl suit out of real girls" (163). Gumb, in other words, aspires to shed his current skin/cocoon for the beauty of a butterfly. Just as the vibrant colors of butterfly wings can function as camouflage to protect against predators or as embellishments to dazzle prospective mates, Gumb seeks to do both. He wants to remain hidden from law enforcement to continue his work, and he convinces himself that an outfit of real skin will transform him into a sexually desirable woman.

In the film, Gumb achieves this illusion by surrounding himself with feminine garments of bright blue, pink, green, and mustard colors. His dressing room is bathed in the yellow-white light of floor lamps, track lighting, and a disco ball. Along with red lipstick, a blonde wig, and even the whiteness of his skin, this mise-en-scène provides a stark contrast with the shadowy filth and blue, ultraviolet light of the remaining dungeon. These contrasting spaces represent the identity he wants to discard and the one he plans to display after his transformation. In this lit space, Gumb dresses as a woman, dances in front of a video camera, and asks, "Do you want to fuck me?" He then holds a large comforter of vivid colors over his shoulders, spreading it out like butterfly wings. Here, Gumb becomes something beautiful. Like the way he has modified his body through tattoos and piercings, he hopes that wearing a suit of real women's skin will free him from the confines of his masculinity. As Tony Magistrale has noted, just as some moths feed on tears,

"Buffalo Bill not only feasts on the wasted 'tears' of his victims who must be destroyed for their 'pelts,' but he is also crying for himself: his own tears of pain and frustration over years of entrapment in a male body" (31–32). Likewise, David Greven argues that Gumb's desire for different skin plays into the film's broader "critique of American masculinity" while mitigating some of its homophobia (91).[38] Yet the underlying fat politics of starving heavy women to place their skin on a thin body offers an important critique of American bodily ideals as well.

Gumb's ultimate failure to metamorphose, however, stems from his rigid view of bodies as the sole means for self-definition. His troubled homosexual affair with Benjamin Raspail, his romance/intimate friendship with Fredrica Bimmel, the first woman he kills for skin (360), and his subsequent fantasies about transsexualism certainly suggest a profound struggle with identity. As Lecter explains to Starling, however, "Billy's not a transsexual, Clarice, but he thinks he is, he tries to be. He's tried to be a lot of things, I suspect" (165). For scholar Judith Halberstam, "the cause for Buffalo Bill's extreme violence against women lies not in his gender confusion or his sexual orientation but in his humanist presumption that his sex and his gender and his orientation must all match-up to a mythic norm of white heterosexual masculinity" (165). As such, Gumb develops an obsession with anatomy itself, with the skin he so desperately wants to obtain. Even Lecter and Jack Crawford entertain the possibility that Buffalo Bill could simply be addicted to surgery. To some extent, their theory proves true—just not in the way they imagine. After every major medical clinic rejects Gumb's application for sexual reassignment, he *becomes* a surgeon of sorts by picking up a scalpel to harvest the skin of real women. The number of sexual reassignment surgeries remained relatively minor in the 1980s, ranging from 9,000 to 12,000 cases,[39] but as noted earlier, the use of cosmetic surgery became increasingly widespread. Liposuction procedures, for example, rose dramatically after this technique made its way from France to the United States in 1982. "By 1984 approximately 55,000 liposuctions had been performed in the United States," and that number nearly doubled in 1986 (Bordo 236). Gumb may be a man biologically, but his desire for surgical alteration aligns him with the plight of "overweight" women at the time. He too struggles to sculpt the "right" figure, revealing his own victimization by contemporary beauty standards. Although his skin suit provides only a temporary solution (akin to tucking or Lecter's use of Pembry's face as a mask), Gumb has stumbled across something that eluded every woman participating in the diet and exercise craze: perpetual youth. If his suit ages or decays, he can simply construct another one with a new round of victims. He can, in effect, appear ageless. As the workout philosophy of Jane Fonda made clear, the call

Gumb's (Ted Levine's) transformation into a moth in *The Silence of the Lambs* (1991). © Orion Pictures.

for women to be thin and beautiful included a tacit warning to appear young for as long as possible. One's beauty and sexual appeal depended on it.[40]

Demme also uses moth imagery to capture Gumb's failed quest for butterfly-like change. When Catherine screams at the sight of a fingernail in the bloody well, for example, Gumb tries to mimic this sound while stretching out his shirt in the shape of her bosom. Like these illusory breasts, his wailing doesn't sound human. What Gumb fails to recognize is that he has already metamorphosed. He has emerged from the cocoon of his humanity into something monstrous. As Starling learns from two scientists at the Smithsonian Museum of Natural History, "The old definition of moth 'was anything that gradually, silently eats, consumes, or wastes any other thing.' It was a verb for destruction too" (106). Gumb has become exactly this—a death's-head moth, burrowed beneath the surface and consumed by the pain he both causes others and feels for himself.[41]

Demme captures this transformation visually during Starling's shoot-out with Gumb. After one of her bullets shatters a basement window, natural light floods the room to reveal blood gurgling from his mouth. This sound, the blue-gray, rag-shag rug beneath him, the position of his hands by his head (palms up and fingers twitching), and the night vision goggles make him resemble a dying moth. His desire for change has robbed him both of his humanity and his life. Even his dying words in the novel point to the problem:

"How . . . does . . . it feel . . . to be . . . so beautiful?" (348). Instead of asking how it feels to be a woman, Gumb focuses on physical beauty, and *The Silence of the Lambs* suggests that America had a similar problem. The cultural imperative for thinness trapped women in potentially self-destructive behaviors—through fad diets, popular exercise trends, and surgery. Instead of helping people pursue a healthy lifestyle, the 1980s tended to present ideal body types as the key for happiness. It encouraged an image-based value system that promoted both self-hatred and the disparagement of others. In this way, Gumb asks the right question in his final breaths. He doesn't need Clarice's opinion on what it is like to be a woman because he already knows the answer. Being a woman is feeling obsessed with one's body. It is feeling the need to change to please others and to do so at all costs.

"A Girl and a Half in All Directions": Diet Culture and Fat Stigma in The Silence of the Lambs

Most fans would probably agree that Ted Tally's award-winning adaptation presents a compelling, more polished version of Thomas Harris's novel. Not only does it effectively streamline various elements of the plot, it also preserves Lecter's sophistication through language—a quality crystallized by the exceptional performance of Anthony Hopkins. Specifically, the screenplay removes the clunky, crass language of Lecter in the book: "No, that's stupid and wrong" (19); "He wants a vest with tits on it" (152); "I'm rather bored myself" (167); "Don't be grabby or we'll discuss it next week" (169); "We'll see what kind of Stoic Crawford is when Bella bites the big one" (226). By contrast, Lecter's linguistic polish in the film helps preserve the illusion of his upper-class civility and makes his acts of physical savagery more unexpected and disturbing.

One important dimension omitted from the film, however, involves the impact of fat stigma and diet culture on women. While the adaptation effectively captures contemporary gender politics, it leaves out Clarice's insights into women's bodies, eating habits, and clothing. These details prove crucial both for tracking down Buffalo Bill and for understanding Harris's critique of modern beauty standards. As Clarice profiles Gumb, she struggles to understand the significance of his preoccupation with heavyset women: "All the victims were big. [. . .] Some were fat, but all were big" (209); "she thought about the poor, fat, sad, dead girl she saw on the table in the funeral home in Potter, West Virginia" (220). Clarice gradually realizes that part of the "sadness" here comes from the way thinness insulates women like herself both from being a target of Buffalo Bill and from fat bias. In other words, she recognizes these women as victimized by both Gumb and modern society.

Catherine Martin, whom he abducts amid Clarice's investigation, offers a powerful example of this dual victimization. Catherine's self-image has been shaped by fat shame, and she describes her naked body as "a show stopper, a girl and a half in all directions" (265). This performance imagery ("a show stopper") alludes to the novel's portrait of women as endlessly scrutinized—for evidence, for erotic desire, and for adhering (or failing to adhere) to mainstream beauty standards. It also reflects the way fatness had become a type of spectacle. In spite of Catherine's efforts, she can neither achieve an ideal weight nor keep off the pounds, and her concerns about size echo those of most Americans by the middle of the decade. In 1986, *Time* magazine reported that "the *average* American male is 18 pounds over his desirable weight, the *average* female 21 pounds over" (qtd. in Bordo 11). Catherine's twenty-pound fluctuation makes her representative of this average: "Catherine had fine, classic clothes in two sizes, made to fit her at about 145 and 165 pounds, Starling guessed, and there were a few pairs of crisis fat pants and pullovers from the Statuesque Shop" (212). Clarice's choice of words is telling. She recognizes weight gain as a "crisis" for women, and despite the national obsession with dieting and aerobics, enough people struggled with weight for Statuesque Shops to thrive: "Every town of any size has at least one store specializing in clothes for fat people" (318). As Clarice's investigation reveals, Catherine's twenty-pound fluctuation has nothing to do with willpower or self-control; instead, it stems from yo-yo dieting. Her "refrigerator was devoted to cottage cheese and deli fruit salad" (210), and these groceries indicate her current efforts to lose weight. Even Gumb notices a change after the abduction: "She looks thinner. He believes she may have been dieting when he took her. [. . .] It definitely has lost weight" (206). Once again, Catherine gets presented as tormented by body size, and in this way, the novel captures the horrors of dieting. Just as Gumb starves his victims to make harvesting their hides easier, his actions become a metaphor for a culture that encouraged a ruthless, self-punishing approach to weight loss.

Fredrica, the first woman Gumb kills for her skin, relies on fad diets as well, and this detail provides another example of fat stigma in the text. Clarice finds evidence of numerous weight-loss programs in Fredrica's home, including "the Fruit Juice Diet, the Rice Diet, and a crackpot plan where you don't eat and drink at the same sitting" (317). This "crackpot plan"—like her participation in exercise fads (she owns "outsized warmups" and the same Juno "fat pants" as Catherine [318])—signals the extent of her desperation. Although Fredrica's socioeconomic background likely prevented her from joining organized diet groups, Clarice notes that two other victims had been members. As a result, "An agent from the Kanas City office, the FBI's traditional Fat Boys'

Clarice (Jodie Foster) alongside Gumb's collection of Polaroids featuring strippers in *The Silence of the Lambs* (1991). Orion Pictures/Photofest. © Orion Pictures.

Bureau, and some overweight police were sent around to work out at Slenderella, and Diet Center, and join Weight Watchers and other diet denominations in the victim's towns" (317). Of course, Clarice hopes that the dieting practices of Gumb's victims will lead to his capture, but they don't. Instead, they only serve as a reminder of an oppressive diet culture.

While investing time, money, and energy in the diet industry, Fredrica also sought outlets for viewing the fat body as beautiful. She owned several issues of *Big Beautiful Girl*, but even this magazine fails to reject American stereotypes about fatness. It invites readers to New York City to meet recent immigrants "'from parts of the world where your size is an asset.' Right. Alternatively, 'you could travel to Italy or Germany, where you won't be alone after the first day'" (317). As Clarice's sarcasm suggests, she likens these marketing ploys to diet fads that capitalize on insecurities. The magazine, which should be celebrating bodily diversity, does little to help women appreciate their own bodies. It accepts loneliness as one of the consequences of fatness, and since American society won't change, one must seek a new cultural framework to find acceptance. The impact of this ideology is evident in the absence of photographs in Fredrica's room. Although posters of popular icons hang on the walls, no images of Fredrica can be found. Her fantasies about looking like Madonna or Deborah Harry cannot be maintained alongside her own image. Without personal pictures, Fredrica can pretend to look like a pop star and

Buffalo Bill's all-American quest for transformation in *The Silence of the Lambs* (1991). Orion Pictures/Photofest. © Orion Pictures.

"cut the fingers off some old gloves of machine lace, to wear them Madonna-style" (317). Fredrica's idealization of Madonna's body, in essence, requires the erasure of her own.

While the film depicts this room a bit differently, including pictures of Fredrica with her father (next to the Madonna poster), a portrait with her friend, and several old family photographs, it does capture Fredrica's struggles to see herself as sexually attractive. Clarice finds erotic photographs of Fredrica hidden in a music box, and although the film omits most of the fat politics of the book, this detail is important on a number of levels. These Polaroids capture Fredrica in her underwear, posing provocatively. We see her kneeling on a bed, grabbing her buttocks, and facing the camera in the style of Marilyn Monroe in *The Seven Year Itch* (1955)—both hands between her legs as if she were trying to keep an imaginary dress from blowing upward. At the same time, her pink hair curlers and the open bathroom door suggest that she has been caught by surprise. She communicates embarrassment about her body by covering her face with her hands, and she appears nervous to be seen without clothes. Someone has coaxed her into a playful moment that exposes a great deal of skin. Presumably these photographs were taken by Gumb, and this spontaneous, intimate exchange alludes to their romantic relationship. In the novel, the FBI discovers correspondence that reveals Fredrica's romance with Gumb before he decided to kill her. Although this detail is absent from the film, these Polaroids and those tacked to the walls of Gumb's sewing room implicate him as the photographer. These pictures also reveal that Fredrica cherished this moment, in part, because she wanted to view her body as erotic.

Just as Harris uses diet culture to critique fat bias, the film captures the broader implication of these Polaroids through the mise-en-scène of Gumb's sewing room. As Gumb stitches together skin with his back to the camera, we see a large American flag covering the wall in front of him and a map of the United States taped to the wall on his left. A number of images have been tacked to the flag: sketches of butterflies, a drawing of a man with butterfly wings, and a motorcycle calendar with a scantily clad woman resting her hands on a Harley Davidson. These images of transformation provide a way to interpret the calendar. Gumb wants to discard the masculinity of motorcycles for the beauty of women in sexy garments. This is further suggested by the Polaroids taped to the doorframe on his left, which show Gumb with various strippers. These images represent the type of woman—the type of beauty standard—he hopes to achieve with a suit of real skin. This contrast between the strippers and Fredrica reinforce an important tension in *The Silence of the Lambs* between the ideal and the real, between self-acceptance and self-hatred. Fredrica's pictures reflect an attempt to find a more tolerant, more realistic framework for bodily diversity and beauty. It is a framework that would have improved Fredrica's life and arguably Gumb's. It is a framework that America needed as well.

Fast Food and Fine Dining: Eating in The Silence of the Lambs

In many respects, *The Silence of the Lambs* is about the worst impulses of consumerism—namely, those that instill an insatiable appetite to remake the self. Like the bodies in Olivia Newton-John's "Physical" that change from fat to thin (and straight to gay), Gumb and his victims seek bodily change to be viewed as desirable. Diet culture, exercise regimens, and surgery certainly promised as much, but the potential for eating too much (or too much of the wrong thing) reveals the tension at the heart of this consumer-driven dilemma. One type of excess often leads to another. Just as moth and butterfly imagery underscore Gumb's inability to transform in the way he hopes, this failure becomes apparent through his diet as well. A mountain of fast-food containers appears on his kitchen table in the film, suggesting how frequently he orders Chinese food and other such meals. Even the "scraps" offered to Catherine get served on a tinfoil plate for fast food. Of course, Gumb's unappealing attempts at cooking might explain some of his reliance on take-out. His rusted stovetop with two pans (one dirty with the remnants of something hastily scraped away) and a pot seem to indicate the type of cooking only a college student could appreciate. Thematically, his failure to make food—to cook and mix ingredients into something nutritious—mirrors a broader failure to change his perspective on the body as the absolute measure of personal worth.

Hannibal Lecter, however, loves to cook,[42] and his sensibility as a foodie—a term that first appeared in print in 1980 and was subsequently used throughout the decade[43]—reinforces his association with upper-class excess. He possesses many of the refinements associated with elite culture, and though many of his "civilized" qualities can queer Lecter,[44] they also reflect his monstrous appetites. Incarceration merely inhibits his diet, but as soon as the opportunity presents itself, he gorges himself. In 1976, Lecter ate the tongue of a nurse, and during his first meeting with Starling, he offers a cautionary tale: "A census taker tried to quantify me once. I ate his liver with some fava beans and a big Amarone" (24). Here, as Lecter's taste in wine suggests, he is a member of the upper class that literally consumes a working-class man. His appreciation of fine dining, classical music,[45] elegant clothing, the arts, education, and international travel offers a stark contrast with most of the other characters. Yet he represents some of the destructive inequalities that characterized the decade. For Adrienne Donald, the tendency to reduce blue-collar and white-collar workers to consumable commodities highlights the "economic narrative of class resentment and aspiration" in the film (353), and Tasker notes Clarice's struggle to escape the stigma associated with her West Virginia upbringing, describing her as a "cross-class cross-dresser" (*Working Girls* 25). Tasker also highlights the fact that Bill "preys on working-class women—women defined by their relative lack of economic power" (*Silence* 83). In these ways, *The Silence of the Lambs* depicts the United States as a place in which the wealthiest and most privileged indulge in the greatest appetites at the expense of everyone else. It is a lesson that the census taker—and the general public—learned too late.

Interestingly, Lecter not only masks his cravings with the trappings of highbrow cuisine, but he also tempts others to partake in the same tastes, to share unknowingly in the same value system. Lecter entices his guests with refined cuisine only to be feeding them the body parts of friends and colleagues in disguise. For instance, when police found the remains of Lecter's ninth victim, a flutist for Baltimore Philharmonic Orchestra named Benjamin Raspail, his body was missing its thymus, pancreas, and part of the heart. "Baltimore Homicide believed that these items appeared on the menu of a dinner Lecter gave for the president and the conductor of the Baltimore Philharmonic on the evening following Raspail's disappearance" (27). While incarcerated, Lecter can no longer give dinner parties, but he can torment people psychologically by feeding them false hope—"to get their hopes up" again and again. As Crawford explains to Clarice, this type of torment is Lecter's "nourishment" (131). He savors the ultimate disappointment and consequences of such manipulation, and this seems fitting for his role as a psychiatrist. In jest, Freud once compared psychoanalysts to cannibals, and critic Barbara Creed uses this notion to link Freud's theories with horror: "Freud theorized the concept of the repressed, conflicted individual: the horror film made the repressed, divided self the subject of its narratives. [...] Both set out to explore beneath the surface, to look into the self, to determine the extent to which the modern subject was able to embrace or recognize the dark, nonhuman, animal self" (192). Such duality characterizes the economic narrative of *The Silence of the Lambs*, which inverts the humanity and civility assumed of the upper echelon, and exposes it as ruthlessly cannibalistic.

Finally, Lecter's inability to control his appetite for human flesh also satirizes America's contradictory eating habits. Just as Gumb wants freedom from what he perceives to be the oppressiveness of being the wrong gender, Lecter longs to eat without restraint and without the condemnation of society. Not surprisingly, he appropriates butterfly imagery at the very moment of his escape.[46] After he eviscerates Lieutenant Boyle, one of the officers assigned to watch him in Tennessee, Lecter stages his body to emulate the flight of a butterfly. Moments before several police officers enter the room with Lecter's temporary holding cell, the shadowy outline of a butterfly appears through the frosted glass of the door. Inside, a low-angle shot reveals Boyle's body high above the ground, his open arms spread wing-like as if in flight. The red-white-and-blue cloth fastening Boyle's body in place provides the illusion of wings, and it suggests that Lecter has now achieved the colorful beauty of a butterfly himself, completing his transformation from captivity to freedom. The colors of the American flag cast Lecter as fulfilling the country's promise for freedom and opportunity, yet against this backdrop, it also presents "the American character, for all its lofty collective and individual aspirations, [. . . as] voraciously murderous to itself and others" (Simpson 42–43). This argument can be applied to food as well. Ultimately, this meal, as well as the meal he plans to make of Dr. Chilton in the closing moments of the film, satirizes the eating desires of many Americans: to eat as much of whatever you want without consequences. This is the freedom that Lecter hungers for. This is the freedom that many Americans sought as they walked down aisles of supermarkets, drove past fast-food restaurants, shopped in bulk, and stared at a seemingly endless array of junk food at almost every convenience store.

American Psycho

"All I Seem to Want to Do Is Workout [. . .] and Secure Restaurant Reservations":
Fine Dining and Killer Bodies in American Psycho

The presidency did not change much about Jimmy Carter. With his reputation for frugality and simple living, it did not surprise people that he purchased a $175 suit off the rack for his own inauguration, that he insisted on cleaning his personal residence in the White House, and that he carried his own suitcases while traveling. Likewise, cabinet members couldn't have been too shocked to learn that having lunch at the White House meant receiving a bill as they left (Kleinknecht 54–55). Such practices aligned with the sentiments of his "Crisis of Confidence" (or "Malaise") speech in the summer of 1979. In response to the energy crisis causing gasoline shortages, long lines for fuel, and skyrocketing prices, President Carter admonished the wasteful materialism that preoccupied American society:

> In a nation that was proud of hard work, strong families, close-knit communities, and our faith in God, too many of us now tend to worship self-indulgence and consumption. Human identity is no longer defined by what one does, but by what one owns. But we've discovered that owning things and consuming things does not satisfy our longing for meaning. We've learned that piling up material goods cannot fulfill the emptiness of lives which have no confidence or purpose.[47]

As the following election and decade would demonstrate, however, Carter could not have been more wrong. His failed bid for a second term signaled, in part, that Americans were not ready to abandon their unwavering faith in consumerism. They still found meaning in material goods and in the promise—no matter how illusive—that anyone could become wealthy. In fact,

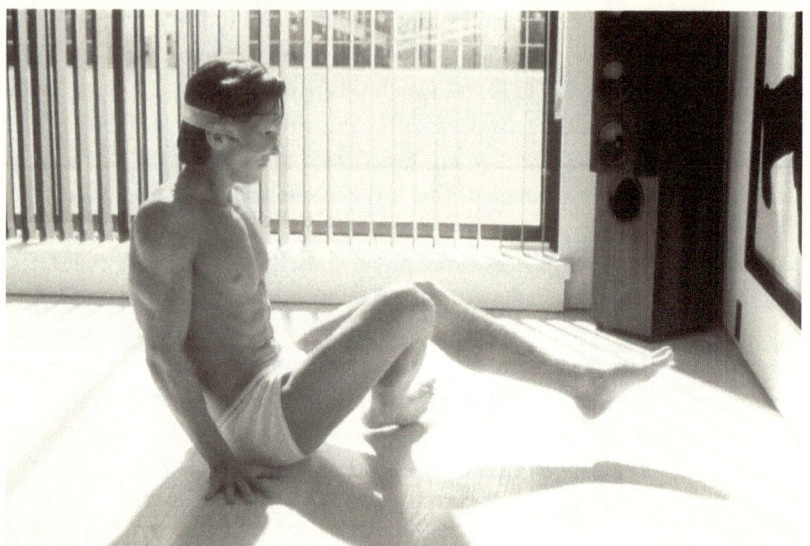

For Patrick Bateman (Christian Bale), one can never do enough sit-ups. Mary Harron's *American Psycho* (2000). Lions Gate Films/Photofest. © Lions Gate Films.

even though a 1983 Gallup poll showed that 70 percent of the public viewed Ronald Reagan as more invested in the rich than in average Americans, they also found comfort in his claims about economic prosperity for all. As he explained during a speech in the same year, "What I want to see above all is that this remains a country where someone can always get rich."[48] This sentiment—along with his film career—shaped the image Reagan projected during the campaign and his presidency. He appealed to a public seeking a leader that embodied optimism and grandeur, encouraged extravagance over moderation, and extoled American exceptionalism.

Ronald Reagan's first inauguration in 1981 certainly announced a dramatic shift in tone from the previous administration. The four-day celebration cost approximately $11 million, and it included 800,000 fireworks, nine inaugural balls (with a ticket price of $250 per person), 14,400 bottles of champagne, 400,000 hors d'oeuvres, and over $13,000 in roses (Mills 16). Nor was this event tailored for modest clothing. Nancy Reagan spent approximately $25,000 on her wardrobe, including a hand-beaded ball gown, "a full-length mink coat by Maximilian, a New York furrier, valued at $8,000 to $12,000; and a $1,650 American alligator handbag by Judith Leiber" (Kleinknecht 55). (She would nearly double these expenses for the second inauguration.[49]) This extravaganza was followed by a costly $44.6 million renovation of the White House and Mrs. Reagan's personal efforts to raise $1 million for redecorating the residence. The First Lady wanted new China dinnerware as well, and "the Lenox pattern with a raised gold presidential seal in the center that [. . . she] chose came to $209,508 for 220 place settings" (Mills 11). No visitor would be billed for a meal at this White House.

Reagan's presidency prided itself on opulence and ostentation. It extoled the virtues of free-market capitalism, deregulation, and self-interest. And it equated money with hard work and power. As historian William Kleinknecht has argued, it sent a message "that the blind pursuit of wealth was not tawdry or immoral but a supreme human virtue" (57). It is not entirely surprising that the yuppie (young urban professional) emerged as the ideal consumer during this era, embodying the president's ethos that making the rich richer would ultimately benefit the economy and trickle down to the middle classes. Conspicuous consumption became the aspirational goal for most Americans, and a figure like Donald Trump in the 1980s, who branded his name on buildings, planes, yachts, and by the twenty-first century food items such as vodka, bottled water, and steaks, became its patron saint.[50]

This valorization of wealth coincided with a denigration of the poor, and the Reagan administration instituted draconian policies to punish anyone it perceived as preferring government assistance to hard work. For Reagan, welfare hindered the unemployed from seeking jobs, and poor people went to soup kitchens simply because the food was free. Not surprisingly, his $41.2 billion cuts to the federal budget in 1982 targeted a wide range of social assistance programs, including aid provided for housing, mental health, unemployment, and food. Approximately 400,000 households, for instance, were no longer eligible for food stamps. Such cuts did not prevent a dramatic increase in military spending and reductions in corporate taxes, however: "Many large companies with huge profits, like General Electric, would pay zero taxes over the next several years, or even get money back from the federal government. By 1983 the portion of the federal tax receipts derived from corporate income taxes would drop to an all-time low of 6.2 percent, down from 32.1 percent in 1952 and 12.5 percent in 1980" (Kleinknecht 29). Likewise, individual tax cuts predominately benefited the wealthiest Americans with the top 1 percent paying 14.1 percent less while the bottom 20 percent paid 16.1 percent more (Farris 332). Yet the image of extreme wealth—particularly its association with success, power, and social value—trumped the reality of socioeconomic inequity, for the wealthy alone were not responsible for Reagan's election and reelection. In fact, the 1984 election gave Reagan and Bush overwhelming victories among the working classes. As Nicolaus Mills notes, "54 percent of blue-collar workers, 59 percent of white-collar workers, and 57 percent of those with incomes between $12,500 and $24,999" voted for

Reagan and Bush. "They were voting for a culture they saw as hopeful and with which they identified, even when it failed to benefit them directly" (28).

Hollywood certainly promoted this economic optimism. *Secret of My Success* (1987) offers one example of the financial fantasy shaping the 1980s. This romantic comedy, about a midwestern college graduate who poses as a Wall Street executive, not only perpetuates the myth that anyone (even a guy in the mailroom) can become a wealthy CEO, but it also valorizes the era's investment in image culture. Brantley Foster (Michael J. Fox) assumes the identity of a newly hired executive, Carlton Whitfield, by taking over an empty office and wearing a suit. Much the same way Superman disrobes in telephone booths (to fight for "truth, justice, and the American way!"), Foster/Whitfield uses an elevator to change between formal suits and casual wear (such as khaki pants, white sneakers, and T-shirts). His move between the mailroom and the boardroom, however, has nothing to do with helping others or fighting for justice. It reflects the American way of the eighties: pursuing wealth for wealth's sake. Casting Michael J. Fox was also a nod to his role on the hit television series *Family Ties* (1982–1989), which garnered Fox three Emmys for Outstanding Actor by 1988. The show revolves around his character, Alex P. Keaton, who embodies the economic values of the Reagan era. Alex is an ambitious yuppie who dreams of amassing a Trump-like bank account, but his family inspires moments of personal insight that humanize Alex, making him recognize familial love as more valuable than materialism. The ties of family, the show suggests, can keep any future Wall Street broker ethically grounded.

The publication of Bret Easton Ellis's *American Psycho* in 1991 offered a radically different vision of 1980s America. It expressed a deep-seated disillusionment with the impact of Reagan's economic and social policies. In the wake of a savings and loan scandal that cost taxpayers an estimated $500 billion and created a federal deficit of $2 trillion (Calavita 1), the excesses of the era inspired Ellis to transform Alex P. Keaton into a cannibalistic serial killer by the name of Patrick Bateman. Bateman, a Wall Street financier with an encyclopedic knowledge of consumer products, wears the trappings of socioeconomic success to mask a xenophobic, racist, homophobic, and misogynistic desire to kill. The sixty-chapter book traces the pointless wanderings of Bateman and his friends, a group of superficial yuppies that care more about wearing the right clothes, sculpting an ideal body, and eating at the hottest restaurants than each other. In this portrait of 1980s New York, image is everything. It seems particularly fitting that Bateman's obsession with seeing his hero Donald Trump never materializes and that the televised appearances of Ronald Reagan and George H. W. Bush can neither be heard nor understood: "The TV is turned to a press conference Reagan's giving but there's a lot of static and no one pays attention" (142); "On the screen now are scenes from President Bush's inauguration early this year, then a speech from former President Reagan [. . .]. Soon a tiresome debate [in the bar] forms over whether he's lying or not, even though we don't, can't, hear the words" (396). The stumbling shift in verbs here—from "don't" to "can't"—implies that Bateman and his Wall Street colleagues simply refuse to hear any renunciation of a president whose policies have ensured their financial success and power.

Bateman not only embodies the benefits of deregulation and tax breaks for the wealthiest Americans, but he has also internalized the ideology shaping Reagan's social policies toward the poor. Bateman notes, for instance, that "beggars and homeless seemed to have multiplied [. . .] and the ranks of the unfortunate, weak, and aged lined the streets everywhere" (278), but this observation does not inspire any sympathy. His ruthless attitude toward them remains consistent throughout the novel, manifesting itself in mockery, chastisement ("I try to lecture her on the merits of getting a job somewhere" [163]), and all types of torment including vivid fantasies about maiming and killing them. In this way, Ellis casts Bateman's serial-killing impulses as a metaphor for a financial system that benefited the wealthiest Americans at the expense of the poor. As Georgina Colby has noted, Bateman's "crimes, in their extreme subjective violence, reveal the true representation of the systemic violence of the [capitalistic] apparatus [. . .] as well as the obscene underside of Republican ideology and the social actuality of the 1980s" (69). Bateman—who specializes in mergers and acquisitions—even refers to his own job as "murder and executions mostly" (206), and according to Leigh Claire La Berge, "this descriptive, metaphorical language of finance [. . .] from 'the killings' to the 'hostile' acts to the 'takeover defenses'" shapes and drives *American Psycho* (124).

By crafting a novel without plot and characterization, Ellis challenges readers to find significance in these vapid characters with their interchangeable bodies, mundane conversations, and exhausting materialism. Bateman's "aesthetics of boredom," as Julian Murphet describes them,[51] lend themselves to the metaphorical, and it quickly becomes clear that Bateman's desire for more products, more workout sessions, and more restaurant reservations embodies the serial appetites of America. As Sonia Baelo Allué has persuasively argued, "*American Psycho* denounces consumerism by portraying the serial killer as the ultimate consumer. [. . .] Bateman's never-ending serial killings mirror our own never-ending serial consumerism" (88). Although Ellis presents these murders with unsettling, realistic detail, basing them on actual accounts of crimes by Ed Gein and Ted Bundy,[52] for instance, they most likely reflect the imaginings of Bateman, a "fantasization of a general class violence toward everything that is not white, male and upper-middle class" (Murphet 43).

When placed in the context of fat and food politics, Ellis's novel also operates as a social document about the cultural anxieties surrounding fitness, fatness, and eating culture at the time. The overriding theme of *American Psycho*, for Jennifer Brown, "is the self-cannibalizing aspects of 1980s capitalism" (182), and Bateman's consumerism, which seeks to preserve his toned, youthful body at all costs, has indeed eaten away his sense of individual identity. Not following the "right" workout routine and eating junk food, therefore, take on great significance for the characters in this book. It becomes tantamount to rejecting the bodily ideals they rely on for self-definition. In this way, Bateman's investment in working out, which reduces everyone to "hardbodies," and his preoccupation with fine dining that devolves into cannibalism capture Ellis's indictment of a culture that commodifies the body, fuels intolerance, and fosters a callous indifference to suffering.

"Mirror, Mirror, on the Wall, Who's the Fairest of Them All?": Hardbodies and Workout Culture

Norman Bates, from Robert Bloch's 1959 novel *Psycho*, hates mirrors. Unlike Anthony Perkins in Alfred Hitchcock's 1960 adaptation, the Norman described by Bloch is a forty-year-old, bespectacled, fat man whose alcoholism exacerbates his schizophrenia and multiple personality disorder. Norman has internalized a value system that fosters a hatred of his own body. He recalls deriving pleasure from looking at his naked reflection until his mother derides this "nasty" habit and strikes him with a silver-handled hairbrush. Subsequently, Norman's discomfort with his own sexuality gets linked with fatness: "It *was* nasty [. . .] to peek at the blubbery fat, the short hairless arms, the big belly, and underneath it—" (91). He also imagines his mother describing him as "a big, fat, overgrown Mama's Boy" (15), and he admits that seeing himself in the mirror makes him wish to be "somebody else. Somebody who was tall and lean and handsome" (91). He wants the type of body mainstream America, including his own mother, finds attractive. By describing her fiancé as "the best-looking figure of a man you ever saw" (92), Mrs. Bates emphasizes the importance of physical appearance over individual character, and this detail reminds Norman of the way his body marginalizes him. Not surprisingly, he develops an aversion to mirrors. He even dislikes his weekly ritual of shaving "because of the mirrors. It had those wavy lines in it. All mirrors seemed to have wavy lines that hurt his eyes" (91). This distorted reflection reveals his fragmented identity as Norman/Norma, son/mother, boy/man, murderer/victim, and fat/thin. His relationship with mirrors and bodily image also adds another dimension to Mary Crane's murder,[53] for just moments before her decapitation, Norman watches her "flaunting" (62) her naked body, her *"damned* good figure" (41), in front of a mirror. The pleasure she takes in her appearance becomes an additional source of rage for Norman. He punishes her for possessing a beautiful body and for being comfortable with her own sexuality.

On the opposite end of the spectrum, Patrick Bateman can't get enough of mirrors. Every glimpse of his reflection validates the carefully constructed image he relies on for self-definition and social importance. At an impromptu dinner party in his girlfriend Evelyn's apartment, for instance, Bateman sees himself "in a mirror hung on the wall [. . .] smiling at how good I look" (11), and moments later he notices Evelyn gazing at "her reflection in the vanity mirror" (13). With his love of mirrors, Bateman is a far cry from Norman Bates, whose violence remains confined to the house/motel and whose "horror [. . .] was in his head" (Bloch 171); Bateman is an "American" psycho. His obsessions, which include working out to sculpt the perfect body, point to a disturbing cultural trend. Self-scrutiny had become the central preoccupation in the eighties, and Ellis uses mirrors to satirize this type of narcissism. Conspicuous consumption had transformed the body into an object that determined one's social value and demanded constant maintenance. It also enabled the misogyny and sexism of Bateman and his ilk. Women get reduced to "hardbodies" just as Bateman is valued for his toned abs, rock-hard chest, muscular arms, and extensive knowledge of sweater vests. For Ellis, this valorization of surfaces enables violence. Whether the violence of an inequitable financial system, racism, sexual assault, masochistic exercise routines, or fantasies about killing, consumerism in the 1980s fueled a monstrous appetite for more at the expense of others.

The mirrors in fitness clubs offer one example of an exercise culture that perpetuates an oppressive preoccupation with the body. Bateman's description of his "health" club, Xclusive, lists its virtues much the same way he talks about consumer goods:

> They carry the latest weight machines (Nautilus, Universal, Keiser), [. . .] ten courts for tennis and racquetball, aerobics classes, four aerobic dances studios, two swimming pools, Lifecycles, a Gravitron machine, rowing machines, treadmills, cross-country skiing machines, one-on-one training, cardiovascular evaluations, personalized programs, sauna and steam rooms, a sun deck, tanning booths, and a café with a juice bar, all of it designed by J. J. Vogel, who designed the new Norman Preager club, Petty's. Membership runs five thousand dollars annually. (67)

This brochure-like catalog reflects Bateman's narrative style, mimicking a marketplace designed to overwhelm one with quantity. While the sheer scope of offerings here is outrageous even by Manhattan standards, this club illustrates the value elite clientele place on excess. Its ten tennis courts, two swimming pools, and four dance studios signal the way American consumerism had become about displaying wealth, not need. The gym simply reminds members of their access to whatever they want whenever they want it. It comes as little surprise that Bateman ends this list by mentioning the architect's name and the club's exorbitant annual fee. Xclusive's primary appeal stems from the social status associated with membership along with its tacit promise of excluding the lower classes. It becomes another named product—a tool for communicating Bateman's elitism.

Inside, conspicuous consumption gets mapped onto the body, and much like the club's decision to remodel three times in two years, the shiny, new equipment reinforces the importance placed on remodeling the self. Bateman can't even enjoy a U2 concert because Bono's body "is not worked out enough, there's no muscle tone" (146). Just as Bateman changes from his "six button double-breasted chalk-striped suit by Ralph Lauren" into "a pair of crow-black cotton and Lycra shorts [. . .] and Lycra tank top, both by Wilkes" (67, 68), workout culture promises bodily transformation through the right equipment and obsessive commitment. Bateman offers almost daily accounts of two-hour workouts (156, 161), "stretching exercises" (26, 73), "abdominal crunches [. . .], push-ups, [. . . running] in place" (76), and "aerobics class" (97). These workouts parallel his hunger for more products and a more perfect body. Not surprisingly, Bateman scrutinizes his appearance in the club mirror *before* entering the gym: "I check myself in the mirror [. . .] and, dissatisfied, go back to my briefcase for some mousse to slick my hair back and then I use a moisturizer" (68). Working out at Xclusive seems predicated on already possessing the perfect body. It is a place to display one's unblemished skin, slicked hair, and muscular form, not to achieve it. In this way, Ellis mocks an exercise ethos motivated by appearance, not health and fitness.

Workout culture spills into other public and private spaces as well, for Ellis's characters constantly surveille bodily "imperfections" such as aging and fatness. Given the premium placed on appearance, a relentless self-scrutiny compels them never to stray too far from a mirror. Bateman notes the way he and his friends frequently "[inspect their] reflections [. . . until] satisfied" at clubs and restaurants (59). In the privacy of his own bathroom, Bateman endlessly studies his "hair line in the mirror" (310) or fixes it "in front of the Orobwener mirror [. . . by smoothing] some mousse into it and then [running] a comb over the mousse" (212). On one hand, he inadvertently equates his hair and skin with consumerism itself. We never see Bateman's natural, untreated skin and hair. Instead, the descriptions of his body primarily come from observations

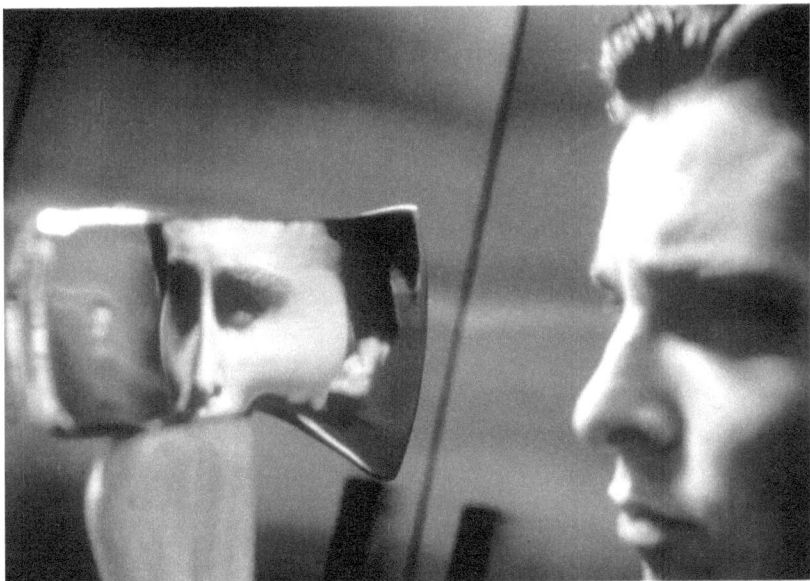

Patrick Bateman's distorted reflection in *American Psycho* (2000). Lions Gate Films/Photofest. © Lions Gate Films.

about his mirrored reflection, and they tend to be presented as an ongoing advertisement for products such as vitamin-enriched revitalizing shampoos, scalp-cleansing agents, thinning-hair supplements, shaving cream, moisturizers, skin lotions, and "anti-aging eye balm" (27–28). Such pedantic lists and didactic advice function as a straw man, focusing our attention not on the individual but on his assiduously constructed image. Many of these items—listed by name—claim to preserve one's youth since dry, flaky skin "makes [the face] look dull and older" (27). For Ellis, they reflect a cultural hostility toward the body that suggests an unnatural attempt to control or eliminate aging.

On the other hand, Bateman's obsession with youth-preserving products parallels his investment in workout culture to achieve another crucial marker for youthfulness—the thin, toned body. Household mirrors not only allow Bateman's social circle to inspect and evaluate their own bodies ad nauseam, but they also encourage turning a critical gaze on others. During Evelyn's party at the opening of the novel, she studies herself in the vanity mirror before scrutinizing Tim Price's reflection:

> "Have you been gaining weight, Tim?" Evelyn asks thoughtfully. She studies Tim's head in the mirror and says, "Your face looks . . . rounder. [. . .] Are you losing your hair? [. . .] Are you gaining weight?" She asks, more seriously this time.

> "Jesus," Tim says, about to turn away, offended. "No, Evelyn."
> "Your face definitely looks . . . rounder," Evelyn says. "Less . . . chiseled."
> "I don't believe this." Tim again.
> He looks deep into the mirror. She continues brushing her hair but the strokes are less definite because she's looking at Tim. (21)

Gaining weight, like losing one's hair, operates as a sign of diminished social value and sexual appeal. While Price appears rounder, it is also rumored that another friend, Van Patten, has stopped working out because he appears "puffy" (50). Such assessments matter to this group because fatness justifies marginalization ("this fat bastard couldn't possibly have gotten into the fucking Groucho Club" [387]). It transforms one into a spectacle ("This morning's topic on *The Patty Winters Show* was People Who Weigh Over Seven Hundred Pounds—What Can We Do About Them?" [283]). And it reveals the potential horror of not working out.

Evelyn's comments about Price's body occur while grooming herself in front of a mirror, and Ellis again uses this detail to reinforce the importance of outward appearance for these characters. Evelyn never speaks to Price or Bateman directly during this scene, only to their reflections, and her words inspire them to withdraw from each other. Price "looks deep into the mirror" (21), and Bateman, after revealing his suspicion about Evelyn and Tim's affair, puts his muscular, thin body on display. Later that evening, while lying in bed with Evelyn and watching the Home Shopping Club on television, Bateman asks why she doesn't date Price since he is rich, good-looking, and "has a great body" (23). Unconcerned with any possible emotional need on his part, Evelyn does not disabuse him of a possible affair. Instead, she matter-of-factly explains that these qualities have become ubiquitous, functioning as prerequisites for success and attractiveness.

Evelyn's problem stems, in part, from the fact that everyone looks like everyone else, so it no longer matters whom she socializes with, dates, or even marries. The physical qualities privileged by her social circle de-individualize them. No wonder they continually misidentify each other: "'The dude who called you Hamilton,' Price says. 'That wasn't Conrad,' I say. 'Are you sure? It looked a helluva lot like him'" (50); "The Chandelier Room is packed and everyone looks familiar, everyone looks the same" (61). The very consumer culture that pressures them to wear the same clothing, use the same skin products, and invest in elite gym memberships has crafted an ideal body type that sacrifices individuality for sameness. They have all become interchangeable, carbon copies of one another, forged by a shared obsession with body types and material goods.

Even though Bateman recognizes this problem to some extent ("I keep studying her face, bored by how beautiful it is, flawless really" [123]), he tries to reestablish his status in Evelyn's life through his body. He places her hand on his torso, "wanting her to feel how rock-hard, how *halved* my stomach is, and I flex the muscles, grateful it's light in the room so she can see how bronzed and defined my abdomen has become" (23). At this moment, he transforms himself into a poster boy for Xclusive or another object on the Home Shopping Club. Yet this investment in image, as Ellis suggests, is as artificial and fragile as the Zirconia and glass dolls being advertised on television (24). Measuring one's worth in terms of youthful muscularity cannot, of course, be sustained, but 1980s America pressured the public to try. As Evelyn reminds Bateman after an unsuccessful attempt at sex, "you can always be in better shape," and "your hairline looks like it's receding" (24). Ellis concludes the chapter with Bateman masturbating, and he admits that he can only come when thinking of "a near-naked model in a halter top I saw today in a Calvin Klein advertisement" (24). Despite all of the efforts Bateman, Evelyn, and their friends put into maintaining "perfect" bodies, no one experiences sensual pleasure in *American Psycho*. No one has mutually satisfying sex or experiences genuine emotion or love. Aloofness and disconnection, as the solipsistic act of masturbation suggests, characterizes their lives. The inauthentic (a model from a print ad) generates more pleasure than the real thing.

This emphasis on appearance points to the dangerous link between objectification and violence. One source of the problem, as discussed earlier, stems from workout culture's tendency to reduce women to "hardbodies." Through this term, Ellis makes clear that the misogyny of Bateman and his cronies has been forged by their investment in physical fitness. They agree unilaterally that "a good personality [. . .] consists of a chick who has a little hardbody and who will satisfy all sexual demands without being too slutty about things and who will essentially keep her dumb mouth *shut*" (91). The reflexive use of "hardbody" signals the way this ideal has made it easier to reduce women to silent, sexualized objects. Though "being too slutty" is not defined here, the context implies any type of female agency when it comes to sexuality such as expressing or acting on desire. "Hardbody" may in fact be the most frequently used word in the novel, appearing forty times, and it does so in conjunction with a pattern of reducing women to body parts such as breasts, buttocks, blonde hair, and "tan and aerobicized legs" (212). Bateman even scoffs at the notion that a woman's breasts can be too large: "The topic [of *The Patty Winters Show*] was Big Breasts and there was a woman on it who had a breast *reduction* since she thought her tits were too big—dumb bitch"

(68). Substituting the word "tits" for "breasts" removes any association with the nourishing function of feeding a baby, and the term *bitch* equates her with a dog in heat.

Additionally, lists of women's physical features often get followed by detailed descriptions of clothing. It seems fitting that only brand names appear as frequently as the term *hardbody* in American Psycho. Body type has become another accessory like Bateman's favorite fashion designer Giorgio Armani, whose products get mentioned forty times as well. For Elana Gomel, *American Psycho* is about "fashion [. . . and] the sociology of appearance," arguing that "brand names constitute the only reality in the world of simulacra. [. . .] This is a world without depth, truth, or knowledge; a world in which clothes and appearances become the only currency of social and epistemological exchange" (50, 52). The currency of high fashion, in other words, represents one's socioeconomic status, ensures sexual desirability, reveals an allegiance to consumerism, and signals an investment in fitness. One needs the "right" clothes to showcase the "right" body, and in the reductionist world of Bateman's America, these surfaces constitute identity.

By contrast, hardbody identity makes any deviation from this standard unacceptable. When checking out one waitress, Bateman observes: "though her knees do support long, tan legs, I can't help noticing that one knee is, admittedly, bigger than the other one. The left knee is knobbier, almost imperceptibly thicker than the right knee, and this unnoticeable flaw now seems overwhelming and we all lose interest" (48). The focus on her knee is telling. Joints can't be altered by a fitness regimen. They serve a critical function, connecting bones, tissue, and muscle to enable movement, and movement is central to one's autonomy. The disgust of these men, therefore, reveals a preference for women to be silent and immobile. While Bateman's clique assumes that women with personality, intelligence, or a sense of humor must be "ugly," female mobility—and by implication freedom—discomforts them unless it functions in the service of attracting men.

Fatness is, of course, the worst deviation from the hardbody, for it suggests a tacit or explicit rejection of 1980s workout culture and an image-based value system. Bateman describes one girl as "dumpy" simply for being five pounds overweight, and two girls from New Jersey get referred to as "cows" (112, 147). Fatness provides just another metric for holding women to unreasonable standards. Not surprisingly, Bateman gets perturbed by the socioeconomic deviation that the fat body tends to suggest. Slightly overweight women, like the "dumpy" girl in her "baggy, nondescript sweater" and another slightly "overweight [woman], wearing a jogging suit—from where, Bloomingdale's?" (112, 84), violate both Bateman's sensibility regarding hardbodies and consumerism. Non-designer, loose-fitting clothes fly in the face of his expectations for sexual attractiveness and elitist taste. If these women cannot afford gym memberships, haute cuisine, and designer clothing, they expose an unsettling economic inequity in the United States. If they invest in a workout regimen without the desired results, their bodies give lie to the promise of perpetual transformation through consumerism.

"I'm Not Really Hungry, but I Would Like to Have a Reservation Somewhere":
Fine Dining, Junk Food, and Cannibalism

Despite the popularity of drugstore lunch counters, lunch wagons, and prefabricated diners during the 1940s, a resurgence in upper-class dining emerged in the 1950s. Le Pavillion, arguably the most prominent French restaurant in the United States, opened its doors on East 55th Street and Fifth Avenue in 1941, and many of its chefs who trained under owner Henri Soulé began opening their own high-end restaurants in the mid-1950s. Increased international travel, made easier by the advent of transatlantic flights in 1959, fueled an even greater interest in French cuisine.[55] Following in the footsteps of James Beard, whose cooking show *I Love to Eat* premiered in 1946, Julia Child's best-selling book *Mastering the Art of French Cooking* (1961) inspired her Emmy and Peabody award-winning television show *The French Chef*, which premiered two years later and ran for ten years in the United States. The 1970s was an important decade in the history of restaurants as well, beginning with the opening of Chez Panisse in Berkeley and the close of Le Pavillion in the same year, 1971. Chez Panisse, though not the first American restaurant to emphasize regionality and local ingredients, changed the way people thought about French cuisine. It abandoned dark décor and stuffy formality for tree-house charm and the sunny, blue skies of Northern California. As Paul Freedman explains in *Food in Time and Place*, "What Chez Panisse accomplished and what has made it so influential is its combination of its social agenda (against the processed foods industry and for attention to where food comes from), delight (in the primacy of taste), and the application of French notions of *terrior* to American agriculture and foraging" (269). This offered a stark contrast to the trend in American restaurants of the 1970s and 1980s, "which was to gloss over the quality of ingredients in favor of variety, complexity, setting, or other diversions" (269).

Despite the decline of French restaurants in the early 1980s (due to economic considerations and competition from other culinary styles), the ostentation and conspicuous consumption of the Reagan era helped make elite dining thrive. Spending money in noteworthy places where one could be noticed became an aspirational goal throughout the decade. It comes as little surprise that Bateman's clique, while shunning French restaurants for being out of fashion (though some places serve dishes influenced by this cuisine), anguish over getting a table at the most exclusive restaurants in New York City. As he explains at one point, "all I seem to want to do now is workout [. . .] and secure restaurant reservations at new restaurants I've already been to, then cancel them" (300). The act of getting and then canceling reservations validates Bateman's sense of superiority. He can showcase his status but also make an equally important display of self-importance by turning down those opportunities. After all the lengthy debates about where to go and the countless phone calls to find a table, these characters seem fundamentally uninterested in food. Restaurants only serve a social function in the text. Certainly the small portions (which often get removed too quickly) don't satiate them. Although Bateman could not be labeled a foodie by any stretch of the imagination, his obsessive need to appear at these restaurants enables him to translate food into another acquisition: popular currency. Being seen at the "right" restaurant becomes an act—much like owning a new stereo system or sports car—that other wealthy, self-important people can witness.

Bateman's social craving for high-end dining mandates a familiarity with the latest restaurant reviews in order to determine where to go and what opinions to have—even before taking a bite. Yet all of the attention Bateman pays to haute cuisine does not help him develop a refined palate or any real knowledge of cooking. He admits at one point that "I can't tell if I'm cooking any of this correctly, because I'm crying too hard and I have never really cooked anything before" (346). He also does not know the difference between broiled and roasted, and neither does one dinner companion who thinks broiled scallops "involve . . . a pan" (107). In fact, not a single meal in *American Psycho* is savored, enjoyed, or appreciated. Despite detailed descriptions of menu items and various dishes, Bateman rarely comments on how something tastes, and even though he notes the aroma of perfumes, blood, human flesh, garbage, and carbon monoxide, he never mentions the smell of food inside restaurants. Only the overwhelming scent of someone's cologne draws his attention to it: "The sickening scent of Drakkar Noir [. . .] floats over near my face, mingling with the scent of the marmalade and cilantro, the onions and the blackened chilies" (140). As a result, these meals, like the places serving them, come across as having no more substance than words printed on a menu. His dry recitations of dishes with unusual ingredients thus have more to do with popular as opposed to physiological tastes, so he simply mirrors the language of restaurant reviews from *New York* magazine and the *Times*—though without the flair and sense of humor (10).[55]

In a 1985 review of Arizona, where the fictional Bateman attends a Christmas party, the pioneering foodie and restaurant critic Gael Greene describes some of the more wacky combinations on the menu: "Jalapeño chutney and sweet-potato fries. Ravioli in ancho-pepper cream. Grilled salmon on warm salad of radicchio, papaya, and jicama. [. . .] And the pounded potato with crabmeat and capered, papaya'd sour cream is an unholy alliance that cannot be tolerated intellectually even though it tastes good" (100, 101). She also admits that "the farfetched matings make you giggle. [. . .] But before storming Arizona, be warned: There are no reservations. The tables are tiny, unbalanced, and close. [. . .] The kitchen can be slow, even . . . very slow" (100).[56] A 1991 *New York* magazine feature on Orso, which Bateman references twice, also emphasizes its popularity, noting people turned away at the door and listing some of the famous personalities who dine there such as Billy Joel, Stockard Channing, Michelle Pfeiffer, and Gregory Peck (David 43). The article even mentions the famed financial banker and mergers-and-acquisitions specialist, Felix Rohatyn: "Liz Rohaytn is here, passing a gelato—right under Felix's nose—to a woman across the table. 'Divine, isn't it,' says one of them with a little gasp of satisfaction" (40). And a 1983 review of Texarkana makes similar observations about its food, crowded dining room, and exotic décor: "The dining room, with walls painted almost exactly the creamy coral color of the restaurant's pungent crawfish etouffee, is reminiscent of the sort of Creole courtyard found in the French Quarter of New Orleans. Those who prefer to see and not to be seen may want tables on the balcony that rims the intensely noisy and jampacked main dining room. [. . .] Enjoy some excellent barbecues based on beef (prime rib steak or peppery tenderloin), veal chops that remain miraculously moist, tender lamb chops and boned chicken, all given a mellow burnishing by the mesquite wood charcoal" (Sheraton). These types of sources explain Bateman's sole interest in haute cuisine. It has nothing to do with eating, and he never mentions actual food as a reason to try or return to a restaurant.

Such reviews inform Bateman's reaction to almost every restaurant in the novel: listing exotic dishes, seeking out celebrities, basking in a place's popularity, expressing frustration over reservations, and complaining about slow service. After studying the menu at Texarkana, for instance, Bateman says, "Hmmm, I see they've omitted the pork loin with lime Jell-O" (215). At Arcadia, Bateman claims to have developed a taste for pilot fish before ordering "the pilot fish with tulips and cinnamon." And he practically goes into a paroxysm when someone describes a simple meal of roasted chicken and cheesecake at a high-end restaurant in Phoenix, Arizona: "'Cheesecake?' I say, confused by this plain, alien-sounding list. 'What sauces or fruits were on the roasted chicken? What shapes was it cut into? [. . .] And the cheesecake, what flavor? Was it heated? [. . .] Ricotta cheesecake? Goat cheese? Were there flowers or cilantro in it?'" To this, his friend replies: "'It was just regular,' he says, and then, 'Patrick, you're sweating'" (107). The shape and garnish matter more than the meal itself. Not surprisingly, Bateman never asks if anyone enjoys the food. This omission distinguishes him from the restaurant reviews on which he relies. He would *never* prefer, as Sheraton notes, to "see and not be seen," and the moistness of veal chops, the temperature of a salad, and the aroma of crawfish stew would go completely unremarked by Bateman. As McDermott notes when they bring him sushi instead of sashimi, "You don't come here for the food anyway" (48). This comment embodies Bateman's entire relationship with elite dining. He cares only about the name of the restaurant and the cost. This pleasureless eating, thus, offers another example of the way conspicuous consumption has robbed him of his humanity.[57]

These meals prove so dissatisfying that Bateman resorts to fast food, junk food, and ultimately cannibalism to feel satiated. This shift—from haute to junk, from meat to human flesh—encapsulates the novel's most searing critique of the consumer impulses that shape eating and dieting practices in 1980s America. When Bateman encounters a homeless man with a sign reading "I AM HUNGRY AND HOMELESS PLEASE HEP ME" (128), he offers money and food only to assault him for not having a job, for violating an ideal body type (with his "heavyset" frame and "triple chin"), and for his poor fashion sense ("polyester pantsuit with washed-out Sergio Valente jeans"; 129). Bateman then uses a knife to maim him, and he compares this sensation to working out or "that first line of cocaine, inhaled the first puff of a fine cigar, sipped that first glass of Cristal" (132). Despite the elitist element of these addictive substances, Bateman does not get a meal at Nell's after the assault (though he is "starving") or a drink at Indochine; instead, "I decide to go somewhere Al would go, the McDonald's in Union Square. Standing in line, I order a vanilla milk shake [. . .] After two more milk shakes my high slowly dissolves" (132). Bateman chooses sugar over alcohol, tobacco, or cocaine here. Along with his earlier decision to snort *Sweet'n Low* instead of cocaine at Tunnel and his preference for Diet Pepsi (over caffeine-free Diet Coke)[58] for "[mixing] better with rum and [having] a lower sodium content" (97), sugar and sugar substitutes are presented as drugs. Together they represent the fundamental tension between excess and restraint in America. For Ellis, dieting culture has trapped people into substituting one type of unhealthy addiction for another. Diet Pepsi and rum, for instance, merely create the illusion of making a healthy choice in the context of something already addictive. Once Bateman imagines crossing the line into violence with the homeless man, he can set aside his own class snobbery to consume fast food. Violating one social taboo (violence) enables another (foregoing his diet).

Cannibalism becomes Ellis's most disturbing image for the satirical target of the novel. Bateman's flesh eating functions as another act of consumption devoid of pleasure, taste, and fulfillment. It is consumption for the sake of consumption, or put another way, cannibalism serves as the logical extension of a marketplace that co-opts bodies. Unlike Bateman, Hannibal Lecter substitutes human flesh for the other meats in French and Italian cuisine. He not only takes time to cook and enjoy his meals, but his savory, aromatic dishes—paired with elegant wines and refined conversation—also enable him to trick people into eating human flesh. Bateman's cannibalism, by contrast, reduces him to a savage, animalistic state: "A pillow props her ass up and cheese, Brie, has been smeared across her open cunt [. . .] and I'm kneeling on the floor beside a corpse, eating the girl's brain gobbling it down, spreading Grey Poupon over hunks of the pink, fleshy meat" (327, 328). Referencing Grey Poupon and brie again reflects Bateman's tireless need to project refinement. Certainly, high-end cheese shops had established themselves in New York by the start of the 1980s. In 1979 the *New Yorker* humorously reported that "every thirty-eight seconds a cheese shop opens in Manhattan."[59] However, no amount of brie and mustard can coat the horrific brutality of his actions throughout these torture-murder sequences. Just as Bateman's savagery remains a mystery to him ("I can already tell that it's going to be a characteristically useless, senseless death" [329]), he gobbles down this "meal" without tasting a thing. He merely feels compelled to eat, not recognizing how this act mirrors his professional and consumer impulses. The literal act of cannibalism, in other words, becomes an extension of the culture shaping him.

Ultimately, even cannibalism leaves Bateman hungry, and once again Ellis uses this as a metaphor for the dangers of consumerism. "Hunger," as Brown notes about the novel, "becomes more than a need for food, it becomes an expression of deep-seated desires for connections and of uneasiness with the modern condition" (177). Bateman's hunger for the trappings of upper-class consumer culture—whether clothing, apartment furniture, stereo equipment, the perfect body, or what and where to eat—casts the modern condition as fostering a perpetual state of desire. Immediately after putting a "girl's femur and left jawbone [. . .] in the oven, baking" (329), for example, Bateman feels the need to dine out, and the next chapter title is "At Another New Restaurant." Earlier in the text, he considers canceling a lunch appointment after looking at the chunks missing from Elizabeth's leg (291), and he intersperses other restaurant outings with acts of cannibalism, noting that he went to Barney's "after a cold, tense brunch with Christie's corpse" (291). All of these details capture both Bateman's unfulfillable hungers and his perverse attempts to align them with elite, upper-class tastes. He often blurs the line between human flesh and the meals served at restaurants. At one point, he even describes his recent victim's stomach as "[resembling] the eggplant and goat cheese lasagna at Il Marlibro or some other kind of dog food, the dominant colors red and white and brown" (344).

No amount of eating, however, will satiate Bateman because eating has never been about sustenance for him. It has always been about social performance and class status to maintain currency in 1980s urban life. In the chapter "Tries to Cook and Eat Girl," he again attempts to consume a woman's flesh but does so maniacally, eating for the sake of shoving something down his throat: "I spend the next fifteen minutes beside myself, pulling out a bluish rope of intestine, most of it still connected to the body, and shoving it into my mouth, choking on it" (344). Though moments later he likens himself to a vampire, Bateman has actually reduced himself to a zombie-like state of indefatigable eating: "I want to drink this girl's blood as if it were champagne and I plunge my face deep into what's left of her stomach, scratching my chomping jaw on a broken rib" (344). Nothing about Bateman's mode of consumption here can be likened to champagne and the refinement of upper-class living. He has become a monstrous consumer. Although all of this occurs in the realm of Bateman's imagination, Ellis presents it in excruciatingly gruesome detail. Understood metaphorically, these horrifying moments intensify the novel's critique of the violence caused by such beauty and body standards in American popular culture. These standards, sold alongside the products to achieve them, ultimately demean and marginalize those who cannot afford to mimic them, wreaking a type of violence on the self and others.

"End of the 1980s" and Mary Harron's American Psycho

Patrick Bateman's disturbing fantasies about torturing, killing, and eating women made *American Psycho* one of the most controversial books of the twentieth century even before its publication. When some of the most horrific sections of the novel had been leaked to the press, the National Organization of Women (NOW) called for a boycott of the book and its publisher, Simon and Schuster. Without any context for this material, such a response is not surprising. Bateman's misogyny enables him to justify extreme sexual violence and murder in the most gruesome detail. Fearing backlash from the media, Simon and Schuster reneged on its contract just weeks before the release date, and even though Vintage quickly stepped into the fray with an offer to publish it, the damage to the novel's reputation had been done. Critics—even without reading the text—likened *American Psycho* to pornography, horror, and snuff films. Not until feminist filmmaker Mary Harron adapted the novel in 2000 did critics—and the public—begin to reassess the text.[60]

Harron, whose other films include *I Shot Andy Warhol* (1996), *The Notorious Betty Page* (2005), and *The Moth Diaries* (2011), adapted and directed *American Psycho* with a keen understanding of the novel's social satire and wicked sense of humor. Despite three moments of explicit violence in the film (the stabbing of a homeless man, the murder of Paul Allen, and Bateman's shooting rampage in Manhattan), Harron only implies Bateman's (Christian Bale's) broader acts of savagery. After showing him stroll down the street with a woman, for instance, the film cuts to some blood-stained sheets that he wants laundered at the dry cleaners. Later, he shares a cab with a blonde woman outside a nightclub, and in the next scene, Bateman sits in his office, playing with long strands of blonde hair. This approach proves effective on a number of levels. First, it alludes to the likelihood that Bateman's violence is a fantasy and nothing more. Harron captures the unreality of Bateman's homicidal behavior most explicitly—and playfully—during a gunfight with police. When two officers begin chasing him for shooting an old woman, Bateman fires back, killing one and causing a police car to explode. Even Bateman looks at his gun in disbelief, mystified by such a dramatic effect. This parody of 1980s action movies underscores Bateman's fantasy world. Like the other details in the film that cast doubt on the veracity of what we are seeing (reality or Bateman's twisted imaginings), Harron presents Bateman as a metaphor for the dark underbelly of Wall Street greed. He and his coterie possess the veneer of sophistication, but beneath the expensive suits lies an absence of humanity characterized by bigotry (against the poor and nonwhites) and misogyny.

Second, Harron's decision to imply much of the novel's violence prevents any voyeuristic interpretation of it. The sex scenes in the film come across as discomforting, not erotic. When Bateman has sex with his friend's fiancée, Courtney (Samantha Mathis), they are both fully clothed, and her body appears engulfed by the bedding and his body—as if she were nothing more than an object to lie on top of. Furthermore, Courtney's excessive self-medication renders her nearly comatose throughout the film, and this makes intercourse a groggy, dissatisfying experience for her. Bateman—dressing as quickly as he can—pays no heed to her emotional or psychological needs here. He stares at himself in the mirror, but when he does turn toward her, we only see him in profile. Harron focuses on Courtney's face instead—her slurred speech and crestfallen expression after seeing his lack of feeling. This focus on women reacting to Bateman provides a vantage point not offered in the novel. It enables the audience to sympathize with the victims of violent rage and/or indifference.

When Bateman hires two prostitutes, whom he names Christie (Cara Seymour) and Sabrina (Krista Sutton), Harron again focuses on the women's discomfort, showing them sitting stiffly on the couch, rubbing their hands together, exchanging nervous glances, and dancing awkwardly as Bateman orders them around: "Christie, take off your robe. [. . .] Sabrina, remove your dress [. . .] Christie, get down on your knees so Sabrina can see your asshole. [. . .] Sabrina, don't just stare at it; eat it!" The film's focus on their suffering, however, underscores his savagery, tearing apart the mask of civility he has worked so hard to craft. When Bateman, with a wire coat hanger in hand, tells the women that the session is not finished, Harron cuts to Sabrina stumbling toward his front door with welts on her back. She turns for the money—her nose bloody and face strained, moments away from weeping. Christie then pushes past Bateman, grabbing the cash without looking back. The horrors of this torture session are left to the viewer's imagination and suggested by Bateman's hard, unreadable face. When Christie reluctantly agrees to return to Bateman's apartment, her dead-pan expressions and mounting fear remain the focus of the camera as the evening progresses. As Murphet has noted, "we are asked here to glimpse Patrick's monstrosity from the outside, and to empathize with a woman who feels obligated to risk torture for a few hundred dollars" (75).

This adaptation of *American Psycho* also recognizes the importance of food and restaurant culture as it relates to the problem of conspicuous consumption. The red substance dripping throughout the opening credits turns out to be raspberry sauce—not blood—and the remaining sequence features bird's-eye shots that glide from one dish to another before the camera focuses on Bateman's table. These elegantly presented meals capture some of the outrageous excesses of the ultra-rich. While the beautifully decorated tables, classical-style music, and waiters with white-jacket tuxedos communicate opulence, the food mostly gets dwarfed by the size of the plates. This detail suggests that the goal here is being part of the restaurant's atmosphere, not satisfying one's hunger. Even the waiters' description of the specials comes across as ostentatious, almost begging to be included in a review of menu absurdities in New York City: "Tonight's pasta special is squid ravioli in a lemongrass broth with goat cheese profiteroles . . . Rare roasted partridge breast in raspberry coulis with a sorrel timbale . . . swordfish meatloaf with onion marmalade . . . and grilled free-range rabbit with herb French fries."[61] When the bill arrives, one of Bateman's friends remarks that the $570 meal seems particularly reasonable, and they all put down identical platinum credit cards. This opening foregrounds the economic politics of the film. All of these men—along with the other diners—are defined by excess and addictive behaviors: patrons smoke cigarettes, alcohol appears at every table, and one of Bateman's friends complains that the bathroom is no good for doing cocaine.

Food has nothing to do with fulfillment or pleasure in this adaptation, and despite all of the time Bateman spends dining out, he never eats. He drinks, pontificates, snorts sweetener, smokes a cigar, and offers Jean (Chloë Sevigny) sorbet. But he never takes a bite of food. At lunch with Detective Kimball (Willem Dafoe), he almost cuts into a steak and nervously shakes salt over it, but only Kimball enjoys the meal. In fact, the audience only sees Bateman sink his teeth into Christie's leg, and this detail alludes to his cannibalism (to which he confesses in a phone message to his lawyer). More significantly, it reinforces the way eating functions as a metaphor for an unchecked, unfulfillable consumerism that reduces people (particularly women) to meat.

Elite restaurant culture links consumerism with misogyny as well. While on the phone with his paramour Courtney, Bateman watches pornography, flips through a Zagat guide to decide which "fabulous" restaurant to call, and offers to take her out for dinner. She only agrees, however, when he promises Dorsia. Bateman fails to get a reservation, but he takes her to Barcadia instead, insisting that it is Dorsia. Courtney, so drugged from a cocktail of "one or more psychiatric drugs," cannot tell the difference. Bateman then selects her meal by citing restaurant reviews: "Courtney, you're going to have the peanut butter soup with smoked duck and mashed squash. *New York Matinee* called it a 'playful but mysterious little dish.' You'll love it. And then the red snapper with violets and pine nuts. I think that'll follow nicely." By having Bateman directly quote this review, Harron captures the way his rhetoric in the novel echoes what he has read of restaurants, albums, electronics equipment, body lotions, etc. Bateman lacks any authenticity, for his tastes are purely mimetic. At the same time, his investment in the social value of restaurants provides another opportunity to display his patriarchal attitude toward women. He tells Courtney both what to eat and how to respond to the food: "You'll love it." Robbing women of their autonomy reduces them to objects that can be treated with callous indifference and violence.

Bateman's objectification of women gets reinforced by his obsession with pornography and horror. He appears to watch these genres exclusively, and both are connected with food. Pornography accompanies his consultation of Zagat's, and later in his apartment, the audience sees a plate of fruit while a woman screams in the background. As the camera moves from a bird's-eye view of this snack to a side view, we see Bateman doing vigorous crunches in front of the closing sequence from *The Texas Chainsaw Massacre* on his television. Both pornography and this film (with the bloodied Sally fleeing the chainsaw-wielding cannibal Leatherface) reduce women to meat—metaphorically and literally. This imagery fuels Bateman's attitudes about hiring prostitutes, asking his girlfriend, Evelyn (Reese Witherspoon), for breast implants, and using Courtney for sex. He also takes cues from his social circle. His friends mock the notion of women having a "good personality," and since physical appearance defines a person's value, they move from body to body with no regard for fidelity or intimacy.

Despite omitting obesity (no fat actors were cast) and junk food (Bateman does not go to McDonald's, discuss Dove Bars, or worry about the sodium level in soy sauce), Harron's choices changed popular and critical responses to the text for the better. It enabled audiences to recognize the rich sophistication of a novel that had largely been marginalized for its controversial content. One final change is worth noting, however. In the closing moments of the film, Bateman and his friends gather at a bar and comment on a speech by Reagan about the Iran-Contra affair. Bryce (Justin Theroux) expresses disgust with Reagan's ability to lie so convincingly, to appear so "cool about it," and Bateman breaks into hysterical laughter. In part, this laughter highlights Bryce's hypocrisy since all of them live dishonestly. They are unfaithful to their fiancées and girlfriends. They misrepresent their professional lives, work ethic, and success. (None of them appear to do any work at all.) And they reveal nothing truthful about themselves, instead striving to project an image of success and belonging at all times. With Reagan's voice in the background, Bryce continues: "he presents himself as this harmless old codger but inside . . . but inside." He doesn't finish his thought, yet Bateman's voiceover explains that the "inside doesn't matter. [. . .] My pain is constant and sharp, and I do not hope for a better world for anyone."

Certainly, these words encapsulate Harron's and Ellis's—as well as King's, Dunn's, Harris's, and Demme's—critique of the superficiality at the heart of 1980s culture. America at the time defined itself by conspicuous consumption, the elite excesses of the Reagan era, and bodily ideals that reduced a person's value to physical appearances. Each of these writers and filmmakers examined the consequences of this social context. Ultimately, the importance placed on surfaces—whether clothing, eating habits, physique, or choice of restaurants—inspired selfishness and unhappiness. As Bateman observes in the closing moments of *American Psycho*, "I gain no deeper knowledge about myself, no new understanding can be extracted from my telling. [. . .] This confession has meant *nothing*" (377). This is the cost of an image-obsessed culture. It fails to provide personal insight and by extension any insight into the lives and needs of others. While Harron ends her film with these words, her use of Reagan's Iran-Contra speech instead of Bush's inauguration carries a slightly different implication. In the novel, the men watch an episode of *The Patty Winters Show* on whether or not "Economic Success Equals Happiness." While Bateman cannot hear the details of the episode, he notes the clips from "President Bush's inauguration early this year, then a speech from former President Reagan" (396). The references to Bush signal both the beginning of the 1990s and the continuation of four or potentially eight more years of the same economic cannibalism of the working and middle classes. Not only is Bateman still out there, but as all of these 1980s works suggest, these ongoing political policies and social attitudes were also far from over.

CHAPTER TWO

A Sharp, Sweet Tooth:
Junk Food, Addiction, and Vampires

Part of America's fascination with vampires in the 1980s stemmed from the country's increasing concerns about addiction. Cocaine and crack cocaine became widespread for the first time. According to the nonprofit organization Drug-Free World, "the number of people who admitted using cocaine on a routine basis increased from 4.2 million to 5.8 million" in 1985.[1] Likewise, government funding doubled the number of alcohol treatment centers between 1980 and 1990, and membership in Alcoholics Anonymous skyrocketed from 907,575 participants to over 2 million.[2] The Reagan administration responded to this crisis, in part, by launching Nancy Reagan's "Just Say No" campaign in 1982. The First Lady visited schools, toured drug rehabilitation centers, and appeared on television shows, billboards, and even movie trailers with Clint Eastwood. In addition to giving forty-nine speeches and over twelve hundred interviews, Nancy Reagan "inspired Americans to found 12,000 'Just Say No' clubs around the country" (Stuart). Her husband supported these efforts by radically increasing the number of nonviolent drug incarcerations through the Anti-Drug Abuse Act of 1986. Since the Reagans attributed juvenile drug use to peer pressure, the problem was a matter of willpower, not addiction. This viewpoint may offer some insight into the broader reluctance in 1980s America to view processed foods in terms of addiction—even as they posed a similar problem.

Fast-food outlets tripled between 1963 and 1983, earning "40 percent of all public eating place sales" (Levenstein 233). By the middle of the decade, Coca-Cola began selling twenty-ounce bottles and encouraged vendors to offer thirty-two-ounce cups. Americans were also consuming 16.7 pounds of candy per year by 1984,[3] and they would be eating three hamburgers and four

General Mills introduced the first chocolate cereal in 1971 with Count Chocula. The art design for the 1987 box featured an image of Bela Lugosi from Tod Browning's *Dracula* (1931). Controversy erupted when Jewish organizations complained that the medallion around the Count's neck resembled the Star of David, suggesting that he was Jewish, but concerns about marketing chocolate cereal to children received little attention.

servings of french fries per week by 2000 (Schlosser 6). Not surprisingly, this burgeoning addiction began to play a prominent role in vampire fiction. In *Our Vampires, Ourselves*, Nina Auerbach has argued that "every age embraces the vampire it needs" (145), and the 1980s did just that. Its vampires reveal the processed food industry to be vampiric, and they portray America as a nation addicted to foods engineered to alter our taste buds and to mask the truth about what we were eating.

Food has recently begun to play an important role in both literary and film scholarship. Gastrocriticism, the study of food in literature, primarily focuses on the way eating choices define the self. As Maria Christou has recently noted, the field tends to approach questions of identity through three categories: historical context, national and political affiliation, and gender. The first typically considers literature alongside contemporary social mores and material culture such as cookbooks, health guides, and diaries. Joan Fitzpatrick's examination of Shakespeare and Robert Appelbaum's interpretation of the early modern period offer two notable examples. Similarly, Denise Gigante's *Tatse: A Literary History* explores eating in nineteenth-century Romantic writing through the lens of British consumerism, and Jayne Archer discusses the issue of food scarcity in England from Chaucer to T. S. Eliot. For Kathryn Dolan, American literature in the mid-1800s "[imagines] alternatives to national policies that prefigure twenty-first-century concerns with issues of globalization, resource depletion, food security, and the relation of industrial agriculture to pollution, disease, and climate change" (4).

The second and third categories examine identity through national affiliation and gender respectively. Wenying Xu's *Eating Identities: Reading Food in Asian American Literature,* for example, uses culinary traditions to explore the way Asian Americans have been racialized in the United States, and his project "treats table narrative [in this fiction] as a dominant site of economic, cultural, and political struggle" (14). Other scholarship in this area includes Tomoko Aoyama's *Reading Food in Modern Japanese Literature,* Parama Roy's *Alimentary Tracts: Appetites, Aversions, and the Postcolonial,* and Allison Carruth's *Global Appetites: American Power and the Literature of Food.* Carruth not only discusses the ability of literature—from Willa Cather to Toni Morrison—to depict the United States as "the main origin of imperialist and unjust practices attending the globalization of food," but she also highlights fiction's unique capacity to "shuttle between social and interpersonal registers" (5). Likewise, feminist food studies in literature have investigated issues of gender identity. Tamar Heller and Patricia Moran's *Scenes of the Apple: Food and the Female Body in Nineteenth- and Twentieth-Century Women's Writing* considers the dynamic between food and feminine identity. And according to Sarah Sceats, food reveals some of the social, political, and cultural issues that impact women. She argues, in part, that food can either reinforce existing patterns in women's lives or signal "deviations from the norm" (184).

Within the study of film, the pioneering works of Gaye Poole, Maggie Dunn, and Cynthia Baron established the foundation for contemporary food studies scholarship.[4] Anne L. Bower's *Reel Food: Essays on Food and Film,* for instance, makes a compelling case for "food film" as its own genre, defining these works as casting food preparation, cooking spaces, consumption, and food itself in starring roles. These narratives "consistently depict characters negotiating questions of identity, power, culture, class, spirituality, or relationship through food" (6). James R. Keller's *Food, Film, and Culture: A*

Genre Study echoes this sentiment through his analogy between directors and chefs, adding that food imagery "mobilizes the audience's appetites" (5). More recently, Tom Hertweck has broadened the scope of these works to include "momentary or less palpable expressions of consumption in film" (xiii), and Laura Lindenfeld and Fabio Parasecoli's *Feasting Our Eyes: Food Films and Cultural Identity in the United States* focuses on the relationship between food and power. Just as "food shapes and is shaped by cultural hierarchies and power structures, providing insights into marginalization and disenfranchisement," food films, they argue, can both challenge cultural norms and "reaffirm effective dominant culture" (20, 23).

The 1980s proved to be an important decade for food studies and film. Cultural anthropologists Carole Counihan and Penny Van Esterik trace the burgeoning of food studies to this decade, noting the rise of food films, food documentaries, scholarly journals, and "the expansion of social movements linked to food" (2). In *Appetites and Anxieties: Food, Film, and the Politics of Representation*, Cynthia Baron, Diane Carson, and Mark Bernard also discuss "the emergence of food films as a discernable genre in the 1980s" (6), and they anchor this discussion in Warren Belasco's seminal study *Appetite for Change: How the Counterculture Took on the Food Industry, 1966–1988*. For Belasco, the rise of naturally produced alternatives to processed foods "[caused] people to wonder about all the brand-name stuff they were buying. [... This] organic paradigm questioned conventional science, challenged the prevailing system of food distribution, and advocated a radical decentralization of population and power" (111). Food corporations ultimately responded by defending the convenience and social benefits of food technology (i.e., the ability to feed large numbers of people). They also coopted language from the countercuisine movement to reposition or rebrand products as "natural" and "healthy"—even when "full of additives and sugar" (219). Consumers in the 1980s thus found themselves torn between the benefits of natural foods and "the ideology of convenience, with its aura of liberation, freedom, and choice" (53). As Baron, Carson, and Bernard explain, these contrasting impulses provide an important context for the way "food films and food documentaries [...] capture the aspirations and the anxieties of people in a consumer society who live with the promise and threat of industrialized food production as well as the promise and threat of slow cooking, organic food, and local sources" (7–8).

Although eating tends to be a central preoccupation in horror, this genre has remained largely absent from these discussions. Shaun Kimber has recently argued for the need to integrate food horror into the field, highlighting its exploration of "food-based diseases and infections; food insecurity and shortages;

and the hidden nature of much of the food system" (126–27). *Reel Food* includes some discussions of food horror such as Blair Davis's essay on 1930s cinema,[5] and Baron, Carson, and Bernard dedicate a chapter to cannibal films, interpreting these works as a reflection of "the fact that food consumption in a consumer society is fraught with uncertainties, people do not know what they are eating, they do not know where their food comes from or where their disposed food will go" (131–32). Yet the first collection dedicated to this topic, Cynthia J. Miller and A. Bowdoin Van Riper's *What's Eating You? Food and Horror on Screen*, did not appear until 2017. It argues, in part, that "Monstrous appetites—desires, passions, requirements or overindulgences—result in the eaters, as well as the substances they consume, becoming objects of horror" (3).

Vampires offer one example of such disturbing hungers, and their attacks on humans typically get "framed in culinary terms: 'feeding' or even 'feasting' on the blood of the living" (Miller and Riper 5). Additionally, scholars Michel Delville and Andrew Norris include vampires in their recent examination of the politics of hunger, positioning self-starvation as central to these narratives: "The most pressing question for the last human is whether to starve or whether to live as something other than human, whether to turn to a food source whose consumption would revoke any vestigial claims to humanity" (106–7). Just as human beings define themselves by what they eat, the same holds true for vampires. Their diets and foodways, according to Alexandra Frank, "not only define them, but carry strong implications for the social, economic, and political identities of the humans in their lives as well" (341). These food choices also prove crucial to half-vampires—humans that have been bitten by a vampire but have not fed on human blood—as they seek to restore their humanity. While scholars have recognized the use of vampirism as a metaphor for addiction, almost no attention has been given to its connection with processed foods. In keeping with Michael Newbury's provocative analysis of the "industrial food apocalypse" in twenty-first-century zombie films (90), this chapter considers eighties vampires to be the fictional counterparts for cultural anxieties about processed foods in America.

Next to blood, fast food and junk food make up the most common meals in these works. For Anne Rice, vampires sired in the 1980s compare blood drinking to "hamburgers and French fries and strawberry milkshakes" (*Queen of the Damned* 44). Tabloid reporter Gayle Clark "sometimes gave in to overwhelming urges for Oreo cookies and Mars candy bars" in Robert McCammon's *They Thirst* (1981). In the film *Once Bitten* (1985), Mark (Jim Carrey) drives an ice cream truck and subsists on a diet of hamburgers, fries, and sodas before undergoing a partial transformation. Tom Holland's *Fright Night* (1985) presents Charley's (William Ragsdale's) late-night stakeouts as fueled by chips, chocolate, and Coke. Mae (Jenny Wright) in Kathryn Bigelow's *Near Dark* (1987) first tempts Caleb (Adrian Pasdar) while eating ice cream, and Tony Scott's adaptation of *The Hunger* (1983) presents McDonald's burgers as a typical meal for its characters. Whether munching on chips, devouring a Big Mac, or slurping down soda, humans use these foods to satisfy hunger, assuage anxiety, provide a needed jolt of caffeine, and pass the time between sunset and sunrise. They are acquired easily and consumed quickly, which makes them pragmatic choices in a world teeming with the undead.

1980s vampires tend to function in one of three ways. First, they can serve as metaphors for the food industry, preying on young and old with products designed to foster overconsumption and addiction. Second, vampires can symbolize the country's addiction to processed foods and the excesses of consumerism more broadly. Their insatiable appetite mirrors the public's perpetual hunger for more—from junk food to consumer goods. And finally, some vampires even emerge as ironic images for healthy eating as they seek a natural, more organic diet than their junk-food-addicted victims. By consuming only what they need to survive, their utilitarian approach to food helps them maintain thin, youthful, vigorous bodies—the aspirational goal of 1980s exercise and weight-loss culture. In each case, these creatures indict an industry that profited from turning consumers into junkies, craving foods that promised heart disease, high cholesterol, and obesity.

Tony Fonesca has argued that the 1980s marked the beginning of "a new generation of highly stylized, esoteric vampire films [. . . that] tended to be more linear and plot driven than stylized and image-driven" (59, 65). The simple narrative of finding, chasing, and killing a vampire no longer sufficed. Instead, as Cynthia Miller notes, these works introduced "the 'human' vampire—vulnerable, flawed, and empathetic—the 'creature of the night' to which diverse cinematic audiences could relate" (281). For Phillips, such horror films reflected the political climate of the decade, "encompassing the strange politics that arose [. . . during] the Reagan revolution" ("You Said" 264). These changes in horror lent themselves to shifting attitudes about food as well, and vampire fiction offers a dark meditation on the dietary transformation already underway in the country. After beginning with an examination of the processed food industry and the efforts by companies such as Coca-Cola and McDonald's to foster addiction, this chapter focuses on characters that wrestle with their own hungers. These struggles typically represent both individual and national concerns about the dangerous allure of fast foods, but the situation was not hopeless. The half-vampires in *The Lost Boys* (1987), *Near Dark* (1987), *Once Bitten* (1985), and *Fright Night Part 2* (1988) fight to regain their humanity. Some of the vampires in Anne Rice's and Whitley Strieber's novels—like the protagonist of *My Best Friend Is a Vampire* (1987) and the vampire community of *A Return to Salem's Lot* (1987)—choose animal over human blood. And these efforts send a clear message about the American diet. 1980s audiences could dine differently, and doing so could save them from the dangers of sugary, processed, and fast foods.

Sugars, Fats, and Processed Foods

With the introduction of high-fructose corn syrup and crystalline fructose, America's relationship with sweetness changed forever. Developed in response to the rising cost of cane and beets, which had been the two main sources of sugar until the 1970s, high-fructose corn syrup appealed to the processed food industry economically and chemically. It was inexpensive, and as a liquid, it could be injected directly into food. According to Pulitzer Prize–winning journalist Michael Moss, this invention offers just one example of the way food scientists engineered products to heighten desirability and to foster addiction. Around the same time, in the early seventies, they discovered the "bliss point": "the precise amount of sweetness—no more, no less—that makes food and drink most enjoyable" (10). Ever since corporations have worked tirelessly, funding research, influencing public policy, and examining market trends,[6] to calculate the exact sugar needed to maximize the sensory pleasure of each product from ketchup to a can of soda. The bliss point, according to one psychologist, not only determines what one eats and drinks, but it also coaxes us into consuming "more than we realize" (qtd. in Moss 11).

In the late 1980s, the introduction of a commercial version of crystalline fructose offered another pathway for achieving this but with added benefits. Since it does not decompose as rapidly as sugar, fructose enables a longer shelf life. It also "delivers an alluring aroma and a crisp, brown surface that mimics the finish achieved in cooking at home, and when frozen, it blocks the formulation of ice" (Moss 130). Most significantly, pure fructose has over twice the sweetness of glucose and nearly 75 percent more sweetness than table sugar. Both this flavoring and its enhanced ability to preserve foods have proven exorbitantly profitable. The corresponding health risks of so much sugar, however, have proven equally devastating for the American public. One 2011 study linked corn syrup and fructose beverages with several major risk factors for heart disease, including heightened levels of LDL cholesterol, triglycerides, and fat-binding proteins. Scholar Robert Albritton has noted that "globally the six-fold increase in cases of diabetes since 1985 almost exactly parallels the global increase in high fructose corn syrup (HFCS) consumption" (344). Other studies have demonstrated a clear connection between sugar and obesity. In 1988, physiological psychologist Michael Tordoff first established a link between soda consumption and obesity, and he discovered that rats given "saccharin solution to drink [. . .] ate 10–15% more food than when given only water" (5). The health risks of processed foods, in other words, not only stemmed from high concentrations of sweeteners but also from their addictive nature. We simply want more of it than our bodies can handle.

No product has been singled out as more dangerous for one's health than soda. Part of this can be attributed to the addictive nature of its ingredients. Coca-Cola, for example, began as a nerve tonic in the nineteenth century as patent medicines became increasingly popular after the Civil War. In the 1880s, a druggist named John Pemberton had been reading about the benefits of coca leaves as a stimulant, digestive aid, aphrodisiac, and even a tool for extending one's life. Scientists believed that coca and its principal alkaloid, cocaine, could also cure opium and morphine addictions, which had become prevalent among wounded veterans.[7] At the same time, the medical community warned "that cocaine might indeed free addicts from morphine—only to enslave them on the new drug" (Pendergrast 24). Pemberton fashioned a medicine that went through several incarnations. Eventually one of his business partners, who came up with the name Coca-Cola for its alliterative quality, recognized that this medicine for headaches and depression could be a popular fountain drink as well (30). In this form, Coca-Cola soon became a highly successful beverage. Nine thousand gallons of the syrup had been sold to soda fountain operators in 1890, and by 1900 the company earned annual profits exceeding $400,000. Although Coca-Cola removed cocaine from its formula in 1903, it kept sugar levels high and substituted another addictive substance, caffeine, to act as a stimulant (89). Perhaps it comes as little surprise that one hundred years after its creation, Coca-Cola had become a domestic and global phenomenon with millions of addicted customers. As company CEO Roberto Goizueta explained to shareholders in 1988, the company had sold 200 billion servings of soft drinks globally, more than twice any other competitor.[8]

One of the more insidious aspects of Coke's success involved the introduction of supersized drinks. In the mid-1980s, it began producing 20-ounce bottles, liters, and 32-ounce cups for its vendors including 7-Eleven. Prior to that, Coke was packaged in 6.5-ounce bottles, but the introduction of the 32-ounce Big Gulp in 1976 changed American drinking patterns. The success of the Big Gulp inspired the introduction of the 44-ounce Super Big Gulp in 1986 and the 64-ounce Double Gulp in 1989 with forty-four teaspoons of sugar (Klara).[9] Furthermore, Coca-Cola came up with the idea of combination deals at fast-food restaurants. It directly approached chains, starting with

An example of the ubiquitous presence of Coca-Cola in the United States. "Vintage Coca-Cola Sign in Downtown Pueblo, Colorado." Gates Frontiers Fund Colorado Collection within the Carol M. Highsmith Archive, Library of Congress, Prints and Photographs Division. Reproduction Number: LC-DIG-highsm-32388.

McDonald's, to sell bundles that included Coke. The company also spearheaded all-you-can-drink beverage bars at these outlets, and the message was clear: the more, the better. According to corporate publications, training films, and chief executives, Coke believed it could sell more product through fast-food outlets and sought to reach more consumers by marketing itself as an indispensable part of such meals (Pendergrast 284). Indeed, consumption rates soared, more than doubling between 1970 and 1997. The annual per capita consumption of soda increased from 35 to 42.5 gallons between 1980 and 1990, which amounted to over 64,000 calories and 4,200 teaspoons of sugar per year.[10]

In addition to sugar, fat has also played a transformative role in the American diet; it adds texture, bulk, and shelf life to products while instilling addictive cravings on the part of consumers. As Moss argues, "If sugar is the methamphetamine of processed food ingredients, with its high-speed, blunt assault on our brains, then fat is the opiate, a smooth operator whose effects are less obvious but no less powerful" (148). He goes on to cite one study by the Brookhaven National Laboratory that shows the brain reacting to processed foods and cocaine in a similar way. Some drugs, it found, "achieve their allure, and addictive qualities, by following the same neurological channels that our bodies first developed for food" (149). Other studies have made similar connections. One scientist, for instance, discovered that the same drug used to combat heroin addiction could suppress the desire to overindulge in snacks such as cookies (156). Yet for the processed food industry, fat is a gold mine. Since we cannot really detect its taste and since fat stimulates pleasure centers in the brain, the human body does not send any signals to stop eating. This helps explain some disturbing trends. For example, the amount of fats and processed sugars in the American diet already averaged 265 pounds in 1979. "This works out to be almost exactly three-quarters of a pound of fat and sugar per person per day" (Mintz 199). Fat-saturated and salt-coated french fries constituted 25 percent of the nation's annual vegetable consumption by the end of the twentieth century, and Americans currently eat three times more cheese today than in 1970 (Albritton 345). Like sugar, all of these fats have serious health consequences. Medical science still considers saturated fat the leading cause of high cholesterol, which puts one at significant risk for stroke or heart attack. It has also been linked with type two diabetes and rising obesity rates.

Next to pizza and cheese, red meat constitutes one of the highest sources of saturated fat, and the average American was eating three hamburgers and four servings of french fries per week by 2000. Not surprisingly, McDonald's remained the largest buyer of beef and potatoes at the start of the twenty-first century, and they were generating 90 percent of the country's new jobs. Although Richard and Maurice McDonald opened their first drive-in restaurant in 1937, they did not simplify the menu (eliminating most items requiring utensils), replace dishes with plastic and paper, serve all hamburgers with the same condiments (no substitutions allowed!), and implement an assembly line approach to cooking until a decade later (Love 12–13). This speedy preparation would revolutionize how and what Americans ate. These hamburgers, for instance, were typically a mixture of beef carcass trimmings collected from various slaughterhouses, and the fattest cuts, known as "fifty-fifties," contained just as much fat as protein (half of each). According to Eric Schlosser, "A single fast food hamburger [in the 1980s and 1990s contained] meat from dozens or even hundreds of different cattle" (204). This fact raised profound concerns about beef safety at the time. With the consolidation of the meatpacking industry, the implementation of massive feedlots, and the use of assembly line production at slaughterhouses, hamburger meat became increasingly unsafe and prone to spreading disease. Cattle in feedlots typically received little exercise, and they lived in filth, standing in mounds of manure all day long. The high cost of grain also inspired the meatpacking industry to alter the natural diet of these animals; 75 percent of cows in the United States were suddenly being fed

The first McDonald's franchise opened in Chicago, just west of the city, on April 15, 1955. The McDonald's Corporation retained ownership of the property, restored an accurate replica of the store, and opened a modern-day McDonald's across the street. "McDonald's Store #1 Located West of Chicago, Illinois." Gates Frontiers Fund Colorado Collection within the Carol M. Highsmith Archive, Library of Congress, Prints and Photographs Division. Reproduction Number: LC-DIG-highsm-12949.

livestock waste—"the rendered remains of dead sheep and dead cattle—until August 1997" (202). They were also fed dead cats, dead dogs, old newspapers, sawdust, and the waste product of chickens. This diet and these conditions made cattle particularly susceptible to disease, which could be passed along to consumers. One early example of these dangers occurred with an *E. coli* outbreak in Oregon and Michigan in 1982 that made forty-seven people ill after eating McDonald's hamburgers. Within the month, an additional twenty-nine cases had been reported (Leiss and Powell 82–83).

Finally, french fries, deep-fried potatoes cut into long, rectangular shapes, may owe its origin to either the cooking technique developed in France in the late eighteenth century or to Belgium peasants one hundred years earlier, but their central place in American restaurants has become emblematic of twentieth-century fast-food culture. McDonald's began using frozen french fries in the mid-1960s, but they maintained their signature taste by cooking them in 7 percent cottonseed oil and 93 percent beef tallow. This mixture, as Schlosser notes, not only provided the fries with their "unique flavor," but they also contained "more saturated beef fat per ounce than a McDonald's hamburger" (120). The corporation did not switch to pure vegetable oil until 1990—after vegetarians complained about not being informed of the ingredients and about increased public concern over cholesterol. McDonald's made this switch only after food technicians could replicate the same taste by adding chemical flavoring to the oil.[11] All of this fat, not to mention the salt, helped make these fries a particularly addictive and unhealthy staple in the American diet.

The Lost Boys

Blood and Junk Food in The Lost Boys

After the success of *St. Elmo's Fire* (1985), Joel Schumacher turned his attention to a story that recast the gangs of 1950s juvenile delinquent films, such as *The Wild One* (1953), *Rebel without a Cause* (1955), and *Blackboard Jungle* (1955), into motorcycle-riding vampires. *The Lost Boys* (1987) not only gives vampires the swagger of Marlon Brando and defiance of James Dean, as Stacey Abbott has noted,[12] but it also depicts junk food as transforming people into vampiric consumers. The film focuses on a family that has just moved to the fictional town of Santa Carla in the hopes of starting over. Following a rough divorce that leaves Lucy (Dianne Wiest) without employment, money, or a place of her own, she takes her two sons, Michael (Jason Patric) and Sam (Corey Haim), to live in her father's rundown farmhouse. Their drive from Phoenix to California parallels Marion Crane's journey in Alfred Hitchcock's *Psycho* (1960), and the father's penchant for taxidermy gets compared to *The Texas Chainsaw Massacre*.

Like the billboard describing Santa Carla as "the murder capital of the world," these allusions preview the dangers awaiting the family. Sam soon befriends two brothers that view horror comics as survival guides for fighting the undead. Lucy begins dating a vampire, Max (Edward Herrmann). And Michael involves himself with a motorcycle gang whose nocturnal shenanigans include hanging from bridges, riding off cliffs, and murdering rival gangs. They also coax him into drinking blood from a decanter, which causes a hallucinatory high that begins his transformation into a vampire. Complete change, however, requires him to kill, and the rest of the film revolves around the attempt by Sam, the Frog brothers (Corey Feldman and Jamison Newlander), and grumpy Grandpa (Bernard Hughes) to restore Michael's humanity. Like the lingering taste for junk food among Santa Carla's teenage

Rebels without a cause in Joel Schumacher's *The Lost Boys* (1987). Warner Brothers/Photofest. © Warner Brothers.

vampires, Michael's near metamorphosis presents these foods as having a vampiric hold on modern America.

Almost every aspect of this town revolves around junk food and its impact on consumers. Aimless teens return to the boardwalk nightly for the same rides and the same sodas, cotton candy, and hot dogs. The local video store owner keeps a bucket of lollipops for customers. And when the Frog brothers meet Sam, one remarks, "If you're looking for the diet frozen yogurt bar, it went out of business last summer." Healthy eating, it appears, doesn't stand a chance in Santa Carla. Junk food is the cuisine of choice, and the film puts a particular emphasis on the adjective "junk." When the family first arrives, Lucy notices two young people scrounging for food in the trash. This dumpster food—found in the Styrofoam containers of take-out restaurants—conflates the meals being consumed on the boardwalk with literal waste. Both are garbage.

"Feeding time" in the vampire's lair proves no different. When the motorcycle vampires share boxes of Chinese take-out and blood-wine with Michael, David (Kiefer Sutherland) uses this meal to torment him, making the rice appear as churning maggots and the noodles as writhing worms. This revolting imagery for fast food suggests that Michael, along with the audience, would be better off not eating such meals at all. Afterward, Michael's new taste for blood is not only linked with addiction (as signaled through

Grandpa's shelf of junk food in *The Lost Boys* (1987). © Warner Brothers.

his daytime naps, bloodshot eyes, and cravings), but it also makes him reject seemingly healthy foods. He refuses to eat a homemade sandwich or to stay for dinner, and when he finally tries to drink milk, he gets violently ill, spilling the container on the kitchen floor. Michael's behavior may be temporary, a side effect of his partial transformation, but he has tasted enough blood and junk food to make recovery—or getting clean—an agonizing journey. This struggle to regain his humanity signals his desire not to be like the vampire gang, which feasts on fast food and blood with equal abandon. Just as these teenage vampires represent and embody the perils of a consumer culture, Michael's experiences signify the painful challenge of freeing oneself of dangerous addictions.

Grandpa most completely embodies the addiction to and risks of junk food in the film. When the boys first arrive, he takes them to the refrigerator to explain some house rules: "We got some rules around here. Second shelf is mine. That's where I keep my root beers and my double-thick Oreo cookies. Nobody touches the second shelf but me." This is the first and presumably most important mandate of the house. He never issues warnings about parties, loud music, drinking, smoking, or other such behaviors. Grandpa only draws the line with junk food. This second shelf, which is covered by a cardboard flap that reads "Old Fart," contains bottles of root beer, a large bag of Oreo mint cookies, and "Peanut Butter Boppers: Peanut Crunch." This box describes Boppers as "New!" and filled with "Creamy Rich Peanut Butter and More," employing a common tactic to manipulate consumers. "More" of what, the box does not say, but it does not matter. Food technicians engineered products to get people hooked on eating more. Double Stuf Oreos became more desirable than regular Oreos, Big Gulps preferable to twelve-ounce cans of soda. Grandpa's diet demonstrates as much. Even his first visit to Sam's room shows him with a large bottle of root beer and a different bag of Double Stuf Oreos—as if he has already worked his way through the mint cookies in the refrigerator.

In a deleted scene from the film, Grandpa and Lucy discuss his diet over a bag of Double Stuf Oreos. "I wish you wouldn't eat this junk," his daughter half-heartedly complains, and he explains, "If I knew I was going to live this long, I would have taken better care of myself." Not only does the film label this food "junk," it also uses his frequent snacking to highlight the addictiveness of these products. It comes as little surprise that the film ends with the family gathered around the refrigerator. Immediately after destroying the head vampire, Grandpa shuffles into the kitchen, reaches for the second shelf, and takes a long sip from a bottle of root beer. He then gives the closing line of the film: "One thing about living in Santa Carla I never could stomach—all the damn vampires." This joke operates on a couple of levels. Grandpa, like the Frog brothers and presumably other locals, has known about and tacitly accepted vampires despite the dangers. The supernatural is as much a part of Santa Carla as processed foods. Similar to the way one must invite a vampire inside, America had already welcomed these risky foods into their lives. Grandpa claims that he cannot stomach vampires, but nothing could be further from the truth. Only when the vampires directly confront his family at home does he act. Otherwise, he stomachs vampires and junk food the same way—disregarding the dangers of both until it is potentially too late.[13]

Grandpa's other compulsive behavior, taxidermy, gets linked with vampires and junk food as well. He dedicates an entire room to this work, and like the second shelf, this space is designated as off-limits. Here Grandpa produces an endless menagerie of animals to decorate the house, give to nearby widows, and adorn Sam's room—startling the boy every morning when he wakes up to a new, menacing creature at his bedside. Taxidermy, the artificial preservation of animals through skinning, stuffing, and chemicals, produces a simulacrum. It mimics something real from a distance or at quick glance, but these creatures remain lifeless and inauthentic. The film implies an affinity between vampires and Grandpa's animals: they are dead but appear alive; they are ageless but frozen in time. The film also connects taxidermy with junk food. In his front yard, Grandpa owns—and may have carved—a large wooden bear guzzling from an upraised bottle of root beer. This statue unites his two passions and signals a general preference for the inauthentic. For instance, his family initially finds Grandpa's body stretched out on the front porch only to discover that he is pretending to be dead. He prefers dead animals to live ones. He uses Windex instead of aftershave. And he lives on a diet of processed foods. These snacks appear to be authentic (they can certainly be consumed), but they are artificially flavored, chemically manipulated, stuffed with preservatives, and loaded with hidden sugars and fats. They have caused consumers to abandon the natural for the artificial. And they too pose a threat to the health of Santa Carla.

By contrast, the only positive moment with food occurs when Lucy prepares a home-cooked meal to introduce her family to Max. Although Sam and the Frog brothers use this opportunity to determine whether or not Lucy's date is a vampire—spilling holy water on him, tricking him into eating a spoonful of raw garlic, and holding up a mirror to catch his reflection—the dinner suggests the virtues of cooking. Lucy uses fresh ingredients to produce a meal that "smells good" and brings the family together for the most part. Even the vampire Max savors the pasta, meatballs, and garlic. This moment aligns with Nicola Nixon's analysis of *The Lost Boys* as "[vaunting] American ideals of normalized family values, of such values in the face of the 'bad' families who represent the potential decay of these ideals" (127).

In the context of 1980s food culture, the scene also helps distinguish between good and bad cuisine, between restraint and excess. Max demonstrates both a hearty appetite and a seemingly refined palate. He dines with Lucy several times, choosing nice restaurants and displaying his own talents as a cook. In some of the deleted footage from the film, one of their dates reveals him to be a food snob. When Lucy orders a fillet of sole, Max playfully tells her that such a meal just won't do, and he insists on ordering for both of them: "We'll start with caviar, Caesar salad, a couple of the best lobsters in the tank, [. . .] and champagne—Dom Perignon '71." When the waiter leaves, he adds, "the '75 is better, but it's just not ready to drink." His ostentation, of course, is designed to impress the working-class Lucy, but his aside about the 1975 vintage suggests equally discerning tastes as a vampire. Just as he doesn't eat fast food, he is not looking for any blood source; he specifically wants Lucy and the idea of building a family with her. She stands in for the '75 Dom Perignon here—an ideal vintage not quite ready for consumption. As these moments suggest, Max's diet appears to have grown healthier, more organic with age, for he has abandoned the addictive culture of 1980s life for refined eating and moderation. He no longer seeks the likes of David to fulfill his bloodlust, desiring instead Lucy and her wholesome sons. He has become, in other words, a discerning eater that eschews mindless excess for quality. As such, when compared with Grandpa's diet, Max's eating habits position vampirism as a disturbingly attractive alternative to the junk-food-fueled lives of the human characters.

Finally, Joel Schumacher's elegant camera work reinforces the film's central themes about addictive impulses. On a literal level, the aerial shots racing across the ocean, over the boardwalk, and through the clouds mimic the awesome power and velocity of vampire flight while capturing their alternative perspective. Vampires view the world differently than humans, in part, because they are frozen in time and development. The motorcycle gang appears doomed to roam along the boardwalk, endlessly performing the same tough-guy routine, spurring the same meaningless rivalries, and taking the same risks for eternity. All of these acts, however, lack real consequences. They cannot die from falling off a bridge or developing diabetes, so very little satisfaction must come from these artificial displays of danger. In a similar way, Max seeks a marriage that will allow him to play the role of a stereotypical suburban dad. Yet he appears to have little influence over his vampire progeny, which highlights an equal hollowness at the heart of his parenting fantasy. This vampire community wants to imitate roles no longer suitable for them, and the performative dimensions of their lives enable the audience to interpret Schumacher's aerial shots another way. All of this camera movement does not signal freedom but comments on the stagnation of vampires as they retrace the same ground again and again in the hope of recapturing their humanity. Apparently, nothing characterizes being human more than addictive behavior.

Another common shot in the film, the bird's-eye view, taps into the audience's fears associated with unseen or unexpected dangers, and these shots further reinforce the analogy between vampires and junk food. Like the perspective in Hitchcock's *The Birds* (1963), the vampires of *The Lost Boys* soar overhead, just waiting to swoop down and yank a victim into the darkness. This vantage point establishes the central tension in the film between complacency and danger. Initially, the camera work establishes a false sense of security for the audience, unfurling beautiful landscapes, showcasing sparkling lights, and offering an escape from the cacophonous boardwalk. These moments of peaceful calm get shattered when the camera moves closer to the ground, and the audience realizes that it has assumed the perspective of a predator. The attacks on a security guard and the couple in a parked car, for instance, illustrate this abrupt shift from distanced calm to sudden violence.

These shots can be understood metaphorically as well. Certain behaviors may seem innocuous at first, but in the broader context of addiction, they are harmful indeed. Processed foods, cigarettes, alcohol, and drugs are often quiet predators, unseen or seemingly innocuous forces that swoop down and take hold with an iron grip. Perhaps, this message comes across most clearly through the challenges of getting clean. Michael's restoration requires the collective effort of family and friends, for the addict needs a supportive community to make healthy, positive choices. He needs help to get and to stay clean. For Grandpa, however, nothing has changed at the end of the film. He has known about vampires all along, and as his sip of soda suggests, he is going to keep stocking that refrigerator. It would seem that it is easier to cure oneself of vampirism than junk food.

Near Dark

Milk and Beer: The Morality of Food in Near Dark

Kathryn Bigelow, the Academy Award–winning director of *The Hurt Locker* (2010), co-wrote and directed *Near Dark* in 1987. Her film, which fuses the genres of horror and the western,[14] functions as an allegory for addiction. It depicts the violent bloodlust of vampire life as antithetical to the values of familial stability and wholesome eating. When Caleb Colton (Adrian Pasdar) becomes infatuated with Mae (Jenny Wright), their first kiss leads to a bite that partially transforms him into a vampire. This tryst provokes Mae's vampire family into abducting Caleb, and they offer him a place in their clan as long as he earns his meals by killing. Caleb refuses, feeding on Mae instead, and this decision makes it morally possible for him to regain both his humanity and his place on the family farm. In the end, Caleb destroys all of the vampires to save his sister and Mae, whom he transfuses with his own blood to bring her back into the daylight. Just as *Near Dark* juxtaposes nomadic vampire life with farming, it contrasts processed with home-grown foods to depict addiction as a destabilizing social force. Whether going out for ice cream or drinking at a bar, the pursuit of addictive substances pulls one away from familial responsibilities that include caring for and cultivating the land. It tempts one to leave the farm for the city, to abandon the home for the local tavern, and it makes one vampiric in the nocturnal quest for pleasure. According to Miller, "the vampires of *Near Dark* participate in a conversation on youth culture, patriarchy, the family, and social class that is iconic of late twentieth-century America" ("Liberating" 276). Food has a central place in this conversation as well, for *Near Dark* situates natural foods at the center of preserving American values. It uses the horrors of vampirism to suggest the need for restraint over excess in a culture that transforms crops into addictive substances and harvests oil to transport goods across the globe.

The film begins by introducing vampirism alongside junk food, tobacco, and alcohol. Initially, Caleb's cowboy boots, pickup truck, lasso, midwestern accent, and penchant for addiction place him in the tradition of the western. Instead of drinking whiskey at a saloon, though, he smokes cigarettes and hangs out at a liquor store in town. One evening, while Caleb roughhouses with some drinking buddies, one of them asks, "What the hell's eatin' you?"

Mae (Jenny Wright) appears as sweet as ice cream in Kathryn Bigelow's *Near Dark* (1987). © De Laurentiis Entertainment Group.

This question not only indicates, as Steven Jay Schneider has noted, "Caleb's own desire—to consume, and to be consumed" (77), but it also signals the importance of eating in the film. When Caleb asks for a can of beer, another buddy replies, "You're going to have to support your own bad habits." As the film shows, bad habits flourish outside of the family farm. Men pass the time drinking—whether in bars or behind the wheel of a truck. Police officers chain smoke and rely on pots of coffee to function. And junk food fills diners, gas stations, and bus stops. Caleb and his friends have been fully indoctrinated in this culture, so when Caleb cannot have a beer, he "feasts his eyes" on a beautiful woman eating soft-serve ice cream:

CALEB: Can I have a bite?
MAE: A bite?
CALEB: I'm just dyin' for a cone.
MAE: Dyin'?

In addition to the playful humor about biting and dying, the two characteristics defining vampire life, this exchange places tobacco, alcohol, and sugar on a continuum of addiction. Caleb's desire for all of them represents Americans' tireless pursuit for narcotics of one kind or another.

This scene also links sexual desire with junk food. His literal craving for a bite of ice cream represents his attraction to Mae, a young woman from Sweetwater, Texas. Like the sweetness of ice cream and the name of her hometown,

Mae's physical beauty gets associated with sugar, and Caleb behaves like an addict in her presence. He lassos her at a horse stable, and he later refuses to drive her home without a kiss: "Maybe I will, but you gonna have to kiss me first." Her kiss not only functions as a substitute for beer and ice cream, but it also leads to his partial transformation into a vampire. Vampirism, in other words, becomes a logical outgrowth of his addictive tendencies and of the culture that fosters them. Caleb's initial resistance to this state merely drives him back to sugar. While waiting for a bus ride home, he notices several vending machines at the station, and the one with an out-of-order sign suggests its extensive use by travelers. Desperately hungry, sweaty, and unsteady on his feet, Caleb buys a candy bar but reacts with disgust after the first bite, spitting it onto the floor. His former cravings for candy have already been replaced by blood here. Like the eating choices that got him hooked on candy, blood is changing his tastes. Caleb cannot survive long without feeding, though, and he scrambles back to Mae, drinking voraciously from her arm until she pulls away. Now he feeds two of his desires—Mae and blood—but as this scene makes clear, these addictions have prevented him from returning home. Selfish need replaces familial and social commitment. In this way, Bigelow casts Caleb's journey from addiction to recovery, from excess to restraint, as emblematic of the food journey needed by the country.

The food politics of *Near Dark* get captured most vividly through the juxtaposition of the Colton farm with the nomadic feeding practices of vampires. The Coltons manage a ranch with cattle, horses, and plowed fields. They do not work for the meatpacking industry or produce crops owned by corporate agriculture. They carry on the tradition of the independent American farmer, cultivating the land and raising cattle to provide food for themselves and to sell locally. In addition to being a farmer, Loy Colton (Tim Thomerson) works as a veterinarian, and the film first shows him tending to a cow, injecting her with a syringe as he wears a stethoscope. After Loy tracks down his son and restores his humanity through a blood transfusion, the family resumes its agricultural life. They sit around the kitchen table for a steak dinner served with glasses of lowfat milk. They partake in mashed potatoes, beans, and water. Although they flavor some of these foods with fat (butter, gravy) and salt, they are consuming natural foods here, cultivated either at home or on nearby farms. These foods represent a wholesome connection to the land and to the labor associated with it. Despite the fats, salt, and possible beer can near the father (though it remains obscured by the milk and untouched during dinner), none of these items gets used in an excessive manner. When Caleb's sister, Sarah (Marcie Leeds), leans across the table to take a second steak, for instance, Loy admonishes her: "Knock that off." Overindulgence is monitored

This wholesome dinner at the Colton farm signals Caleb's (Adrian Pasdar's) restored humanity in *Near Dark* (1987). © De Laurentiis Entertainment Group.

and curbed here. That is what stable families provide—an environment that encourages good health, good eating habits, and restraint.

Life on the road, however, gets characterized by unchecked hungers and foods designed to foster overconsumption. While Loy and Sarah search for Caleb, they interview people drinking soda at gas stations. They eat in diners with fast-cooked hamburgers and soda. And most significantly, at the Godspeed Motel, Sarah leaves her room at five in the morning to buy Coke from a vending machine. This predawn soda highlights the food industry's vampiric impact on consumers, for this sugar craving literally endangers her life when a vampire named Homer (Joshua Miller) approaches. He entices her to come to his room with the promise of watching color television, and these desires—for Coke and television—make her vulnerable. Once inside, Sarah meets the rest of Homer's family as they play cards, smoke, and crack wise. When Severen (Bill Paxton) sees her, for instance, he asks, "Who ordered pizza?" Equating her with delivery fast food not only functions as a joke about people as the diet of vampires, but it also reinforces the film's presentation of such meals as instilling dangerous appetites. It keeps families from natural, home-cooked foods, and it enables a rootlessness that is antithetical to rural life. After Homer turns on the television, the screen shows an American flag fluttering in the breeze, but moments later the signal breaks, producing only static. This image invites viewers to think about this scene in terms of American culture. Whether through tobacco, gambling, soda, or fast food, Bigelow

Caleb and America feed their respective addictions in *Near Dark* (1987). © De Laurentiis Entertainment Group.

depicts the country as increasingly susceptible to addictive vices. These cravings, which have already led Sarah and Caleb into danger, threaten the stability of the family.

In this context, Caleb's battle with bloodlust functions as a metaphor for the nation's struggles with addiction. Mae first tries to introduce Caleb to killing when they hitch a ride with a trucker. While the man sips beer behind the wheel, Caleb drinks and smokes as he considers murdering him for food. Ill from hunger and moral apprehension, Caleb insists on getting out of the truck, and he falls to the ground clutching his stomach. The driver then asks jokingly: "What's the matter, boy? You can't drink and drive?" Once again, vampirism gets aligned with other forms of substance abuse (drinking and smoking), and though Mae has advised Caleb to disregard any moral qualms about killing, his resistance establishes the fundamental dichotomy of the film between right and wrong, restraint and excess. Instead of feeding on the driver, Caleb drinks from Mae as she stands in front of oil rigs churning up and down, sucking the black, viscous fluid from the earth. Oil not only enables the itinerant life of these vampires (as they endlessly drive cars across the country), but it also provides the means for transporting processed foods, alcohol, and tobacco. It enables the supply of America's various addictions while mirroring the country's vampiric hunger for oil in the 1980s. Like the rigs that never stop drilling, Caleb takes so much of Mae's blood that she warns he might kill her. This is the danger that Caleb and the country face more broadly—cultivating a self-destructive appetite.

It seems fitting that the clan—after issuing an ultimatum to Caleb—takes him to a roadside bar for drinks. They order whiskeys and beers, and Jesse (Lance Henriksen) eventually fills a mug with the blood of a waitress. Alcohol and blood become interchangeable here. After Severen bites into a man's neck, he burps as if drinking too much and sucks the blood off his fingers, proclaiming, "It's finger lickin' good!" This famous advertising slogan for Kentucky Fried Chicken captures Severen's wicked sense of humor and points to the ubiquitous presence of fast food in America. The slogan—much like the signs for Marlboro cigarettes, Bud, Hamms, and other beers in the bar—reminds the audience of the nearly inescapable presence of addictive substances in consumer culture. After Severen's meal, the young man intended for Caleb jumps through a window and runs into a field behind the bar. Caleb catches up with him beneath a billboard reading "Because clean hay pays." Clean hay and natural farmland starkly contrast fried chicken, alcohol, and other snacks elsewhere in the film. "Clean hay" implies farming without pesticides, and the slogan suggests both a tangible and intangible reward for responsible decisions. Caleb's choice between vampire and human becomes emblematic of the choice facing Americans between healthy eating and processed, chemically altered foods. Just as Caleb and Mae will try to embrace a natural, balanced diet in the closing moments, the film invites audiences to do the same.

Laughing All the Way to the Grave: Junk Food and Vampire Comedies

> I don't want to be a vampire. I'm a day person.
> —*Once Bitten*

Following the financial success of *Love at First Bite* (1979), a reworking of Bram Stoker's *Dracula* that brings the Count to New York City to pursue his infatuation for a fashion model and to discover the wonders of disco, filmmakers in the 1980s wanted to capitalize on the appeal of horror comedy. These genres may not seem like natural bedfellows, but as Mary Hallab has noted, horror and comedy share numerous affinities. They both deal in "surprise, shock, and incongruity, but most importantly, the abrupt reversal of accepted beliefs and commonplace expectations" (139). Humor is also "tolerant and open-minded toward new ideas, new people, new creatures," and it

Mark (Jim Carrey) contemplates his transformation in Howard Storm's *Once Bitten* (1985). © The Samuel Goldwyn Company.

has the power to get audiences to laugh at their own shortcomings. Vampire comedies in the eighties became the ideal vehicle for mocking the country's addictive tendencies. As the Count himself explains in *Love at First Bite*, "How would you like to dine on a warm, liquid protein diet, while all around you people are eating lamb chops, potato chips, Mallomars, Chivas Regal on the rocks with a twist?" Such temptations proliferated in the following decade, and numerous films including *Once Bitten* (1985), *My Best Friend Is a Vampire* (1987), *A Return to Salem's Lot* (1987), *Fright Night* (1985), and *Fright Night Part 2* (1988) critique the processed food industry by presenting vampires and half-vampires as choosing a healthier, more natural diet than most humans. Ultimately, this contrast between fast food and vampirism paints America's quick-fix mentality—for sex, food, and even maintaining a youthful appearance—as morally and socially harmful.

Once Bitten (1985), which cast Jim Carrey in his first leading role and features some of the physical comedy that would characterize his career, uses junk food as a central image for its critique of casual sex. For centuries, the Countess (Laura Hutton) has maintained her youthful appearance by feeding on the blood of a young male virgin three times a year, but finding a virgin has proven particularly difficult in the 1980s. Once she meets Mark Kendall (Carrey), a teenage boy desperate for his first sexual experience, his seduction begins to transform him into a vampire. The connection between junk food and casual sex gets established most notably through his part-time job driving an ice cream truck. As his only mode of transportation, this vehicle

Mark (Jim Carrey) ponders his desires for fast sex and fast food at Burger Circus in *Once Bitten* (1985). © The Samuel Goldwyn Company.

embodies his addiction to harmful foods as well as his susceptibility to making "bad" choices. Mark eats a great deal of junk, and even the healthy options in his life get transformed into something questionable. One breakfast at home consists of orange juice and cookies, and his favorite morning meal is an "egg burger"—a concoction that appears to be a beef patty, fried eggs, and two slices of bread. Given Mark's penchant for sweets, it makes sense that he would try to indulge his sexual hungers in the ice cream truck. At a popular make-out spot in an oil field, he awkwardly tries to convince his girlfriend, Robin (Karen Kopins), to have sex with him, but she doesn't consider the front seat a fitting place for her first time. Mark's efforts get stymied even further when a heavyset teen knocks on the window to request "a cream sickle." Like the oil drill pumping tirelessly in and out of the ground, this customer and the couples having sex in nearby cars depict teenagers as driven by mechanical urges, not intimacy. Sex for them is no more meaningful than eating ice cream.

The role of fast food reinforces the film's message about the risks of casual sex. After school, Mark's best friends, Jamie (Thomas Ballatore) and Russ (Skip Lackey), work at a hamburger stand, and this place becomes a metaphor for their gung-ho attitude about one-night stands. While eating a hamburger, munching on fries, and slurping Pepsi, Mark complains about both his sexless relationship with Robin and his undercooked (though clearly charred) burger. The desire for fast sex and fast food (something too hastily cooked) is conflated here, momentarily reducing Robin to a piece of meat. The failings of this mentality get underscored when Jamie turns up the grill and scorches everything. This quick fix requires an extinguisher to quell the grease fire, covering the meat patties with goop. On one hand, the humor comes from the sexual overtones of this squirting white fluid after a conversation about sex. On the other hand, it satirizes restaurant chains such as McDonald's and Burger King. Jamie merely wipes off the toxic foam with a dishtowel in order to sell the burgers. Later in the film, he and Russ cut onions with the skin on and get "Burger Circus: Secret Sauce" from a plastic vat that resembles an industrial paint container. Even the design of the stand, which places the service counter between the lips of a gigantic clown, implies that the real fools are those who fill their mouths with this food. Such unsanitary conditions and carelessness suggest the risks of fast food, but the boys—like most Americans—eat it anyway. By contrast, Robin does not share the heated impatience of the boys. Just as she seeks the "right" time and place for sex, she also does not eat fast food or sweets of any kind, embodying a healthy alternative to their diet. Her reluctance to have sex as quickly as one might turn up the flames on a grill offers a different vision for intimacy—one that the film presents as safer and arguably more satisfying than quickly extinguished flames.

The link between women and food further highlights the dangers of a fast-food mentality toward sex. As the boys drive to a dating club in Los Angeles, the city gets depicted as a carnival of consumerism. Exclusive stores, movie theaters, palm readers, and ritzy cars appear alongside flirtatious women that dance spontaneously on the streets and take pet lions for walks. (Yes, pet lions.) Mark and his friends also notice an array of eating options including all-you-can-eat lunch buffets, the pricey Hard Rock Café, and Glitter Restaurant. In the display window of Fred Segal's Café & Eats, for example, a Roy Lichtenstein poster shows a blonde woman on the phone with speech bubbles: "What shall I wear?" and "I'll see you Sunday for Brunch!" Fashion, female beauty, food, and technology intersect here, and this image—like this montage of Los Angeles—suggests that anything can be acquired quickly in modern America. The Phone-A-Date club, however, proves to be as satisfying as a slice of Wonder Bread (which is prominently advertised on a tour bus during the montage). The trio receives no pleasure from several rounds of beer, and Mark gets seduced by the Countess here. At her mansion the next morning, he recalls nothing but a dream about fruit juice: "You know those little packets of fresh fruit juice? You know ... made out of tin foil where you stick the little straws in them to open them? [...] Well, I think I dreamt that I was one of those." This detail certainly offers a funny image for what the vampire has done to him while referencing the popular drink Capri Sun, which first appeared on US shelves in 1981. In effect, the Countess has reduced Mark to processed food.

It is worth noting that the juice described in this dream has little or no nutritional value. Juice concentrate, for instance, is produced by peeling fruit (removing fiber and vitamins), extracting juice from the pulp (removing more fiber), adjusting the sweetness, and evaporating the water. This process converts it into "stripped juice" or pure sugar while allowing the industry to advertise it as healthy; i.e., fruit (Moss 134). It makes sense that Mark can only think to give the Countess one thing when he leaves the mansion—not a kiss, hug, or affectionate gesture but a Nestlé Crunch bar from his truck. Like a treat that will melt or in this case go uneaten, a one-night stand has not proven as meaningful as Mark had hoped. It has not cured his anxieties about sex; instead, it leaves him hollow as an empty juice container, guilty for cheating on Robin and transformed into a partial vampire.

By contrast, the eating habits of vampires come across as a positive alternative to the American diet. After her experiences with Mark, the Countess considers seeking virgins elsewhere, but her butler protests, "Are you suggesting we invade suburbia? Bowling alleys? RVs? Chicken McNuggets?" Certainly, his elitism corresponds with the Countess's sense of socioeconomic privilege. Working-class individuals, such as peasants and shepherds, have been exploitable resources to her for centuries, and Mark is no different. Nevertheless, her quest for the pure blood of a virgin suggests that McDonald's fast food would compromise the quality of this diet. (She keeps bottles of "Whole Blood" in her refrigerator, after all.) She needs something pure and untainted, which directly contrasts most of the food in the film. Robin echoes a similar sentiment when she learns of Mark's infidelity: "Where did you find her? A 7-Eleven? A bowling alley?" The analogy between junk food and infidelity casts both as dangerously irresponsible.

The Countess's diet may have some merits for a vampire, but she is not immune to the temptations of modern consumerism. Though she laments that "being a vampire in the twentieth century is a nightmare," her frustration with the hedonistic impulses of Los Angeles appears tempered by her complete immersion in conspicuous consumption. She sleeps in a plush coffin, exercises on a treadmill wearing workout clothes in the style of Jane Fonda, and lives in an elegant mansion with modern décor. The need to surround herself with the trappings of upper-class privilege reflects her hunger to stay young, thin, and sexually desirable. Nothing horrifies this vampire more than aging, and her attitude offers a parody of America's valorization of youth culture. Modern society does not make room for the natural progression of things such as aging, sexual experience, and cooking. When the Countess fails to feed, her body begins to age, and she pleads, "Call a plastic surgeon!" This moment suggests that the allure of consumerism—whether through surgery, material goods, or meals—has the potential to make one vampiric, and this risk faces Mark literally and figuratively. His gradual change represents the dehumanizing impact of a culture that objectifies women and promotes instant gratification. Though Robin decides to have sex with Mark at the end of the film to save him from the Countess, the future is less clear. They both smoke in this scene, and while the cigarettes serve as an obvious gag, Mark still appears stuck in a cycle of substituting one addiction (junk food, sugar, alcohol, sex) for another (tobacco). Like Mark, it seems America has a long way to go before breaking loose from the fangs of consumerism.

Sweets have dangerous implications in *My Best Friend Is a Vampire* (1987) as well. They tempt one to eat outside of the home (away from mom's cooking and a refrigerator filled with fruits and vegetables). They get linked with sexual temptation for the "wrong" woman, such as predatory vampires and cheerleaders, and they eventually need to be offset by a healthy diet. The film revolves around teenager Jeremy Capello (Robert Sean Leonard) and his romantic attraction to a nerdy classmate, Darla (Cheryl Pollak). Things gets complicated, however, when a sexual encounter with a vampire begins to change him. Faced with this new identity, Jeremy realizes that maintaining some connection with his humanity (and Darla) requires fighting his newfound urges. In many respects, *My Best Friend Is a Vampire* centers around questions of what to eat. After opening with Jeremy's erotic dream about the girls' locker room, the camera shows his mother standing next to a cookbook and frying eggs. Jeremy's hunger for Darla—the only girl he wants to kiss in the dream—gets equated with home cooking here. It casts Darla as a healthy choice for Jeremy, and he will need a truly virtuous diet in order to be with her. This breakfast of eggs, toast, and orange juice also signals Jeremy's supportive family. His parents manifest their care for him, in part, by encouraging healthy eating, so when Jeremy stops partaking in family meals ("I'm just not hungry"), they know something is wrong. Even Jeremy's changing tastes reveal the value placed on good foods in the Capello home. While making a protein shake, for example, he modifies the ingredients by putting a raw, bloody steak into the blender. This concoction horrifies him at first, and though it reflects his burgeoning nature as a vampire, it says something about the type of eater Jeremy has been. He considers protein shakes, instead of Doritos, a viable late-night snack. While he does not eschew junk food, he never consumes it onscreen. This detail fits into the film's broader presentation of natural or homemade foods as a symbol for living a balanced, moral life.

Jeremy has plenty of exposure to sugary snacks, and these foods almost always signal trouble. His part-time job at a grocery store gives him access to sugar on a daily basis. Its shelves contain a wide range of processed foods including Velveeta cheese, Ruffles potato chips, soda, Minute Maid juice, and Five Alive. At the start of one shift, Jeremy pauses at the checkout counter to grab some candy from a box between the Milk Duds and Tic Tacs. The presumed consumption of sugar (we don't actually see him eat) precedes his delivery to a vampire named Nora (Cecilia Peck). Inside her home, Jeremy nervously drops the groceries on her dining room table, and she picks up a spilled apple just before sucking his recently cut finger. For her, groceries function as a pretext for getting access to a warm body, but the substitution of one type of food (apple) for another (blood) reflects the choice many teens in the film are making between natural foods and junk. In the following scene, Jeremy tells his crass best friend about Nora over burgers, fries, and Cokes, and later Jeremy and Darla order a "Garbage Can Pizza" on their date—a name that advertises its unhealthiness with campy glee. These details link eating choices with a broader tension between instant gratification and moral behavior. What one eats signals what one values, and the temptation for bad food mirrors the potentially dangerous consequences of bad decisions about sex.

Jeremy finds himself tempted by another woman associated with junk food—a high school cheerleader named Candy (Lee Anne Locken). Much like candy itself, this girl is enticing but not a healthy choice for Jeremy. As his father remarks, "your mom said a girl named Candy called today. . . . That's a great name, Candy. It sounds yummy." The misogynistic humor reinforces one of the gender critiques of the film as the pronoun "it" refers to both her name and the tendency among men to objectify women. Not surprisingly, his father—who keeps an open container of Whoppers on his desk at home—enjoys junk food. In both cases, vampire Nora and Candy represent the wrong choice. They signify Jeremy's lust, and though he does not want to view sex this way, his buddy's advice about a carefree fling prods him into a late-night liaison with Nora. Afterward, Ralph (Evan Mirand) is puzzled by Jeremy's refusal to drink a cherry Coke: "I thought it was your favorite." While the film uses these moments to reveal Jeremy's changing tastes as a nascent vampire, they also fit into a pattern of associating junk food with making poor decisions. Jeremy pays a steep price for this brief ethical lapse. At one point, he protests the seeming injustice of it all: "Why is this happening to me? I've been good—no drugs, no alcohol. I do my homework. Why me?" In the moral

Healthy choices for 1980s vampire in Jimmy Huston's *My Best Friend Is a Vampire* (1987). © Kings Road Entertainment.

economy of this film, however, doing one's homework and avoiding drugs are not enough. Healthy eating represents the ability to act morally. Meaningless sex, by contrast, becomes akin to a diet of cherry Coke and Milk Duds.

My Best Friend Is a Vampire reinforces this message about choosing the "right" foods most explicitly after Jeremy's transformation. His desire to maintain human friendships and to nurture his affection for Darla demand a socially responsible diet. With the help of a vampire mentor and the advice book *Vampirism: A Practical Guide to an Alternative Lifestyle*, Jeremy learns that Whole Foods Market surreptitiously sells pig's blood to vampires. He first purchases some from a store butcher whose cap reads, "USDA Choice: Grain Fed Beef." After drinking the blood, Jeremy accepts his new identity as a vampire and begins stocking his refrigerator with an array of pig products: "Pig's Blood. 100% All Natural. No additives, preservatives, salts, starches, yeast, sugars, or flavor enhancers. Keep refrigerated. LOW FAT, NO MSG." Some of the other items include Pig's Blood soda, Pig's Blood Light, and wine from Chateau la Swine. It appears that vampires worry about the dangers of processed foods as well. Like the butcher's hat, which reminds customers about the poor quality of most processed meat in America, these products promise beverages without sugar, preservatives, or flavor enhancers such as MSG.

Pig's Blood Light helps vampires know what they are getting, but the same cannot be said for most humans in this film. At one point, Grimsdyke (Paul

Wilson), the fat, clumsy sidekick for famed vampire hunter Professor McCarthy (David Warner), tries to save himself by telling a suspected vampire: "You don't want me. I'm old. My blood is polluted with cholesterol!" American eating habits had become so bad that vampires would be advised to turn elsewhere for sustenance. Jeremy ultimately consumes the "right" foods— foods that enable him to maintain his friendships, to be Darla's boyfriend, to assuage his parents' fears about his possible homosexuality,[15] and to live the wholesome life of an undead teen. Just as Jeremy's food choices as a vampire define him, the film suggests that the same is true for the audience.

Larry Cohen's *A Return to Salem's Lot* (1987), though not a comedy per se, offers a similar critique of the American diet by presenting vampires as eating more responsibly than humans. Salem's Lot, a town overrun by the undead, takes its cues from a master vampire that decides to hire anthropologist Joe Weber (Michael Moriarty) to write a history that will change the way outsiders perceive their race. Joe grew up in the town, and his nostalgic attachment to the place tempts him to accept the assignment. Eventually, he discovers that the vampires breed drones to protect their graves, to corral the occasional victim, and to maintain the façade of normalcy by operating the town during the day. Except for the occasional holiday, the vampires of Salem's Lot no longer feed on human prey. Instead, they raise cattle. As the master vampire explains, cattle farms enable them to maintain a steady food supply and to ensure quality: "We're all dairy farmers in these parts. You outsiders grow stock for meat. We grow 'em for blood. See . . . human blood is still the best, but the way things are going nowadays it's not quite good for you—what with drugs, alcohol, hepatitis, and this AIDS virus going around." Human addictions have become so prevalent and destructive that even vampires fear feeding on people.

Furthermore, these eighties vampires assert an ethical high ground when it comes to eating. In addition to controlling their urge for human blood (most of the time), they consume cows in a more humane way than the "butchering you outsiders do." These dairy-farming, cattle-raising vampires grow what they consume but refuse to kill. They merely drain some of the cow's blood so that within a week's time it can be replenished naturally. This detail makes the critique of the American food industry clear. Through its mass production of meats and the proliferation of scientifically altered foods, modern eating habits have become more horrifying, less healthy, and far less natural than those of vampires.

In the closing moments of the film, Joe must battle the master vampire for literal and, arguably, gustatory freedom. As they tussle on the floor of a toolshed, Joe's son, Jeremy (Ricky Reed), lances the vampire with an American flag pole, and the flag covers his body while the creature turns to dust. The heavy-handed imagery invites audiences to read the central conflict of the film as one between captivity and freedom. The vampires' freedom is predicated on the enslavement of others—most notably the mindless, unfeeling drones—and Joe's coercion along with Jeremy's abduction places humans in the same category of servitude. They become expendable resources for a master race. Certainly, the film's repeated references to Nazism, including a Nazi hunter that helps save Joe and Jeremy, reinforce its warning about ideological threats to democracy. Destroying the head vampire and the town of Salem's Lot thus functions as a way to reassert the value of individual freedom—even the freedom to make the wrong choices about love, family, and food. Joe has been tempted by nostalgia and the seductiveness of a teenaged vampire. Jeremy, a fashionably dressed juvenile delinquent, has been enchanted by a beautiful girl, the idea of perpetual youth, and a community that appears to promise stability. And like the son's addiction to smoking and swearing, Joe craves soda when he first gets to town. As they drive away from the burning town, Jeremy accepts Joe as his father, and he even views aging as a natural process: "All of a sudden I'm not in such a rush to grow up. [. . .] I guess getting old isn't so bad either." The closing shot focuses on cattle grazing in the lush green hills outside of town. This emphasis on the natural—of biological family and of aging—gets aligned with the natural diet of animals. We don't know if Joe and his son will return to the habit of drinking sodas, but the closing image suggests that they will try to find something healthier.

Lastly, *Fright Night* (1985) and *Fright Night Part 2* (1988) share similar concerns in their joyful, campy celebration of horror. In a 2008 interview, Tom Holland, the writer and director of *Fright Night*, recalls "laughing the entire time [he wrote the script], literally on the floor, kicking my feet in the air in hysterics," and he considers the film a valentine to the genre: "There is only love for the fans and love for the horror movies of that time."[16] This love helps explains the unexpected success of the film, which became the third most lucrative horror movie of 1985;[17] it laughs good naturedly at Charley Brewster (William Ragsdale) while treating the vampire mythology seriously. Horror has value in the world of *Fright Night*. It enables Charley to recognize vampires, and the solutions for defeating the undead come from fans, not books. "Evil" Ed (Stephen Geoffreys), for instance, gives Charley advice on protecting himself from his vampire neighbor in the first film: "Start with this [a cross], but you must have total faith in it for it to work. Then get some garlic. [. . .] Then, of course, there is holy water. [. . .] But your best protection right now, Charles, is that a vampire cannot enter your house without being

Charley (William Ragsdale) indulges his passion for horror, junk food, and voyeurism in Tom Holland's *Fright Night* (1985). © Columbia Pictures.

invited by the rightful owner first." Likewise, Peter Vincent (Roddy McDowall), a second-rate horror actor and current host of the late-night television show *Fright Night*, uses props from his films such as stakes, vials of holy water, and pocket mirrors to do battle. In the sequel, Charley even argues passionately for the artistic value of horror: "Did you see *Bloodsuckers from Beyond*? Then you don't know what you're talking about, do you? God, it makes me mad when people do that. [. . .] There happens to be some great literature from the field. Did you ever read *Dracula*? It's a great book [. . .] a great book!" Ultimately, the knowledge derived from the genre inspires heroism and save lives. It rewards fans for their passionate investment.

In keeping with the social commentary at the heart of the genre, *Fright Night* and *Fright Night Part 2* also warn against the dangers of addictive behaviors, and they link horror with junk food to suggest that both have the potential to foster unhealthy obsessions. Horror may be crucial for defeating the forces of evil, but like eating too much junk food, an obsessive relationship with it can be harmful. Horror—whether watching old B-films or peering into the windows of suspected vampires—prevents Charley from emotional and physical intimacy. *Fright Night* begins with Charley expressing frustration over his girlfriend's unwillingness to have sex, but as soon as she invites him to bed, he gets distracted by some men moving a coffin into the basement next door. Largely oblivious to her feelings, Charley begins a stakeout of sorts, watching his neighbor's house through binoculars. These evenings are accompanied by horror films on television and an array of junk food. During one vigil, the camera shows the remnants of Charley's snacks on the floor—a bag of chips, a Coke, a candy bar, and some other wrappers strewn across a pornographic magazine. Moments later, he sees a prostitute undressing next door just before his neighbor bites her neck. Junk food, pornography, and horror get equated here, and all of them contribute to Charley's disconnection from others. These foods presumably help him stay awake, but as the centerfold (whose face is covered by the bag of chips) and his observation of the prostitute suggest, he continues to substitute something artificial for something real. Pornographic images and voyeurism take the place of his girlfriend, and such substitutions, the film suggests, hinder personal growth and maturity.

Fright Night Part 2, which takes place three years later and presents Charley in a state of arrested development through his tastes in film and food, reinforces this message. Once again, he has a girlfriend, Alex (Traci Lind), reluctant to have sex with him. His problems with intimacy stem from his limiting attitudes about female sexuality. Charley's absentminded insensitivity to Alex's emotional needs can be attributed, in part, to his taste in film. After years of psychotherapy designed to convince him that vampires do not exist, Charley has abandoned the tools for fighting the undead, throwing out his collection of stakes, crosses, hammers, and garlic. His passion for B-horror films, however, has merely been replaced by B-erotica. Movie posters of the latter cover the walls in his college dorm room: *Women's Prison*, *Pushover*, *Sex Kittens in College* (with the tagline "Never has the screen had so much fun with a student body"), and *Teenage Caveman*, which features a naked woman and a scantily clad prehistoric man battling a Tyrannosaurus Rex. These images suggest that Charley has replaced one type of fantasy for another. Both horror and campy erotica tend to objectify women, and in this way, little has changed for Charley since high school.

The same goes for food. After a string of bumbled dates, he apologizes to his girlfriend with roses and a promise to bring her dinner in the library. The meal, which he purchases from a deli, consists of two sandwiches, pickles, packets of mustard, and two large chocolate milk shakes. One milk shake has two straws, and the other has been emptied to serve as a makeshift vase for the flowers. Though one wouldn't expect a college student to cook in a dorm, to have the budget for high-end cuisine, or to bring something particularly refined to a library picnic, the performative aspect of this dinner reflects Charley's ongoing struggle to be true to himself. The red-checkered tablecloth remains unused. The vase has no water in it. And the content of the sandwiches remains obscured by large slices of white bread. The only thing the audience sees clearly is the milk shake, a prominent image for his love of sweets. Furthermore, the shortwave television he brings to broadcast a live concert of Bach's music (appealing to Alex's taste, not his) ends up showing only *Fright Night*. These details remind the audience of Charley's core passions for horror, junk food, and clichéd notions of romance.

Through his gradual transformation into a vampire, the film uses Charley's true cravings for food to reinforce its message about psychological and emotional balance. After noticing the necks of women on campus, he rushes off to get a slice of pizza. He stands impatiently at the counter as the saleswoman lauds its quality: "All natural ingredients. We made the tomato sauce fresh this morning, none of that canned crap. Freshly grated parmesan and Romano. The leanest sausage in town. Baked with no nitrates in it. Organic artichoke hearts. Oh yeah, and my special, secret ingredient . . . a whole bulb of garlic on each pizza." Charley has already taken a bite at this point, and with these words, he spits out the food. Of course, this reaction to garlic signals his new vampiric nature, but the desire for pizza—like chocolate milk shakes—represents something authentic about him. He craves it, just as he craves horror fiction. This "healthy" pizza becomes a humorous image for the challenge of striking a balance between restraint and overindulgence. The saleswoman's pitch happens while she smokes a cigarette, and the pizza place, located inside a college bowling alley, features racks of potato chips, dispenses Coke products from a soda fountain, and serves beer. It seems unlikely that any student comes here for quality food. Even when the vampires subsequently feed on her and the heavyset owner, the audience cannot help but think of that meal as equally unhealthy.

These details in *Fright Night Part 2* are not designed to demonize junk food or horror. The audience only catches glimpses of the way processed foods characterize modern life, and its celebration of Bram Stoker's novel as "great literature" alongside the music of Bach and Mahler are in keeping with *Fright Night*'s celebration of the genre. What Charley learns is that he does not need to stop eating sugar and watching horror to live an emotionally and psychologically healthy life. He just needs to balance his gustatory and artistic tastes. In the closing moments, Charley and his girlfriend appear on a blanket amid a sweeping rose garden with a real picnic basket at their feet. Outside, beneath the sunlight, they discuss a future together. As Charley explains, "We go on with our lives. [. . .] We rent an apartment together. Maybe get married. Maybe make some babies. Maybe buy a farm." Charley's insularity and his appetite for sex without the complications of intimacy have been replaced with an image of marriage and family. His penchant for junk food has been replaced with a picnic basket and dreams of buying a farm. As the roses and the cross around his girlfriend's neck suggest, they will remain fans of horror and watchful of future vampires. They might be dining on clichéd fantasies at this moment, but the film presents both of them as trying to live (and eat) authentically.

The Queen of the Damned

*"So Sweet . . . It Can Be Fatal": Addictive Hungers
in Anne Rice's* The Queen of the Damned

Between 1976 and 2016, Anne Rice published twelve volumes of the *Vampire Chronicles*, a series of novels featuring Lestat de Lioncourt, an eighteenth-century French nobleman turned vampire. These books have arguably made Rice the most influential writer of vampire fiction since Bram Stoker. Her first novel in the series, *Interview with the Vampire* (1976),[18] revolutionized the genre by dispelling some of the traditional tools used against these nocturnal creatures, most notably garlic, crucifixes, and wooden stakes through the heart. It also introduced, as Simon Bacon has noted, the "first, mainstream, self-loathing vampire" in Louis de Pointe du Lac (49). Most of Rice's vampires are male, bisexual, and devilishly handsome. As one ancient vampire in the series remarked, "Was nobody ugly ever given immortality?" (*Queen* 277). They establish communities, get involved in passionate relationships, build up frequent flyer miles, acquire vast riches, raise offspring, and remain "refined enough not to irritate each other throughout eternity" (Auerbach 154). They also wrestle with addictive appetites. Unlike Lestat, who overindulges in killing, feeding on "humans all the time, sometimes two or three a night, sometimes more" (41), Louis dines on small animals in *Interview with the Vampire*: "I believed I killed animals for aesthetic reasons only, and I hedged against the great moral question of whether or not by my very nature I was damned" (72). Although this existential crisis determines what and how he eats, similar concerns preoccupy many of Rice's vampires at one time or another. Even the narcissistic Lestat experiences some moral qualms about his hungers by *The Vampire Lestat* (1985) when he decides "not [to] drink innocent blood" (11). Although Rice prefers to focus on origin stories and sweeping histories, she does comment on 1980s American culture in the frame of *The Vampire Lestat* and throughout *The Queen of the Damned* (1988), which she originally intended to be the final volume of the *Vampire Chronicles*.[19]

Scholar George Haggerty has noted of the series that "If not the record of the cultural experience of the United States since the 1980s, they at least offer a précis of some of the nation's most deeply held cultural assumptions" (185). While he focuses on Rice's failure to challenge homophobic ideology in the late twentieth century,[20] the cultural assumptions surrounding food, consumption, and the dangers of excess shape her portrait of the decade as well. For Rice, addictive foods contribute to the vampiric consumerism and

Queen Akasha (Aaliyah) returns to punish men's appetite for violence in *The Queen of the Damned* (2002). Warner Brothers/Photofest. © Warner Brothers.

perpetual dissatisfaction that characterize contemporary life, dehumanizing people to such an extent that they can no longer recognize the difference between themselves and vampires. The contemporary frame for *The Vampire Lestat*, which also serves as the starting point for *The Queen of the Damned*, makes food an important part of Rice's examination of American life. Lestat's music has made him "a Rock Superstar" in 1984 (*VL* 1). It has also given him a notorious reputation within the vampire community, for his celebrity and song lyrics violate a sacrosanct rule against revealing the existence of vampires. When Queen Akasha returns to life and takes Lestat as a lover, promising to make him a god, she reveals her plan to fashion an Eden on Earth by destroying those most responsible for violence—men. As she explains, "A new era is coming when those males who glorify death and killing shall reap their reward, and the era of peace shall be yours" (297). The Queen's eventual demise prevents the mass killing of men (and the annihilation of vampires), but through her character, Rice crafts an origin story that keeps the literal act of eating and the dangers of excess central to vampire lore. *The Queen of the Damned*, thus, becomes a cautionary tale about eating too much of the wrong thing. Whether through fast food, alcohol, blood drinking, or cannibalism, overconsumption serves as a metaphor for the monstrous appetites of a country that has lost its sense of balance, restraint, and compassion. It is a country, in other words, where the undead feel right at home.

Many of Rice's vampires have been roaming around for centuries, far too long to have developed a taste for McDonald's, but her portrait of the 1980s emphasizes the nation's cravings for fast foods, sugar, and alcohol. In the opening moments of *The Vampire Lestat*, Lestat wants to pass among the living, and this requires external sleight of hand only. Fashionable clothes and makeup enable him to craft an outward appearance that mimics current trends, and he implies a similar approach to eating: "I decked myself out in the shimmering dream skins of the fashionable shops. I wore white turtleneck shirts and crisp khaki safari jackets, or lush gray velvet blazers with cashmere scarves. I powdered down my face so that I could 'pass' beneath the chemical lights of the all-night supermarkets, the hamburger joints, the carnival thoroughfares called nightclub strips" (11). Whether wearing velvet blazers in a nightclub or turtleneck shirts in a fast-food restaurant, Lestat recognizes that passing demands the "right" clothes and the appearance of consuming the "right" foods. The most notable examples of this come in the form of processed foods in supermarkets and hamburgers.

Of course, Lestat has a history of imitating eating rituals to put people at ease. In *Interview with the Vampire*, he and Louis perform evening meals in front of Lestat's blind father: "Lestat and I sat down to dinner each night with the old man and made nice noises with our knives and forks, while he told us to eat everything on our plates and not to drink our wine too fast" (49). Just as he offers his father a reassuring parody of family life, he uses the pretext of dining to lure female victims into his home: "Lestat pretended to dine . . . you would be surprised how people do not notice that a vampire is only pretending to eat" (77). He flirts with two women here, inviting one to sit on his lap before draining her blood and claiming that she "has no head for wine" (78). Her perceived overindulgence serves to deflect his own.

Rice has Louis make a similar analogy between blood and sugar in *Interview with the Vampire*. When Louis explains that "a fresh young girl was [Lestat's] favorite food," he likens them to sugar (41): "I shall give you a perfect example of what Lestat liked. Up the river from us was a Freniere plantation [. . .] which had great hopes of making a fortune in sugar, just shortly after the refining process had been invented. I presume you know sugar was refined in Louisiana. [. . .] This refined sugar is a poison. It was like the essence of life in New Orleans, so sweet that it can be fatal, so richly enticing that all other values are forgotten" (42). Sugar functions as a metaphor on several levels here. First, the sweet fatality of this substance alludes to the violent consequences of the plantation system. The destructive impact of slavery on African identity appears throughout the early part of the novel, and a slave revolt ultimately reduces Louis's home to ashes. The country's addiction to sugar fueled its addiction to forced labor, making African lives and freedom the cost for maintaining the nation's sweet tooth.[21] Louis's observations about sugar also link it with a vampire's craving for blood. Both reduce one to bodily impulses. When faced with these urges, other values such as personal restraint and empathy (for the treatment of slaves) often get abandoned. Rice uses these details to establish an affinity between vampires and sugar, casting both as dangerous for humanity.

Though Rice never shows Lestat drinking a Coke or ordering a Big Mac, she does depict new vampires—those created in the 1980s—as associating bloodlust with fast foods and sweets. Baby Jenks in *The Queen of the Damned* becomes part of a vampire biker gang, the Fang Gang, after they turned her into a vampire in 1983. At the time, this fourteen-year-old girl was high on heroin and bleeding to death from an abortion. Her history of drug use—much like her work as a prostitute—makes her a victim of an addictive culture. She gets high, in part, not to care about what happens to her body while being operated on or while servicing men. She and the Fang Gang also capitalize on their victims' thirst for alcohol, luring men "out of the roadside beer joints" to feed. One addiction mirrors—and enables—the other. Baby Jenks even associates her newfound cravings with processed foods: "Oh, the blood was good, yum, it was so good, even now that she was alone and had to work up the nerve, the way it had been this evening, to pull into a gas station and lure the old guy out back. Oh, yea, snap, when she'd gotten her hands on his neck, and the blood came, it had been just fine, it was hamburgers and French fries and strawberry shakes, it was beer and chocolate sundaes. It was mainline, and coke and hash. It was better than screwing! It was all of it" (44). Her catalog of addictions begins with fast food, ice cream (both shakes and sundaes), sugar (chocolate), and alcohol. Sugar, along with the fats and saltiness of these meals, has the same allure as drinking or drugs. She equates them with the physical pleasures of sex as well, but Rice quickly undercuts these analogies. As a prostitute, sex was rarely a source of pleasure for Baby Jenks. Her father's alcoholism fueled his abusive treatment of her, and drugs merely provided a coping mechanism for personal trauma. Junk food, therefore, functions as another self-destructive, short-term fix.

At moments of anxiety, most notably when she fears that the Fang Gang has been destroyed, Baby Jenks thinks first of sugar and processed foods, and Rice contrasts this with the natural hungers of vampires: "It's bad enough now not being able to walk into a 7-Eleven under those lights without people looking at you. Who wants to look at the white marble?" (47). This self-consciousness about her pale skin offers a humorous reminder of image culture in 1980s America. (Perhaps it is not surprising that Rice's vampires can see themselves in mirrors. Even vampires need to look their best in the eighties!) The references to 7-Eleven present the store as a kind of drug dealer. Heroin or a Big Gulp? It doesn't matter since both provide a fix. When her vampire companion points out the absurdity of her craving ("Baby Jenks, you don't need anything anymore from the 7-Eleven" [47]), this moment positions the vampire's diet as a positive alternative to this junk habit. Members of the Fang Gang eat based on need; they don't engage in needless consumption. Rice thus uses this chapter to direct that message to the audience as well: we don't need—and ought to avoid—this kind of food.

Rice's portrait of human character Daniel Molloy, the unnamed boy who interviews Louis in *Interview with the Vampire* and returns in *The Queen of the Damned* as the lover of Armand, again highlights the addictive behaviors prevalent in America. The vampire Armand relies on Daniel as a guide to modern life ("You will tell me everything about this century" [93]), but it turns out that there is not much to learn. The modern era privileges two things: consumer excess and addiction. Daniel provides the most immediate example, consistently eating and drinking too much both to assert his humanity (Armand cannot do these things) and to cope with his despondency over not being a vampire: "He had started eating, lustily, furiously—a little fish, a little everything, put it all together, what did he care, and Armand had been so delighted, laughing and laughing like a schoolboy as he sat watching, with folded arms. [. . .] He got drunk as fast as he could" (88). Eating everything on the menu represents Daniel's approach to hunger and longing. He consumes in excessive quantities to fill certain voids in his life. By contrast, Armand's diet appears far healthier. He controls his urges (never drinking from Daniel). He does not wantonly create new vampires. And he does not behave in self-destructive ways. Unlike Daniel, he is not a creature driven by addiction and overconsumption.

Not surprisingly, with Daniel as his model, Armand's decision to commit to the twentieth century means committing to consumerism: "When Armand said he was ready to enter the century in earnest, he understood enough about it now. He wanted 'incalculable' wealth. He wanted a vast dwelling full of all those things he'd come to value. And yachts, planes, cars—millions of dollars. He wanted to buy Daniel everything that Daniel might ever desire" (97). Armand does not do these things for himself, which distinguishes him from Lestat, but his acquisition of wealth does reflect a distinct American sensibility. Specifically, Armand builds a mall named Night Island off the coast of Miami, stocking it with every imaginable consumer good. With "five dazzling glass stories of theaters, restaurants, and shops, [. . .] You could buy anything on the Night Island—diamonds, a Coca-Cola, books, pianos, parrots, designer fashions, porcelain dolls. All the fine cuisines of the world awaited you. Five films played nightly in the cinemas. Here was English tweed and Spanish leather, Indian silk, Chinese carpets, sterling silver, ice-cream cones or cotton candy, bone china, and Italian shoes" (100). The presence of haute cuisine alongside such high-end goods makes sense, but the reference to soda and junk food ought to be absurd. Yet its serious presentation here makes Rice's point clear. Drinking Coke, buying Italian shoes, and collecting porcelain dolls stem from the same impulse. They all play an integral role in a marketplace that wants to instill a bottomless desire for more. Fittingly, all of this stuff does not make Daniel happy. He continues to drink himself into oblivion, and only when alcoholism has destroyed his body ("'You're dying,' Armand said softly" [107]) does Armand relent and make his companion a vampire. From soda to shoes, alcohol to blood, vampirism becomes a mirror for the nation's worst impulses.

Rice crafts an origin story for vampires as well that raises moral questions about this culture of overindulgence. Eating functions as the central historical tension in *The Queen of the Damned*. The marriage of King Enkil of Kemet (later known as Egypt) to Akasha created a national conflict over food. Akasha's urban sensibility, education, and royal upbringing put her at odds with some of the cultural practices of the King's rural subjects—most notably cannibalism. She observed that "they tended to neglect [farming] to hunt, to make war for human flesh" (314). These people not only eat human flesh, but they forego their responsibilities as well as a natural diet to indulge in the violent gamesmanship of cannibalism. Eating meat and the pleasures of warring for it, in other words, had become an addiction among these people. Not surprisingly, when Queen Akasha bans the practice, instituting severe consequences for disobedience, the people become enraged: "Tribes who had hunted for flesh for generations were infuriated that they could no longer enjoy this sport, but even greater was the fury of all the people that they could not eat their dead. Not to hunt, that was one thing, but to commit one's ancestors to the earth was a horror to them" (315). The Queen's edict violates a practice that functioned as a source both for pleasure (for flesh-eating and war) and for honoring the dead.

Akasha also uses it as a pretext to arrest the most powerful witches in the region—Maharet and Mekare—in order to coopt their ability to communicate with spirits. For these twins, cannibalism functions solely as a funereal rite, and they consider other forms of it offensive: "the savage people [of the Nile valley] made war as they had always done upon the jungle peoples south of them. [. . .] For not only did they devour their own dead with all proper respect as we did, they ate the bodies of their enemies; they gloried in it. They believed the strength of the enemy went into their bodies with the consumed flesh. Also they liked the taste of the flesh" (313). The tempting "taste of the flesh" has justified an almost perpetual state of war ("as they had always done"), and as such, the condemnation of the celebratory and gustatory pleasures of cannibalism gets linked with the novel's critique of excess more broadly. Not all cannibalism is wrong among these ancient tribes, but there is something wrong with compulsive, destructive acts of consumption.

Intersecting the history of vampirism with both cannibalism and the 1980s invites readers to view American appetites in similar terms. No wonder Lestat and his ilk enjoy this decade so much; their near insatiability aligns perfectly with contemporary attitudes toward food and material goods. As Doane and Hodges argue, "these vampires are completely at home in late twentieth-century America as she constructs it. This America is a world of leisure, of inhabitants devoted to consumption [. . .]. When Lestat wakes into the America of the eighties, he finds himself in a utopia" (437). Lestat's desire for fame, for "strutting before the hot lights and the camera lenses," for visibility, and for conspicuous consumption reflect the central ethos of the period. Even the ancient Khayman, one of the first vampires, becomes momentarily enamored with the possibilities of so much excess: "He liked the blood of his victims, of course. [. . .] He felt no great need for blood anymore, but he wanted it. [. . .] He could have feasted upon three or four mortals a night" (120). Contemporary life taps into such impulses, inspiring him to want excessive amounts of what he does not need. As such, the vampires' affinity for 1980s America reinforces Rice's message about the dehumanizing potential of consumerism and the dangers of addictive foods.

Perhaps Rice shies away from the contemporary era because she cannot have it both ways. Every time she claims one final installment of the *Vampire Chronicles*, another book appears, for the very impulses driving Americans to buy processed foods, supersized sodas, and consumer goods inspire a craving for another installment of her work. The film industry, which has capitalized on the popularity of horror since the early twentieth century, has tried to do the same with Rice's vampires as well. The success of *Interview with the Vampire* in 1994, however, did not lead to immediate adaptations of her subsequent Lestat books. In fact, the disappointing adaptation of Michael Rymer's *The Queen of the Damned* in 2002 may have stalled such projects. Its decision to omit the backstory of the twins, to gloss over Akasha's (Aaliyah) origins, and to obscure its portrait of 1980s America make for a confusing and somewhat vapid film. It replaces homosexual love and passion with a hackneyed heterosexual relationship between Lestat (Stuart Townsend) and a paranormal investigator named Jesse (Marguerite Moreau). Apparently, the only thing an angst-ridden, gay vampire needs is the love of a good woman. Its monstrous depiction of Akasha without any backstory also ends up reinforcing negative stereotypes about African American women as hypersexualized. As Zélie Asava has argued, the film offers "a damning portrayal of Africans as cannibalistic, evil and anarchic, which, of course, is a cinematic tradition going back to *Birth of a Nation*" (101). And though Lestat feeds on groupies and Akasha, food and the politics of eating are absent from the film.

In fact, other than the backdrop of Goth metal music, this film largely erases the very historical context that inspired Lestat to reenter the world. Scholar Ken Gelder has argued that the camera work in *The Queen of the Damned* is equally deceptive. With its elaborate establishing shots, diverse locations (despite being filmed entirely in Australia), and sweeping camera movements, the film exposes the limited mobility of the vampire, not its freedom. For Gelder, the modern vampire "is immensely constrained in terms of movement and adaptability. [. . .] Rather than demonstrate the 'ease' of contemporary movement, the film ties it to a binary of excess (the modern) and restraint (which may also be modern, since it is something Lestat comes to learn about) that it is unable to resolve" (26). After the Queen disintegrates, Lestat returns to a vampire life of anonymity. Indulgence is not an addiction here, just a flirtation. It is something the vampire or alcoholic or sugar addict can retreat from. This notion of vampires as trapped can also be applied to the absence of cultural context. Once the social and political implications of homosexuality, interracial sex, and food in Rice's late 1980s novel get removed, its vampires remain trapped outside of history. Driven by whim and with no understanding of themselves, they lose any metaphoric significance, and these one-dimensional creatures rob Rice's novel of its richness and cultural commentary.

The Hunger

I'll Take Some Blood with That Hamburger and Coke: Fast Food and The Hunger

In its exploration of the various hungers characterizing American life at the start of the decade, Whitley Strieber's best-selling novel *The Hunger* (1981) equates vampirism with both the overconsumption of fast food and the desire for healthy eating in a world teeming with processed foods. The story focuses on the literal and metaphoric hungers of two female protagonists, Miriam Blaylock and Sarah Roberts. From the crowded streets of ancient Rome to 1980s America, Miriam has spent centuries feeding on human blood and trying to mitigate the loneliness of immortality by finding human companions

Miriam (Catherine Deneuve) and John (David Bowie) contemplate the addictive appetites that enslave them in Tony Scott's *The Hunger* (1983). MGM/UA/Photofest. © MGM/UA.

whom she infuses with her blood and entices with false promises of everlasting life. In truth, Miriam can only offer a stay of execution, extending the lives of her lovers for a few hundred years before their bodies decompose with rapid violence. As critic Mary Pharr has noted, Miriam's lovers "degenerate into hideous things caught between life and death in a state of perpetual starvation. During their deterioration, they become grotesque monsters, desperate to feed but unable to absorb the blood of their victims" (100).

This state between hunger and insatiability highlights the novel's broader concern about eating the wrong things. Strieber's human and half-human characters try to satisfy their compulsive hungers either by consuming too much or by consuming something harmful. The second protagonist, Sarah Roberts, falls into this pattern. As a scientist researching the aging process, she has become obsessed with "seeking the cure for man's most universal disease—old age" (52). Sarah hungers for professional success within a patriarchal profession, but this drive threatens her romantic relationship with Tom. This tension typically inspires the couple to turn to food for satisfaction, and when Sarah gets infected by Miriam's blood, she longs for a supersized McDonald's meal above all else. For Strieber, America's relationship with junk food exposes a culture that tries to turn every hunger into an addiction. It also reveals the processed and fast-food industries to be part of a predatory marketplace that sought to cultivate addiction and to create a sense of perpetual dissatisfaction.

Strieber includes four meals between Sarah and Tom to establish the novel's warning about the dangers of overconsumption. Early in the text, Tom uses the promise of a home-cooked dinner to coax Sarah into focusing on him instead of her research at the laboratory. He hopes copious amounts of food and alcohol will immobilize her: "Salad, pasta, veal. Fruit and cheese afterwards. Plenty of wine. By dinner's end she'd probably be so close to sleeping that she wouldn't try to go back" (60). The soporific qualities of the wine and heavy foods reveal Tom's insecurities about both their relationship and the inversion of conventional gender roles. Tom's culinary abilities relegate him to the kitchen, and he is the only one in their relationship who cooks. Tom copes with this gendered anxiety, in part, by taking pleasure in her professional failures, particularly the budget cuts that threaten to eliminate her research funding: "There, he felt it again—that ugly little stab of glee. Soon enough her nights would belong only to him" (59). This possessiveness points to a larger dissatisfaction on his part. Throughout the novel, his relationship with Sarah—much like his position at the clinic—is characterized by lack. Neither provides enough fulfillment, and in this way he embodies a culture marked by insatiable desire. There is simply never enough love, power, prestige, food, or wine.

Their second meal introduces Strieber's use of fast food as an image for addictive impulses and dissatisfaction. All of the characters in the novel hunger for something. Miriam, for instance, searches endlessly to recapture lost moments of passion ("She had searched eternity for a better moment" [37]). John resents his newly discovered mortality, which has made his insatiable hunger for blood intolerable. For Tom, the "warm sweetness" of Sarah's lips creates an almost insatiable sexual desire for her (113). And Sarah wonders if love is simply "an urge to containment, a hunger to fill oneself with another, [. . .] a desire to fill the hollowness inside" (127–28). A Chinese fast-food dinner becomes as an image for such hollowness: "[Tom and Sarah] were hungry and they ate all of it even though she had as usual ordered too much" (116). The pattern of overeating mirrors their bottomless hunger for emotional reassurance. Just as an emptiness remains at the center of their relationship, this meal fails to satisfy them: "They had had wine with the spicy Chinese food and then spent a restless night" (126). The following morning they both turn to other addictive substances to fill the void. Sarah makes coffee, and Tom craves a cigar. When he tells her that he "needs" a cigar, she quips: "So eat one. [. . .] You're on your way to neoplasm of the mouth. Anyway, a cigar will make you sick on four hours of sleep" (127). The conflation of eating and smoking reinforces both as sources of addiction with, as her comments about cancer and insomnia suggest, serious health consequences. Tom admits later in the novel that he enjoys cigars, "feeling the warmth of the smoke in his lungs, [. . .] All forbidden, all dangerous. It was so typical of the human predicament that something as pleasurable as a cigar would have to be so damn unhealthy" (227). Strieber clearly includes foods and alcohol in this category, suggesting that one dangerous craving simply fuels another.[22]

The next eating scene involves two meals that highlight the dangers of excess, particularly for women. After Tom invites Sarah to a Mexican restaurant in celebration of her ongoing research funding and his new position as director, he is startled by her hunger: "Sarah ordered the biggest dinner on the menu; she normally subsisted on nibbles and snacks. Sometimes he thought a handful of birdseed a day was all she really needed" (237). This characterization contradicts the eating habits displayed by Sarah and Tom up to this point in the novel. Sarah not only eats and drinks heartily, but she also has a pattern of overdoing it. Likening her appetite to a bird's thus reflects Tom's fantasies about her as domesticated and hungry with sexual desire for him, not her actual relationship with eating. Interestingly, Sarah soon becomes self-conscious about the meal, and the idea of overindulging makes her consider the potential consequences in terms of bodily transformation: "I'll be as plump as a pigeon in a few years. [. . .] Tonight I want to eat. There's nothing the matter with that. [. . .] I'm ravenous as a matter of fact. A second ago I felt like taking a salad right off that tray" (237). Sarah's ravenous appetite, which stems from the blood transfusion she has unknowingly received from Miriam, marks her gradual change from human to nonhuman, while her fears about weight gain highlight society's view of fat as a monstrous transformation—something to avoid at all costs.

Tom reinforces this sensibility by condemning her for ordering another enchilada: "An appetite was fine, but she was going to turn into a sausage if this kept up" (237). The sausage image, like that of the pigeon and his subsequent description of her as eating "like a hippo" (239), equates fatness with a loss of one's humanity. A single moment of excess is too much for women because it only takes one extra bite of fatty, salty foods to gain weight. Likewise, tasting a single drop of human blood for a half-vampire signals the end of his or her humanity. As Sarah continues to consume every last morsel of dinner, Tom returns to bird imagery: "She paused, ate a couple of bites with birdlike speed" (238). Now Sarah's birdlike qualities suggest the way addictive foods can inspire one to eat too much, too quickly. It also functions as a metaphor for uncontrolled American appetites. As Sarah walks home from this meal, she passes Chinese, German, and Greek restaurants. The city offers an abundance of choices, and in addition to the supernatural dangers of vampires, unfettered access to so much food gets presented as equally predatory and dangerous.

After her Mexican meal, nausea, and subsequent sickness, which Tom attributes to either salmonella or "just plain overeating" (239), Sarah fantasizes about McDonald's, and her subsequent trip there reinforces the novel's warning about the dangers of fast food. She describes her appetite for "a Big Mac and double fries and a huge, cold Coke" as both "disgusting" and a "temptation" (243). She disavows this type of meal both by noting that "she hardly ever ate that sort of stuff" and by using the term *stuff* instead of "food." Nevertheless, when confronted with her most intense cravings, her body desires McDonald's presumably for the taste and, as the adjectives "huge," "double," and even "Big" suggest, for the portion size. Her medical background and upper-middle-class status contribute to her perception of McDonald's as unappealing. She likely knows that these selections would minimally have 1,350 calories including 50 grams of fat and 1,410 milligrams of sodium,[23] yet precisely this fat, salt, and sugar (in the soda) drives her craving. Her lingering addiction to these foods comes from pervious exposure to them, which her observations about its quality suggest: the "hamburgers seemed unusually good, rich with flavor, aromatic, cooked just right. Better than Big Macs usually were. Even the Coke and fries were wonderful. What did this place do—serve gourmet junk food after the moon went down?" (244). Although she no longer eats as much fast food as in the past, she has consumed enough to evaluate its quality. The blurring between junk and gourmet highlights the evolution of her tastes as a fledgling half-vampire, but the idea of "gourmet junk food" suggests that her healthier, more refined tastes have not quelled an underlying addiction to "junk."

Despite the occasional McDonald's meal, Sarah does not typically find herself eating there at 2:30 in the morning, and the crowd surprises her: "In fact the place was humming. She had to spend five minutes in line, finally all but hopping from foot to foot with hunger. She ordered two Big Macs, double fries, a pie and a jumbo Coke" (244). To some extent, this business in the early morning hours underscores the addictive impulses at work here. There never seems to be a time when Americans don't want to eat. Sarah soon realizes that most of the customers are transvestites and drag queens, which serve both as a reminder of her own vampiric transformation and the transformative possibilities of eating too much fast food.[24] When Sarah leaves, she begins thinking about breakfast with "eggs and hot spicy sausages and a mountain of buttered toast, and maybe pancakes on the side" (245). Her hunger may be driven by the supernatural, but in the context of a fast-food nation, it represents a country that cannot stop thinking about and eating food.

Through Sarah's final acts of eating and hunger, Strieber underscores his critique of American food culture by presenting pure vampirism as a natural approach to consumption. Her ongoing transformation into a half-vampire makes her insatiable for familiar foods ("all she could think of was eating" [296]), yet she gradually realizes that her body craves a different type of nutrient: blood. Later in the novel as more of this change has taken hold, she passes the ventilation system of a restaurant and finds the cooking odors repulsive: "People were willing to eat garbage these days. Her mind seized on the familiar image of the peaches they used to get from their backyard tree down in Savannah. They had been rich and yellow-red. She wished she had one now" (307). She not only likens contemporary cuisine to waste, but she also imagines eating naturally, tasting the peaches from her backyard in Georgia. She recalls their rich flavor and vibrant colors, and this description starkly contrasts the processed, fatty, salty, and sugary foods she has been consuming to this point. The closer she gets to vampirism, in other words, the more naturally she wants to eat. In this way, Strieber takes another jab at modern food by positioning vampirism as inspiring a hunger for something natural. Vampires primarily eat organically, and according to Miriam, they follow a tightly restricted approach to food: "we never kill more than we need. [. . .] You'll need to feed only once a week at most" (342, 348). This measured approach is antithetical to the excesses characterizing the American diet.

Furthermore, Sarah's hunger operates as a reflection of her consumer sensibility. Miriam—the only pure member of her species—understands the biological need to feed and to "Sleep," yet her relationship to eating is never characterized by extremes. Only her half-human "pets" (most notably her deteriorating companions John and Sarah) feel tempted to overindulge, and this detail highlights addiction as something fundamental to human nature. John, for instance, overeats when he begins to die. He "gorges" himself on one victim (91), and while killing Alice (Miriam's perspective replacement for him), he drinks wine: "The wine had been a fitting complement. Unlike other food, alcohol remained delicious to him" (100). Likewise, Sarah compares her newfound hunger to a loss of control: "Sarah didn't want food. This felt like some kind of addiction. Hunger" (298). When she finally tastes Miriam's blood, Sarah likens it to cocaine: "Sarah and Tom had occasionally taken a little cocaine. It lifted one, in the first instant, to what had up until now seemed the pinnacle of pleasure. It was nothing compared to this" (308). Whether through cocaine or a Big Mac, such compulsions stem from a culture that facilitated addiction and indulgence. Thus, it would seem that Miriam's failure to sire pure vampires comes from the lingering humanity in her victims. Some come to terms with the "cannibal life" (91), but none can shed their addictive nature. It is an impulse, exacerbated by late twentieth-century life and facilitated by the food industry, that eventually consumes them.

In 1983, Tony Scott directed his first film, an adaptation of *The Hunger* starring Susan Sarandon (Sarah), David Bowie (John), and Catherine Deneuve (Miriam). The visual style with its billowing curtains, lighting, and even the pigeons in Miriam's attic draws heavily from his brother's science fiction masterpiece *Blade Runner* (1982). Nevertheless, these details give *The Hunger* a hallucinatory quality that invites the viewer both to accept the supernatural in a world defined by scientific rationalism and to experience the altered consciousness associated with blood drinking. While this adaptation takes significant liberties with the story, it does retain the novel's central preoccupation with eating. The presence of fast food in the film, for example, contributes to its portrait of addiction as central to American culture, making vampirism a metaphor for these dangerous impulses. While the film omits Sarah's visit to McDonald's, it presents Tom and his colleagues as regular fast-food eaters. Tom first appears with a McDonald's coffee and a bag of hamburgers, announcing cheerfully to his coworkers in the laboratory, "Big Macs!" While eating, they study footage of a monkey in their sleep experiment that has become increasingly erratic and violent after not sleeping for fifty-six hours. It then kills another monkey and eats her. On one level, this fast food saves time for scientists who are literally trying to save time for humanity. Their research hopes to slow the aging process and extend life, and their professional dedication leaves them few opportunities to cook for themselves. On another level, these eating habits signal their own addictive tendencies. Like Sarah's reliance on cigarettes throughout the film, consuming Big Macs (none of them questions the choice or hesitates to eat the hamburgers) has become a familiar routine. The harmful characteristics of fast food, coffee, and nicotine will likely shorten their lives, and this irony highlights the film's message about the choices confronting modern-day Americans: to succumb or to break free from its various addictions.

Scott's version modifies another important scene with food in *The Hunger*, replacing Tom and Sarah's cheese-drenched, fatty Mexican meal with a steak dinner at an upscale restaurant overlooking an indoor pool. Moments earlier, Sarah has sex with Miriam, an encounter in which they bite into each other's veins and exchange blood. As blood slides down Miriam's skin onto the white bedsheets, the film makes a jump cut to a steak being carved in half, its blood oozing onto a white plate. We then see Tom and Sarah at the restaurant. Glasses of red wine are featured prominently on the table, and Sarah smokes nervously as they speak:

TOM (speaking while chewing): "You ordered it rare."
SARAH: "I know."
TOM: "So, what's the problem?"
SARAH: "Nothing."
TOM: "And you sent back the clams."
SARAH: "I'm just not very hungry."
TOM: "Well, then why order it if you're not hungry? Why order the steak at all?"
SARAH: "I thought I wanted it."

All forms of addiction are on display here. Sarah orders too much food, and as with the impulses driving supersized meals and thirty-two-ounce cups of soda, she feels compelled to have more than she needs. She also smokes and drinks too much, admitting to a glass of sherry with Miriam even though it gives her a headache. And her erotic thoughts of Miriam, which get interspersed with images of the women in the swimming pool, reveal her new desires for this woman and for blood. Just as Sarah smokes more and more heavily throughout her transformation, this hunger for blood mirrors the physiological responses of withdrawal. At one point, panicked, shaken, and sweaty, Sarah is mistaken for a junkie by two thugs at a phone booth. Tom, too, deals with his increasing anxiety about Sarah's well-being by smoking and drinking beer in his apartment. Once again vampirism becomes an extension of human impulses. Whether through drug use on the street, cigarettes, fast-food take-out, alcohol, or haute cuisine, every aspect of American culture provides an opportunity for overindulgence. These excesses, however, do not lead to happiness but to a state of perpetual dissatisfaction. After Sarah becomes ill that night, Tom reports to the medical team the next day: "She's ravenous, and she can't eat." America had become a place of ravenous yet insatiable appetites in the 1980s, and *The Hunger* uses the violence of vampirism to warn of the personal and social dangers of addiction.

Dracula, Addiction, and the 1980s

There is really one person to blame for America's (and arguably the world's) bloody mess of an obsession with vampires: Bram Stoker. The publication of *Dracula* in 1897 unleashed a character that would captivate audiences and become synonymous with this mythology in ways that continue to overshadow his predecessors and followers.[25] This popularity cannot be understood apart from the Golden Age of Hollywood horror—the label most scholars use for the monster movies between 1931–1948.[26] Not only was *Dracula* (1931) the first major Hollywood horror film, but it also catapulted the figure of the Count to worldwide fame. The success of Tod Browning's *Dracula* inspired countless sequels and adaptations in its wake, beginning with Universal Studio productions of *Dracula's Daughter* (1936), *Son of Dracula* (1943), and *House of Dracula* (1945). Ever since, whether through films, novels, short stories, television, comics, cartoons, operas, plays, musicals, or video games, the public's appetite for these sexy, undead creatures has been insatiable. Dracula in particular maintains an almost hypnotic hold over this mythology—particularly as costumed and performed by Bela Lugosi. Children and adults still wear Lugosi-inspired Dracula costumes for Halloween. Anne Rice's egomaniacal Lestat complained in 1985 that "everybody was sick of Count Dracula"—despite the penchant among her vampires to wear clothing inspired by him (*The Vampire Lestat* 13). The film industry continues to bring Dracula back from the dead for the occasional blockbuster, such as Terence Fisher's *Dracula* (also known as *Horror of Dracula*) in 1958, Stan Dragoti's *Love at First Bite* (1979), Francis Ford Coppola's *Bram Stoker's Dracula* (1992), Genndy Tartakovsky's *Hotel Transylvania* (2012), and Gary Shore's *Dracula Untold* (2015). The crowded field of vampire television owes a great debt to Dracula as well, and despite the short-lived NBC series *Dracula* (2013–2014), his occasional guest appearances remain a testament to this allure. In the fifth season of *Buffy the Vampire Slayer*, for example, Buffy (Sarah Michelle Gellar) gets a chance to tussle with the legend, and she stakes him—only to discover that he can come back to life again and again. The message is clear: nothing can rid us of Dracula. Even scholars seem to have an unquenchable thirst for this creature. One critic has recently lamented that "it appears seemingly impossible [. . .] to talk about the vampire without making at least tacit reference to *Dracula* as a pivotal text."[27]

The continued proliferation of Dracula also reveals the audience as vampiric in its constant need to consume, reproduce, retell, and adapt his story. Our hunger for Dracula and vampires more broadly, suggests that we share the addictive qualities of these creatures, that we possess similarly dangerous cravings. This trend has only intensified into the early twenty-first century. In the summer of 2016, for example, two Orlando police officers pulled over a sixty-four-year-old man for a minor traffic violation: he failed to make a full stop before exiting a 7-Eleven parking lot. While questioning him, the officers noticed a "rock like substance" on the floor by his feet, and they asked permission to search the vehicle. Several more chunks of this material, which they surmised to be drugs, were found inside his car as well. The driver protested: "'That's . . . glaze from a doughnut.' . . . They tried to say it was crack cocaine at first, then they said, 'No, it's meth, crystal meth'" (Stutzman). He explained his routine of buying a Krispy Kreme doughnut every other Wednesday, but both field tests on the material read positive for methamphetamine. The man was arrested for possession. When a police laboratory subsequently determined the substance not to be a narcotic, however, the state attorney's office dropped the case. This incident happened just a few weeks after the *New York Times* reported that 21 percent of drug evidence listed by the Florida Department of Law Enforcement "as methamphetamine turned out to be something else" (Stutzman). While this doughnut-meth mix-up pointed yet again to the questionable reliability of portable drug-testing kits, it also raises some other troubling questions: What exactly is in the foods that we eat? How could doughnut glaze be mistaken for drugs in any context? And if it can, shouldn't the Florida Police Department be investigating Krispy Kreme?

Of course, this news story was not reported as a cautionary tale about junk food, but mistaking doughnut frosting for drugs points to the addictive nature of the American diet. While this Florida man learned "never to let anyone search [his] car again," the experience did not change his eating habits. By all accounts, he continues to enjoy Krispy Kreme doughnuts every other week. America behaved much the same way in the 1980s. A doughnut or meth? It did not matter for corporations that could legally design addictive foods. It did not matter to a public that had developed a vampire-like hunger for sugar and processed foods.

In the 1980s, Nancy Reagan could just have easily launched a "Just Say No" campaign about eating as millions of Americans found themselves increasingly hooked on junk food. Supersized meals characterized much of restaurant culture. Massive drinks and an endless array of snacks crammed grocery store shelves. And it seemed nearly impossible to eat a meal unaccompanied by some type of sugar. Vampire fiction and film in the 1980s found these excesses and the cultural fears they inspired to be fertile ground for the horrific. Whether depicting the food industry as vampiric, casting Americans as vampire-like addicts, or presenting vampires as healthier, more natural eaters than humans, these works used the audience's appetites as a way to shed light on some of the more disturbing aspects of the American diet. They challenged audiences to think about their own addictive tendencies—drawing explicit analogies between drugs, alcohol, cigarettes, and junk food in order to highlight the harmfulness of such meals. They raised questions about the dangers of fast foods—inviting people to see their own eating habits as monstrous. And they equated vanquishing the vampire—and its hungers—with a call to change what and how we eat.

CHAPTER THREE

Eat Your Heart Out: Zombies, Overpopulation, and the Environment

When the *Exxon Valdez* struck a reef in Alaska's Prince William Sound on March 24, 1989, it released approximately 11 million gallons of oil into the sea, tainting 1,300 miles of coastline and making it the worst spill in US history at the time. The initial clean-up efforts did little to contain the damage. The primary chemicals used for the task, Exxon's dispersant Corexit 9537, Exxon's experimental fertilizer Inipol EAP22, and the household cleaner Simple Green, posed serious hazards to marine and human life.[1] According to the *Exxon Valdez* Oil Spill Trustee Council for the State of Alaska, over 250,000 seabirds, 2,800 sea otters, twenty-two killer whales, hundreds of bald eagles and seals, and billions of salmon and herring eggs perished.[2] Images of animals covered in thick black oil appeared in newspapers and on television screens across the country. The problem did not stop with the ocean and coastline, though. Much of the waste collected by spill workers ended up at incineration sites to be burned, releasing it into the atmosphere.[3] The scope of the accident and damage not only served as a vivid reminder of the nation's addiction to oil, but it also exemplified the environmental harm of consumer culture.

Contemporary zombie fiction explored these concerns as well, often associating the undead with apocalyptic fears about pollution and overpopulation. From the perspective of ecocriticism, 1980s zombies function as an image for an overpopulated country that devours too many resources at the expense of the planet and generates too much waste. A number of powerful tropes have shaped ecocritical writings, but none has been more influential than the apocalypse. Lawrence Buell views the apocalypse as "the single most powerful master metaphor [. . . in] the contemporary environmental imagination" (*Environmental Imagination* 285). Whether through depictions of

Zombies cross barren fields and depleted farmland in George A. Romero's *Night of the Living Dead* (1968). Continental Distributing Inc./Photofest. © Continental Distributing Inc.

post-apocalyptic life in *Silent Spring* or science fiction and horror, this imagery challenges audiences to take responsibility for destroying nature. "Apocalyptic rhetoric," as Greg Garrard explains, "seems a necessary component of environmental discourse. It is capable of galvanizing activists, converting the undecided and ultimately, perhaps, of influencing government and commercial policy" (113). Not surprisingly, this trope's popularity in the horror genre has contributed to the rise of ecohorror studies. This branch of ecocriticism tends to focus on literature and film in which the environment—through animals, insects, or plants—attacks humans responsible for harming nature. Lee Gambin considers the 1970s the starting point for films in which "the real evil that will ultimately destroy us [. . . is] nature itself" (18).[4] More recently, Stephen A. Rust and Carter Soles have suggested broadening this definition. Instead of merely focusing on horror that depicts a wrathful nature (or "revenge of nature" motif) such as Steven Spielberg's *Jaws* (1975), ecohorror should include "texts in which humans do horrific things to the natural world, or in which horrific texts and tropes are used to promote ecological awareness, represent ecological crises, or blur human/non-human distinctions more broadly" ("Living in Fear" 509–10). Robin L. Murray and Joseph K. Heumann have taken this call to heart in *Monstrous Nature: Environment and Horror on the Big Screen*, and their discussion of zombie films examines the way the genre "provides a stage for addressing some of the negative effects humans have had on their environment" (100). They do so, in part, by considering "what might happen if we continue down a dangerous path that includes nuclear warfare, ineffective toxic waste disposal, or unchecked chemical and biological experimentation" (101).

In zombie fiction of the 1980s, overpopulation and toxic contamination emerge as the primary ecological threats to the planet. Most of these zombies tend to be indefatigable, mindless eaters (despite the occasional dance routine in Michael Jackson's *Thriller*). Their bottomless hunger puts them on a perpetual quest for food, and the danger they pose to the living comes not from speed or outward expressions of viciousness but from numbers. In this way, they offer a visual reminder of American consumer excess and the relentless competition for limited natural resources. This chapter begins with a discussion of the apocalyptic fears surrounding overpopulation, ozone depletion, food production, and toxic waste at the end of the decade. It then examines George A. Romero's original zombie trilogy and the works he inspired in the eighties. Zombie outbreaks in this fiction typically comment on public concerns about the destruction of the planet. Some function as cautionary tales about consumer excess such as *Day of the Dead* and several stories from *Book of the Dead* (1989) including Chan McConnell's "Blossom," Robert McCammon's "Eat Me," Stephen King's "Home Delivery," and Stephen R. Boyett's "Like Pavlov's Dogs." Others focus on acid rain and toxic waste, like the *Return of the Living Dead* series, *Toxic Zombies* (1980), *Surf II* (1984), and *Redneck Zombies* (1989). Ultimately, the environmental devastation in these works can be attributed to both overpopulation and overconsumption, offering a searing critique of America's appetite (for food, housing, oil, chemical products, weapons, etc.) and the capitalistic marketplace fueling it.

The End of Nature: Apocalyptic Panic in the 1980s

An environmental apocalypse loomed large by the end of the 1980s. On January 2, 1989, *Time* magazine substituted its annual "Man of the Year" issue with "Planet of the Year" after the news organization hosted a conference with over two dozen scientists, politicians, and administrators. Thomas A. Sancton's lead story reads a bit like an ecohorror film, arguing that 1988 witnessed Mother Nature's wrath. A three-month, nationwide drought destroyed 31 percent of the country's grain harvest. It killed thousands of livestock and helped facilitate the largest wildfires in the history of Yellowstone National Park.

For seven weeks, a heatwave kept temperatures above 100 degrees across the country, and according to the National Centers for Environmental Information (NCEI), somewhere between 5,000 and 10,000 people died as a result.[5] Beaches—awash with raw sewage and medical waste—provided little respite for the public. Air conditioners, aerosol cans, and automobile exhaust continued to deplete the ozone layer, making skin cancer more likely. And "perhaps most ominous of all, the destruction of the tropical rain forests, home to at least half the earth's plant and animal species, continued at a rate equal to one football field a second" (27). In his overall assessment, Sancton describes 1988 as a year of "freakish weather and environmental horror stories" (27). Inaction, as the entire issue argues, would only lead to rising temperatures and sea levels, and he reminds readers with the subtlety of a jackhammer that significant climate change has always accompanied mass extinctions: "Unless mankind embraces that cause [a universal crusade to save the planet] totally, and without delay, it may have no alternative to the bang of nuclear holocaust or the whimper of slow extinction" (30).

With a similar flair for the apocalyptic, William McKibben's *The End of Nature*, published in 1989 and credited as the first book about climate change for a general audience,[6] examines the dangers of overpopulation in terms of chlorofluorocarbon production and the food supply. The global population tripled in the twentieth century, and he cites China's increasing fertility rates as an imminent threat to the planet. "China, which has the largest coal reserves and recently surpassed the Soviet Union as the world's largest coal producer, has plans to almost double her coal consumption by the year 2000" (13). The use of fossil fuels concerned American scientists and environmentalists as well. The population of the United States grew 9.8 percent (by approximately 22 million people) in the 1980s, and California continued to be the most populated state with over 29 million residents.[7] As the vast freeway system of the Golden State illustrated, Americans loved cars. This romance began with Henry Ford's Model T in 1908 and flourished during the 1950s and 1960s with massive gas guzzlers like Elvis Presley's pink Cadillac. The Arab oil embargo in 1973 may have stalled the auto industry, inspiring consumers to buy smaller, more fuel-efficient vehicles, but as sales rebounded, Americans "drifted back to larger cars" by the early eighties (McCarthy 223). Soon the SUV became one of the most popular cars in the nation. As McKibben reminds readers, these cars were causing irrevocable damage to the atmosphere: "The average American car driven the average American distance—ten thousand miles—in an average American year releases its own weight in carbon into the atmosphere" (6). The Environmental Policy Institute already warned that 25 percent of the ozone layer could be depleted within sixty years. "If ozone levels declined 20 percent, two hours in the sun would blister exposed skin" (44). McKibben makes clear that the public could not reverse the damage; it could only hope "to avoid the most gruesome" consequences of climate change by reducing the emissions of chlorofluorocarbons (67).

Both *Time*'s "Planet of the Year" issue and McKibben also include a discussion of the environmental ramifications of food production. In "Overpopulation: Too Many Mouths to Feed," Anastasia Toufexis notes that 90 percent of the population growth in the twenty-first century would occur in poor, developing nations—the places least equipped to provide necessary food, housing, and fuel for its citizens. The decade of the 1980s already witnessed widespread starvation and malnutrition across the globe. The Indian government, for example, reported that 37 percent of its own people could not afford enough food to survive, and one Indian official believed that "'We may well be on the way to producing a subhuman kind of race where people do not have enough energy to deal with their problems'" (48). McKibben sounds a similar alarm about global food shortages, but he first discusses the relationship between food production and carbon dioxide output. Whether stemming from cow flatulence (the planet's 1.2 billion cattle released millions of tons of methane gas into the atmosphere annually) or the exhaust from tractors, the visible effects of global warming in 1988 demonstrated the fragility of the food supply. The drought reduced the US corn crop by 2.6 billion bushels (125). When farmers finally harvested what they could, seven states reported corn contaminated by a carcinogen linked with liver cancer. Seventy cornfields in Texas alone produced inedible corn, and forty nearby dairies were forced to "dump milk from cows fed with infected grain" (126). For McKibben, the prospect of ongoing food shortages would lead to the breakdown of civilization. "Such a world—a world where people shoot each other in the streets of Boston over a loaf of bread—is not unimaginable" (147).

While McKibben concerns himself with shortages, Paul Roberts's *The End of Food* focuses on the dangers of overproduction, which began with the high-volume, low-cost food model in the 1980s. For Roberts, the combination of Fritz Haber's invention to "fix" nitrogen (or pull it from the atmosphere into a usable molecule) and plant breeding technologies transformed the global food supply. Known as Haber-Bosch (Carl Bosch commercialized the idea), this development enabled farmers to cheaply and easily add ammonium nitrate to dirt. Farmers no longer needed to rely on animal fertilizer to grow crops, nor did they have to worry about depleting nutrients in the soil. They could dedicate more land to food production (as opposed to grazing for animals), and they could grow year round. At the same time, a new emphasis on uniformity by plant breeders revolutionized farming as well. Hybrid corn of the same size, for example, could be harvested faster and more efficiently by machine, displacing the majority of farmers.[8] This mass production model and the ability to replace farmers with fuel-consuming technology, however, exacerbated the pollution associated with agriculture. According to Michael Pollan, the natural gas in fertilizer and the fossil fuels required of pesticides, tractors, and crop transportation meant that "every bushel of industrial corn [required] the equivalent of between a quarter and third of a gallon of oil to grow it—or around fifty gallons of oil per acre of corn" (45). Some of the nitrogen in this fertilizer poisoned the water table, contaminated streams and rivers, and evaporated to acidify rain. Not only did these efforts fail to alleviate world hunger, but they also taxed and poisoned the environment.

Another ecological danger associated with overpopulation is trash—from household garbage to toxic waste. Rotting landfills, McKibben argues, expel vast amounts of methane gas, and leachate, the polluted liquid produced by rainfall that passes through landfill, contaminates groundwater. In 1979, a landfill in New Castle County produced 170,000 gallons of leachate per day, compromising an important aquifer, and in "Islip, Long Island, a thirty-nine-year-old landfill had developed an underground plume that extended 1,300 feet wide, 170 feet deep, and one mile long, accounting for the destruction of one billion gallons of water" (Brown 100). For most Americans, however, the primary concern was space. In 1987, the *New York Times* reported on a Long Island garbage scow that had no place to unload. The vessel had traveled over 6,000 miles to various ports in Central America and Mexico, and after being denied entry everywhere, it returned to New York to bury its cargo on Long Island (Pellow 55). This floating refuse heap was emblematic of a national crisis. At the time, the federal Environmental Protection Agency already warned that 50 percent of cities and towns would run out of landfills within a decade (Shabecoff). The problem stemmed, in part, from the massive amount of garbage being produced by Americans. As David Pellow explains in *Garbage Wars*, the National Council of Public Works Improvement noted that "between 1960 and 1984, the average per capita rate of waste generation in the United States increased from 2.32 to 3.08 pounds per person per day, a rise of 33 percent" (55). The most common solution to this problem at the time, waste incinerators, assuaged some concerns about space, but they also raised the alarm for environmentalists who warned about the dangers of toxic ash and fumes.[9]

Fears about toxic waste and unscrupulous disposal practices became particularly acute in the wake of the Love Canal tragedy. After purchasing the canal for landfill in the 1940s, Hooker Chemical Company began unloading fifty-five-gallon barrels of toxic sludge into that site, and it would ultimately dump the equivalent of 20,000 tons of waste there. The company stopped using the land in 1952 when the Niagara Falls School Board approached them about buying it. The dump was then sealed in order to build schools and a suburban community on top of it. The construction of the LaSalle Expressway in the 1960s, however, damaged some of the sealant designed to contain the waste, and the community of Love Canal began noticing unusual changes in the environment. Chemical landfill seeped into basements and the groundwater, and "benzene, a known cancer-causing agent in humans, had been readily detected in the household air up and down the streets" (Brown 17). Children needed medical attention for chemical burns after playing in fields. Numerous birth defects resulted as well as severe illnesses, including asthma, liver damage, leukemia, and respiratory failure. In 1978, after a two-year investigation, the state of New York recommended evacuating *some* of the one thousand families living there. According to Richard S. Newman, this moment made Love Canal "an emblem of toxic waste nightmares regionally, nationally, and even globally" (107).

Michael Brown, a journalist for the *Niagara Gazette*, reported on the Love Canal events and began investigating similar practices throughout the United States. In *Laying Waste: The Poisoning of America by Toxic Chemicals*, he chronicles such incidents across the country, presenting toxic waste as an ongoing national disaster. A Hooker Chemical facility in Montague, Michigan, for example, regularly leaked pesticidal fumes and chlorine gas into the atmosphere (82). Groundwater contaminated with trichloroethylene and trichloroethane, "two compounds [. . .] in solvents used as degreasers, as refrigerants, and fumigants in organic synthesis," could have contributed to New Jersey having the highest cancer rate in the country between 1950 and 1970 (133). Petro Processors dumped vast quantities of oil sludge and chemical waste into swampland in Baton Rouge, Louisiana, destroying over 540 acres of land (158, 161). And 3.7 million cubic feet of commercial nuclear waste, packaged in fifty-five-gallon drums or wooden and cardboard boxes, was buried in Maxey Flats, Kentucky. Gradually, these radioactive particles, including tritium, strontium 89, cesium, and plutonium, migrated from that site; it "infiltrated surface runoff, penetrated the groundwater, or seeped through rock fissures and joints to surface outside the disposal grounds" (277).

For 1980s commentators, many of these problems—whether from waste, acid rain, contaminated water, rising temperatures, depleted ozone, or limited food production—could be traced to overpopulation. The realities of a planet with too many people competing for limited resources took on an apocalyptic quality in the writings of journalists, scientists, and environmentalists. Michael Brown's harrowing portrait of toxic waste concludes with this final warning: "And only then [when society conforms to the needs of nature] will we be sure that what rises from the ground or what is in our air and rivers will be, as it ought, the source of life and good health—and not the agents of an untimely death" (335). Not surprisingly, fiction writers tapped into such fears, and the zombie genre seemed to literalize this image of agents of death rising from the ground. Zombies presented a vision of consumer appetites out of control, of spaces crammed with too many bodies, of food shortages, and of lands contaminated by toxic waste. They became both the logical outgrowth of America's greedy, wasteful consumption and a fitting punishment for its abuses of the planet.

George A. Romero's Original Zombie Trilogy

Too Many Mouths to Feed: Overpopulation and Zombies in the Late Twentieth Century

Zombie films typically get divided into two periods: 1932 to 1967 and 1968 to the present.[10] The first zombies stumbled across the silver screen during the thirties and forties as images for either the abuses of slavery or the limitations of vengeance. *White Zombie* (1932), *I Walked with a Zombie* (1943), and even elements of the comedy *King of the Zombies* (1941) attribute zombification to Caribbean voodoo in order to comment on colonial exploitation. By contrast, films like *The Walking Dead* (1936) and *The Man They Could Not Hang* (1939) feature scientists that animate corpses to avenge someone's death. None of these zombies eats their victims, however. They have simply been trapped by social, economic, or psychological forces, such as the plantation system or petty impulses like greed.

A new type of zombie emerged in the late 1960s, and most scholars consider George A. Romero's *Night of the Living Dead* (1968) the starting point for this second phase. His films place a zombie outbreak at the heart of American capitalist society, suggesting that every aspect of the country—from its urban centers to the most remote farmhouse—has embraced a consumer ethos corrosive to both humanity and the environment. As Michael Newbury observes, "no voodoo sorcerer produces these figures; rather, beginning with Romero in the late 1960s, zombies tend distinctly to be imagined as products of modernity, the result of environmental contamination, nuclear fallout, or rogue scientists experimenting on anything from microbes to genetically modified organisms" (99). Others have cautioned against drawing too stark a distinction between these two periods. Certainly, Hollywood continued to

The zombie masses seek one final meal in George A. Romero's *Day of the Dead* (1985). United Film Distribution Company/Photofest. © United Film Distribution Company.

employ the voodoo trope after 1968. It appeared in zombie films throughout the 1980s, including *Dead and Buried* (1981),[11] *Zombie Nightmare* (1987), and *Serpent and the Rainbow* (1988). Likewise, Sarah Juliet Lauro traces its present-day popularity back to Haitian mythology, particularly the country's history with captivity and resistance. For Lauro, whether through Caribbean plantations or "a different kind of servitude, under advanced capitalism and its culture of consumerism," rebellion and enslavement have always played an integral role in the genre (97).

This tension between slavery and resistance certainly resonates with Romero's depiction of both consumerism *and* environmental apocalypse. Steven Shaviro has argued that zombies serve as an allegory for capitalism; namely, its exploitation of labor, regimentation of the workplace, and efforts to generate an "artificial, externally driven stimulation for consumers" (83). He then adds another crucial point—that "their menace lies in numbers. [. . .] Their slow-motion voracity and continual hungry wailing sometimes appears clownish, but at other times emerges as an obsessive leitmotif of suspended and ungratified desire" (84). While their hunger represents this marketplace desire, the idea of numbers plays a central role in Romero's films in a way that has received little critical attention. His characters constantly try to calculate how many zombies gather outside a farm, lurk in a mall, cling to the perimeter of a shelter, or crowd together in a nearby city. Counting helps determine the risk associated with an escape plan or a supply run, and it allows Romero to comment on the dangers of overpopulation in the modern world.

Overpopulation—as depicted by the ever-growing ranks of the rising dead—places an unsustainable demand on natural resources. It literally creates too many mouths to feed. Since zombies eat with reckless abandon, not considering balance (no vegetables come with that meat!) or where the next meal will come from, they feed until the food supply has been completely used up, and Romero suggests that Americans have been doing the same.

These zombies also get presented as vehicles for environmental resistance: they emerge from contaminated earth, have been animated by natural phenomenon (such as radiation), and turn on the species most responsible for harming nature. Soles has argued for the need to view *Night of the Living Dead* in terms of ecohorror, considering the film a meditation on the causes of environmental collapse in the wake of Rachel Carson's *Silent Spring*. For Soles, Romero "[locates] the blame for the environmental apocalypse with the U.S. government, the scientific establishment, and ultimately, the American people writ large" ("And No Birds" 528). I would like to extend this reading to include the significance of overpopulation, for the sheer volume of zombies in Romero's films, crowding every space and endlessly reaching for more, reminds the audience of the imminent danger people pose to the planet.

The origin of *Night of the Living Dead*, a film about a group of strangers taking refuge in a farmhouse to protect themselves against reanimated corpses, can be traced to a lunchtime conversation over provolone sandwiches and beer. Several friends, including Romero and John Russo, agreed to contribute $600 a piece to make a low-budget horror film. After debating who would direct it, they agreed on Romero—a decision that would irrevocably shape his career (Gagne 21). While Romero has famously disavowed any political agenda for the film, particularly with regard to casting an African American as the lead, he admits that in 1968 "*Everybody* had a 'message.' Maybe it crept in. I was just making a horror film, and I think the anger and the attitude and all that's there is just there because it was 1968. We lived at the farmhouse, so we were always into raps about the implication and the meaning, and stuff like that" (qtd. in Gagne 38). Indeed, commentary about American culture crept in and became more pointed with each installment. The trilogy as a whole explores a wide range of issues including misogyny, racism, consumerism, the nuclear family,[12] and the consequences of environmental devastation. For the latter, the zombie masses in *Night of the Living Dead*, *Dawn of the Dead* (1978), and *Day of the Dead* (1985) become an unnerving image for unchecked population growth and for a marketplace that encourages excess at the expense of nature.

Zombies only appear gradually in Romero's films, but as their numbers multiply, they raise concerns about what happens when too many people compete for too few resources. *Night of the Living Dead* introduces a single ghoul to Barbra (Judith O'Dea) and her brother, Johnny (Russell Streiner), at the cemetery. It wears a suit and moves almost casually among the headstones until it attacks. Once Barbra flees to a nearby farmhouse, she looks out the window several times and notices two more in tattered clothes. Within moments, the original ghoul stumbles into the shot as well, making three. The undead will increase in number throughout the night, and this will become one of the central preoccupations of the characters. When Ben (Duane Jones) first arrives at the house, he immediately tries to quantify the threat: "Don't worry about him. I can handle him. They'll probably be a lot more of them as soon as they find out about us." He then asks Barbra for a count, and this type of calculus happens repeatedly. Ben later describes ten or fifteen ghouls chasing a gasoline truck and another fifty or sixty surrounding Beekman's Diner. The radio refers to the killers as "a virtual army of unidentified assassins," while each exterior shot reveals more and more of them around the farmhouse. Tom (Keith Wayne), who has been hiding in the cellar with his girlfriend and the Cooper family, asks for an estimate, too, but less than a minute later, a higher number gets counted: "about eight or ten out there now." Likewise, Mr. Cooper (Karl Hardman) insists on remaining hidden because "There's not going to be five or even ten. There's going to be twenty, thirty, maybe a hundred of those things. As soon as they know we're here, this place is going to be crawling with them." He later complains that "there could be 15 million of those things out there!" By the end of the film, the farmhouse that once appeared safe for human life has been overrun. It teems with zombies crammed together, clawing at the living and pounding against the walls. Just as the sheer volume of bodies overwhelms the characters, they overwhelm the space onscreen through close-ups, low-angle shots, and tightly cropped frames. This camera work proves central to Romero's environmental critique. The visual logic of *Night of the Living Dead*, as well as *Dawn of the Dead* and *Day of the Dead*, comes from showing the audiences that there are too many of them and, by extension, too many of us.

    The role of gasoline and food, a primary concern for both the living and the dead, further reinforces Romero's warnings about unchecked population growth and the depletion of natural resources. The film opens with Johnny and Barbra driving a 1967 Pontiac LeMans. They have traveled three hours, undoubtedly refueling along the way, and they will need to do the same for the return trip. Almost immediately after the outbreak, gasoline proves to be an endangered resource. One tanker truck explodes after being attacked by zombies. Ben's pickup runs out of fuel, and the pump behind the farm catches fire, burning Tom and Judy (Judith Ridley) to death. On one level, its volatility and limited supply suggest the risks of humanity's reliance on crude oil and fossil fuels. On another level, gasoline serves as a reminder of the resources needed to transport food for human consumption. The tanker truck explodes outside of a diner where people have driven for dinner, and when Johnny parks at the cemetery, he asks, "Is there any candy left?" Dressed in their Sunday best, eating junk food, burning gasoline fumes, and passing several American flags in the cemetery, these siblings represent the nation's thoughtlessness about the environmental costs of so much consumption. Even the setting of the farmhouse—a place that should represent the cultivation of land—reveals nature to be more dead than alive. Dry grasses, empty fields, and several dying trees surround the property, and the ghoul in pursuit of Barbra lumbers across a wide, barren pasture. Nothing grows here. Though the place has furniture, food, a radio, and a television set, it no longer appears to be an active farm. In this way, Romero presents a glimpse of nature that can no longer sustain the demands of human life.

Night of the Living Dead also establishes an important link between human and zombie appetites. Ben initially rummages for food in the farmhouse, and later, when confronted by the belligerent Mr. Cooper, Ben explains, "I'm fighting for everything up here. The radio and the food is part of what I'm fighting for." He dismisses Mr. Cooper's protests that they, too, have a right to this food. Instead, Ben asks if anyone there owns the house. This moment raises several important questions: What rights do they have to food? If so, does that abdicate any responsibility for preserving nature? Do they have more eating rights than zombies? None of them, in fact, "owns" the land, and if the dead fields around the farm offer any indication, people appear to have devoured these resources much the same way the ghouls plan to devour them. Additionally, the radio reports punctuating their conversations disclose that "the killers are eating the flesh of the people they murder." This revelation equates the farmhouse occupants with the food they have been fighting over. They, too, are food. They, too, have become a limited resource that can't possibly satiate the appetites of such voracious consumers.

These zombies get associated with natural phenomenon as well, evoking the "revenge of nature" motif in ecohorror. As R. H. W. Dillard has noted, the creatures "have no identities and are really no different from any other natural disaster; Tom specifically compares them to a flood, and he is right" (21). In fact, the first zombie appears after the start of a thunder and lightning storm at the cemetery, and this detail connects zombies with nature's destructive power. Even the source of the outbreak implies nature's wrath. When a news anchor indicates that NASA has recently destroyed a radioactive satellite returning from Venus, he poses the question: "Could that radiation be somehow responsible for the wholesale murders we are now suffering?" Radiation, however, occurs naturally in the universe. It can be found in water, air, and soil. It can be found in space emanating from supernovae and other sources. Yet these natural phenomena tend to become dangerous when manipulated or abused by mankind. The destroyed satellite, which deposits radiated particles into the atmosphere like nuclear fallout, can thus be viewed in terms of nature's vengeance. It confronts humanity with an environmental crisis of its own making.

Romero's examination of the environmental consequences of consumer culture and overpopulation continues in *Dawn of the Dead*, a film about four people who take refuge in a shopping mall during a zombie outbreak. Much like Franz Kafka's portrait of Gregor Samsa in *The Metamorphosis* (1915), Romero suggests that the zombification of America happened long before this epidemic. Almost every detail in the film highlights the zombie-like tendencies of consumers.. When pondering the behavior of the walking dead, for example, Stephen (David Emge) believes that they gravitate toward the mall from "instinct. Memory. What they used to do. This was an important place in their lives." Later, one of the S.W.A.T. officers concludes that "They're us. That's all." These observations imply that consumerism has become an instinctual behavior of the utmost value in America—so much so that even in death people push shopping carts, wander the floors of the mall, press up against window displays, and wear outfits marking their former identities as security guards, handymen, mechanics, nurses, and members of the middle class. Even nuns choose the mall over church, and one Hare Krishna appears to abandon vegetarianism and proselytizing for an eternity of shopping. To some extent, these details cast consumerism as America's primary religion, equating one's humanity and national identity with the ability to shop.

Numerous scholars have examined the role of consumerism in the film, and such readings provide a crucial backdrop for any environmental reading of Romero's work. Critic Andrew Loudermilk, for example, has noted that the real apocalypse in *Dawn of the Dead* is the end of capitalism with its "consumer citizenry [. . .] literally zombified by those who once were us" (85). Shaviro views these zombies as "a positive expression of consumerist desire. [. . .] The zombies mark the dead end or zero degree of capitalism's logic of endless consumption and ever-expanding accumulation, precisely because they embody this logic so literally and to such excess" (93–94). Likewise, Kyle William Bishop views 1970s Americans as "the true zombies, slaves to the master of consumerism" (130), and in *The Cinema of George Romeo: Knight of the Living Dead*, Tony Williams argues that "Human and zombies become equal partners in a goal of conspicuous consumption dominating personal behavior. While the zombies graphically devour bodies of their living victims in spectacularly gory fashion, their human counterparts inside the mall mechanically indulge in their own form of consumerist consumption" (92). Matthew Bailey also considers the way Romero "uses zombies to tell the story of the mall's place in American society, and to question the impact of its promulgation of conspicuous consumption" (105).

In the context of ecocriticism, these depictions of consumerism enable *Dawn of the Dead* to meditate on both the social and environmental problems of overpopulation, and it does so most powerfully through its portrait of three spaces—urban public housing, the countryside, and a suburban mall. The tenement building in Pittsburgh provides the first glimpse of overpopulation in the film. Its tiny apartments, low ceilings, narrow hallways, and crammed staircases function as a microcosm both for crowded urban life and for the vast scope of poverty in America. Inside, only one zombie appears at first. Lying on a kitchen floor with a missing foot, it seems to pose little danger until two more attack. Numbers, once again, prove to be the real threat. In an echo of *Night of the Living Dead*, one S.W.A.T. member remarks: "Just as long as there aren't too many of those things around, we can handle them easy." Inevitably, however, zombies overwhelm the building. The ethnicity of these former tenants—mostly African Americans and Hispanics—also highlights the link between poverty and race in America. Despite Officer Wooley's (Jim Baffico's) racist rants about "fancy hotels" ("How the hell come we stick these low-life bastards into these big-ass fancy hotels, anyway? Shit, man, this is better than I got."), this place, with its peeling paint and cheap furniture, is clearly unsuitable for both the living and the dead. Wooley's biases thus reflect a broader failure on the part of white America to understand the way race informs poverty. Just as there are too many people in this building, there is too much economic inequity based on skin color.

Racism characterizes the countryside as well. While the four protagonists flee the city, they witness roving bands of white Americans hunting zombies under the bemused, watchful eye of the military. The helicopter crew refers to them as "rednecks," reacting with disgust as the hunters take pleasure in the sport of shooting zombies. With a seemingly endless supply of ammunition, coffee, and beer, they treat the entire experience like a tailgating party. The only African Americans here appear in uniform, for the countryside is the domain of whites. Its open fields represent the possibilities offered to them at the expense of immigrant labor and racial injustice. Their cowboy hats and hunting paraphernalia mark them as working class, but their skin color provides freedoms denied to nonwhites. They engage fearlessly with law enforcement and fire weapons with impunity—privileges not granted to the public housing residents. As the disabled priest explains to a white officer at the outset of the film, "You are stronger than us [gesturing to himself and by extension his nonwhite congregation], but soon, I think, they [the dead] be stronger than you." These comments link the apocalypse with a social system that uses race to determine one's access to power, and as Williams has persuasively argued, they "[articulate] the need for a new philosophy to replace ideologic capitalist, racist violence" (*Hearths* 151). Immediately after this scene in the tenement building, Romero shows zombies falling under the rifle fire of white hunters, and multiethnic groups of soldiers work alongside them with a shared purpose. This image of a pluralistic community would be hopeful in almost any other context, but within *Dawn of the Dead*, it becomes a reminder of racism so deep-seated that it requires the end of the world to stop it.

The act of hunting further encapsulates Romero's environmental message about excess and waste. As suggested by the hunters' equipment (from rifles to clothing) and playful attitude, these men enjoyed this pastime long before the zombie outbreak. Here, they relish the opportunity to hunt without permits, quotas, or restrictions, and this behavior, which includes blowing up cars for the sake of amusement ("Git the gas tank!"), is accompanied by a country-style song that celebrates men as self-entitled and narcissistic ("'Cause I'm a Man").[13] Throughout the scene, no animals other than hunting dogs appear, and this equates the undead with more traditional game such as deer or elk. It is fitting that zombie meat does not provide any sustenance, for Americans have relegated hunting to a sport. The safari-themed gun store in the mall underscores this point. Its romanticization of hunting—through background music (drum beats, chanting), sound effects (screaming monkeys, roaring elephants), and the mounted heads of African animals including a rhino, impala, wildebeest, and Thomson's gazelle—is undercut by an obvious inversion. Humans have become the endangered species in a zombie world—victims of equally irresponsible and voracious consumers. Peter (Ken Foree) and Stephen even take note of the creatures looking down on them as if to say, "This is where you're going to end up." These moments capture Romero's warning about humanity's wasteful relationship with nature and natural resources.

The mall—particularly after the spacious countryside—allows Romero to return to his commentary on overpopulation. Zombie consumers press impatiently against its doors and windows, and the demand becomes so great that the survivors must barricade the entrances with trucks. Once the biker gang gets inside, however, the mall becomes overwhelmed with greedy eaters. The bikers take things sporadically as they turn the space into a kind of carnival, hollering, riding motorcycles, shooting guns in the air, and even throwing pies in the faces of zombies. This gleeful expression of consumer desire and waste (taking a mere fraction of the mall's goods and effectively destroying the rest) mirrors the amusement-park antics of the protagonists' earlier efforts to secure the building. They ran past endless racks of clothes, converted an escalator into a slide, and sprinted through clusters of zombies, knocking them to the ground. After the Hare Krishna zombie tries to bite Fran (Gaylen Ross), for instance, Stephen hopes to console her with consumer goods: "You should see all the great stuff we got, Franny. All kinds of stuff. This place is terrific. [. . .] All kinds of things. We've really got it made here." Neither group (the helicopter crew nor the biker gang) uses these supplies systematically or with any thought for the future beyond the mall. Clearly, the zombie apocalypse has not changed their consumer ideology. They still believe more goods, more malls can be found. Yet the arrival of the bikers suggests otherwise. Soon, the zombie masses overwhelm both the gang and the original inhabitants. Over a dozen zombies pile onto one biker leaving the building, and those inside share a similar fate. The destruction of the mall turns the remaining humans into consumer items for the undead, and the film ends with Fran and Peter flying away, leaving the mall zombies to search for sustenance that is no longer there.

In a genre preoccupied with eating, it is not surprising that food plays an important role in Romero's portrait of consumer wastefulness and ecological neglect. Food motivates most of the action in the film. Throughout the chaotic opening, one scientist explains that zombies "kill for food. They eat their victims. [. . .] That's what keeps them going." A similar drive motivates the helicopter crew's search for shelter: "We don't have food. We don't have water. We don't even have a radio." If, as Romero establishes, zombies imitate former human behavior, their eating habits fall into this category, too. One scientist explains that zombies "use maybe 5% of the food available in the human body. With that small amount, the body is usually intact enough to be mobile when it revives." This practice may help propagate the species, but it also comments on America's attitude toward natural resources. Eating only 5 percent of a meal mirrors the behaviors on display at the mall. Once the helicopter crew secures the structure, food becomes just another consumer pleasure like dressing up, listening to music, ice skating, shooting basketballs, and playing video games. They "shop" for food in restaurant refrigerators and from high-end grocery stores, filling shopping bags with items such as salami, bread, dried fruits, nuts, crackers, candy, Columbian coffee, spices, and cheese. The advertisement playing on the mall's sound system, which can be heard while Fran puts on makeup, makes this connection explicit: "Attention all shoppers.

If you have a sweet tooth, we have a special treat for you. If your purchases in the next half hour amount to five dollars or more, we'll give you a bag of hard candies, free!" Consumption becomes the reward for consumption, and every aspect of the mall encourages excess, extravagance, and "commodity consumption run wild" (Shaviro 91). Just as candy encourages one to eat more sugar and fat, the crew tends to eat randomly and poorly, munching on crackers and drinking whiskey. No one prepares for future food shortages. No one considers rationing or measuring the quantity of perishable items. And only after being there for over three weeks does Stephen load two boxes into the helicopter (one of which is labeled "ammo"). In fact, they treat food the same way they try on clothes and decorate their living space like a suburban home—as if it were endlessly renewable.

Like their suburbanized kitchen and living room, the mall itself encapsulates Romero's broadest critique of consumerism as shut off from the environmental ramification of its practices. The survivors have sealed themselves inside the building, and this insulates them from one of the most pressing problems of the apocalypse—food shortages. One scientist even argues that the country has only two options left: eating the dead or using nuclear weapons: "I'm showing you a way that we can up the food supply twenty times. [. . .] What else are you going to do with them? [. . . Alternatively,] since they seem to congregate in heavily populated areas and since we have not touched upon our nuclear resources, why don't we drop bombs on all the big cities?" On one hand, he advocates turning the nation's penchant for meat-eating to the next logical source—the undead. Romero plays with this image when the crew piles dead zombies into a refrigerated unit with large cuts of beef that later become dinner for Fran and Stephen. Just as America has eaten its way into a problem (facilitating a meatpacking industry that taxes the environment and contributes to human health problems), the film wryly posits that the country could try eating its way out of this new problem. On the other hand, the suggestion that the government use nuclear weapons on cities offers a perverse solution to the dwindling food supply: "They won't run out of food. They won't run out of food while we are still alive." Such an act might finish off the zombies by finishing off most of their sustenance, but it would surely destroy the environment as well. There is not much hope for nature or humanity in a country filled with shopping malls and nuclear weapons.

The final installment of Romero's original trilogy, *Day of the Dead* (1985), takes place in Florida five years after the outbreak, and it offers a powerful continuation of these themes. A hodgepodge group of survivors—namely, soldiers, scientists, a helicopter pilot, and a civilian radio operator—have taken refuge in a defunct mine used for storage. The soldiers have been assigned the task of procuring zombies for scientific research, which puts them at ongoing physical and psychological risk, and the lead scientist, Dr. Logan (Richard Liberty), has descended into madness. The film culminates in the total collapse of this underground installation as zombies get inside and tear apart the living. Only Sarah (Lori Cardille), John (Terry Alexander), and McDermott (Jarlath Conroy) seem to survive, escaping to a presumably deserted island. Though the dream sequences framing the film cast some doubt about the end, one stark reality remains: zombies have taken over the planet, leaving little to no hope for humanity. Robin Wood credits this trilogy as "one of the most remarkable and audacious achievements of modern American cinema" (287), singling out *Day of the Dead* as its finest installment. For Wood, the film challenges the ideology of Reagan's America, the depiction of hypermasculinity in 1980s action films, and the ethos of capitalism: "all good capitalists are conditioned to live off other people, and the zombies simply carry this to its logical and literal conclusion" (289). This message about consumerism gets communicated most clearly with the revelation that a zombie "has no stomach. It can take no nourishment from what it ingests. It's working on instinct." Romero keeps audiences focused on the literal implications of so much eating through close-ups of zombies devouring human bodies. They ingest for the sake of ingesting, and as Williams has noted, these "zombie residual (learned) instincts parallel those conditioned by capitalism" (*Hearths* 269). Like the previous films, *Day of the Dead* ultimately presents nature as striking back against consumer excess. It reduces people to a limited resource for an overpopulated species and denies its bounty (sunshine, the ocean, fish, meat) to survivors too fearful to step outside for more than a few moments a day.

The film opens with a helicopter crew searching for human survivors, and Romero juxtaposes the end of capitalism with the persistence of nature here. Empty store fronts and an abandoned movie theater line the streets. Automobiles have either been wrecked, damaged, burnt out, stripped, or rendered unusable in some capacity. Human waste fills garbage cans and covers the ground. And outside the National Bank, piles of money scatter in the wind, rendering the very thing motivating consumerism as meaningless. Like the other garbage, these items have become monuments to the detritus of consumer excess, and they recall the vast environmental resources once needed to support it. At the same time, Romero highlights the impressive beauty and strength of nature. Palm trees grow, and though dead branches litter the ground, they only appear out of place on artificial surfaces (asphalt, cement). Crabs feed on corpses, a tarantula crawls on the shoulder of a zombie, and an alligator stands guard in the doorway of the National Bank, as if to indicate nature's determination not to allow this destructive economic system

Eat Your Heart Out

The lingering waste of consumerism in *Day of the Dead* (1985). United Film Distribution Company/Photofest. © United Film Distribution Company.

to return. The environment has proven more tenacious than capitalism, and the zombie outbreak has functioned as a corrective. Additionally, when compared with the flimsy fence surrounding the military installation, the surrounding forest appears lush and dense. Trees fill most of these shots. No sky can be seen through the thick greenery, and it appears to be pressing against the chain-link fence along with the zombies, threatening to reclaim this space. Nature has reasserted its power.

Numbers again play an important role in assessing the extent of the outbreak and in highlighting Romero's warning about the dangers of overpopulation. The peaceful depiction of nature at the outset gets undercut by the image of a solitary zombie. First, its shadow appears across fallen palm tree branches and a sheet of newspaper. Then its upper body, still covered in a faded suit, fills the screen, blocking the sun and revealing a face with a rotten, hollowed-out jaw. Like the trash at its feet and the obscured sunlight, the decimated mouth implies the harm humanity has done to itself and the planet for the sake of "devouring" suits, merchandise, cars, and entertainment. Soon the shadows of two more zombies can be seen, and the camera introduces a host of undead Floridians: a movie ticket salesman, a marching band player, a utility worker, and tourists. Within moments, zombies crowd the streets, stumbling toward the noise being made by the helicopter crew. Their collective, harrowing moan can be heard above the sound of the helicopter's engine, and this din communicates both their vast numbers and the depth of their hunger. When the crew returns to base, one soldier notes that there are "more and more of them every day," and John complains about their overwhelming numbers as well: "There are hundreds of them out there. Thousands. A million of them." As Dr. Logan later explains in the mess hall, "They have overrun us, you know. We're in the minority now. Something like 400,000 to one by my calculations. I haven't eaten. Is there food?" All of these numbers become a reminder of the way humans consumed too many environmental resources to feed its various hungers prior to the outbreak. Now, nature has inverted the dynamic. The same phenomenon reanimating the dead has made human beings the primary object of consumption, and like humanity before them, this new species continues to deplete its own food supply by eating too much, too quickly.

Day of the Dead's juxtaposition of sunny Florida with the tomb-like conditions of the mine also encapsulates Romero's message about environmental exploitation as having apocalyptic consequences. As Paul R. Gagne explains in *The Zombies That Ate Pittsburgh*, Romero used "a 125-acre limestone mine in Wampum, Pennsylvania, a town some thirty miles northwest of Pittsburgh," for the setting of his film (155). "Actively mined until just after World War II, the eerie, charcoal-gray labyrinth is now used as a storage facility for everything from recreational vehicles (boats, golf carts, and Winnebagos) to surplus powdered milk and feature-film negatives (including that of *Gone with the Wind*). [. . .] If the Monroeville shopping mall is a temple to the consumer society Romero pokes fun at in *Dawn of the Dead*, then this is its tomb" (155).[14] It is also important to recognize the literal implications of this setting. As a mine and storage facility, it illustrates two aspects of the environmental harm associated with consumerism: resource depletion and waste production. Since the mine's previous function never gets identified in the film, it represents all efforts to excavate finite planetary resources for the sake of consumer culture. Whether limestone to build shops or coal to provide them with electricity, this mine has nothing more to yield, suggesting the overuse of nature prior to the outbreak. Furthermore, its function as a storage facility—for unused vehicles and a hodgepodge of human artifacts—reduces it to nothing more than an underground landfill. Humanity first exploits the land and then fills it with garbage.

This resource depletion becomes a catalyst for nature to protect itself. As John explains, the mine contains countless documents: "They got official accounts of [. . .] volcano eruptions and earthquakes and fires and floods and all the other disasters that interrupted the flow of things in the good old U.S. of A." He even warns Sarah that her scientific work will lead nowhere:

"You ain't never gonna figure it out. Just like they never figured out why the stars are where they're at. It ain't mankind's job to figure that stuff out." On one level, he associates the zombie apocalypse with both natural disasters and the beauty of the universe. As with fires, floods, volcanic eruptions, and even stars (which eventually collapse or explode), the most destructive aspects of nature tend to be followed by periods of recovery and restoration. Not surprisingly, John offers a vision of starting over with Sarah, suggesting that they have babies together on a deserted island. This fantasy of renewal, however, stems from humanity's failed responsibility to the planet: "We've been punished by the Creator. He visited a curse on us, so we might get a look at what hell is like. Maybe he didn't want to see us blow ourselves up and put a big hole in the sky. Maybe he just wanted to show us he was still the Bossman." The reference to "Bossman," much like Dr. Logan's nickname of "Frankenstein," reinforces the film's warning about scientific overreach. Yet given the nearly nonexistent role of religion in the characters' lives, one might also attribute this wrath to Mother Nature. Either way, the zombie outbreak functions as a punishment for destructive environmental acts such as harnessing nuclear energy for weapons and tearing apart the ozone layer.

In many respects, the survivors experience two types of hell in the film: their confrontations with the living dead and their exclusion from nature. They become Edenic outcasts of sorts, denied the beauty of and any connection with the natural world. Since they fear drawing too much attention from zombies to stay outside, they have sealed themselves in a dungeon, leaving them only glimpses of sunlight. Trees must remain at a distance, and beaches can only be viewed from a helicopter cockpit. Romero presents this banishment as the ultimate price for abusing the Earth. He does so in part by contrasting the beautiful, fleeting shots of Florida's coastline with the grim, claustrophobic setting of the mine. He also uses pumpkins in this fashion. The film begins with Sarah looking longingly at a photograph, not of her family or friends but of a wall calendar. The month of October features a pumpkin patch with lush green grasses and carefree people deciding which orange globes to take home for Halloween. This image exemplifies both nature's bounty and the public's wastefulness before the zombie apocalypse. Most carving pumpkins, first designed in the early 1970s for their color, size, shape, durability, and long stem, end up discarded and uneaten by Americans, adding to already crowded landfills and producing greenhouse gases from the decomposing matter.[15] This seasonal pastime recalls the consumer culture surrounding Halloween, a holiday defined by eating excess quantities of processed sweets. It recalls a time when ghouls, monsters, and zombies existed only as costumes, not realities. And it recalls a time when nature's fecundity appeared boundless enough to support a vast crop for mere decoration. Sarah touches the picture with her fingers, wistfully, and suddenly the arms of dozens of zombies burst through the wall to grab her. Taken together, the squandering of natural resources as evoked by the picture offers another example of the way Romero's zombies serve as a referendum on humanity. Sarah wakes up from this nightmare to find herself in a helicopter, safe from the dangers on the ground but removed from the natural world.

Toxic Terror: *The Return of the Living Dead* Series, *Toxic Zombies*, *Surf II*, and *Redneck Zombies*

The ecohorror film *C.H.U.D.* (1984) offers one example of the way toxic waste played a prominent role in 1980s cinema. It uses the vast sewer and tunnel system beneath New York City as a metaphor for public blindness about the environmental harm of industrial, nuclear, and everyday waste. Much like the street cleaner in the opening moments of the film, burying waste beneath New York creates the illusion that it poses no real threat to the planet. Both acts (street cleaning and depositing chemicals underground) remove the visual consequences of producing so much garbage. Only the transformation of the subterranean homeless community into C.H.U.D. (Cannibalistic Humanoid Underground Dwellers) forces residents and local politicians into action, uncovering a plot by the Nuclear Regulatory Commission to illegally dump radioactive materials. The film's focus on the homeless also highlights the class implications of such practices in America. As many environmental scholars have noted, poor, nonwhite communities typically have greater exposure to harmful pollutants.[16] Ultimately, *C.H.U.D.* presents photojournalism as a possible solution to these problems. The pictures taken by George Cooper (John Heard) offer irrefutable evidence that can convince naysayers, expose conspiracies, galvanize the public, and hold government officials accountable. They can force Americans to recognize—and literally to see—social and environmental injustices.

Just as these infected homeless people have emerged from beneath the surface to feed, zombies often rise from some contamination that the government tries to cover up. In films such as *The Return of the Living Dead* (1985), *The Return of the Living Dead Part II* (1988), *Toxic Zombies* (1980), *Surf II* (1984), and *Redneck Zombies* (1989), overpopulation still functions as an image for environmental harm as the undead overwhelm victims by numbers, but government conspiracies become the focal point as zombies represent uncovered truths about toxic waste, the human cost of exposure, and the environmental harm of so much pollution.

Suicide's (Mark Venturini's) exhaust-spewing car in Dan O' Bannon's *The Return of the Living Dead* (1985). MGM/Photofest. © MGM.

Dan O'Bannon's *The Return of the Living Dead*, loosely based on the novel by John A. Russo,[17] recasts *Night of the Living Dead* as a story about the consequences of toxic contamination. In the opening scene, Frank (James Karen), a foreman for a medical supply company, tells his nephew that Romero based his film on an actual incident with a pesticide that leaked into a military morgue. The US Army tried to cover up the truth, placing the infected bodies in sealed drums, but a shipping snafu landed them in this warehouse. In a display of bravado, Frank damages one container, releasing a noxious gas that infects the men and reanimates a dead corpse (along with a few split dogs and several mounted butterflies). He and his boss, Burt (Clu Gulager), try to manage the situation by chopping up the reanimated corpse and using an incinerator to destroy it. When the zombie's contaminated ashes drift into the atmosphere to generate acid rain, however, the downpour scorches the earth, burns the skin of teenagers partying in a cemetery, seeps into graves, and revivifies the dead. At the end of the film, the army destroys part of the town with a nuclear weapon, considering the mission a success for killing only four thousand people, but the fallout also acidifies the rain. As it seeps back into the ground, the dead begin to rise once again. Using acid rain as the vehicle for the zombie outbreak enables *The Return of the Living Dead* to link its environmental message with one of the most pressing concerns of the 1980s. Whether from chemical agents, ash, nuclear waste, or car exhaust, acid rain illustrates the apocalyptic consequences of such pollution and reminds viewers that the survival of humanity depends on the well-being of the planet.

The clownish antics of the characters provide much of the comedy in the film, but their actions also highlight the dangers of America's failed responsibility to the environment. Greed and fear of embarrassment motivate Frank and Burt, and the military behaves no differently. As suggested by the black-and-white poster of Richard Nixon in the warehouse basement, a culture of dishonesty and absence of personal responsibility permeate American life from its most powerful figure to a working-class guy. All of this has serious consequences for nature. Darrow Chemical, the maker of the pesticide 2-4-5 Trioxin, manufactures poisonous agents. The government uses weapons with callous indifference to nature and to human life. Frank harms the atmosphere by releasing the contents of the drum and using an aerosol can. Incineration and nuclear fallout turn the rain acidic. Even the residents of Louisville mistreat the landscape. Spray paint appears on buildings, walls, and gates. Suicide's car coughs up filthy, thick clouds of exhaust. Garbage litters city streets as well as the graveyard. Toxic materials such as paint cans and acetone fill the basement of the medical supply company. And one of the teens even goes by the name "Trash." All of these details offer vivid reminders of human wastefulness.

In addition to the ugliness of this pollution (from exhaust fumes to graffiti), the film's playful use of signs reinforces its warning about these behaviors. "No future" has been scrawled on the gate of the cemetery, and Suicide (Mark Venturini) has painted his name on the car's hood. Both suggest that America's treatment of the environment will bring about its own demise. The signs inside the medical warehouse function in a similar way. Beneath a disability parking sign hangs several others: "Toxic," "Keep Out: Quarantined: Chicken Pox," and "Quarantined," which gets obscured by the lid of a crate being used to ship a skeleton. This progression implies that toxicity leads to communicable disease (whether chicken pox or zombification), quarantine, and ultimately death (skeleton). Even the disability parking sign plays with the idea of toxic contamination disabling both people and the planet.

The Return of the Living Dead modified the traditional diet and speed of zombies to reflect its environmental message as well. These zombies hunger for brains, not flesh. As one explains, this meal mitigates "the pain of being dead; I can feel myself rot. [. . . Eating brains] makes the pain go away." As far as explanations go, this one does not make much sense on a literal level. Why would brains lessen the pain of decay more than flesh, blood, or a decent aspirin? Metaphorically, however, this emphasis on brains raises questions about the intellectual choices of the characters—particularly those that hide the truth about toxic waste. The moaning refrain of "Brains," in other words, can be heard as a challenge for the audience to "Think!" Think about the consequences of producing dangerous waste. Think about the future condition of the planet. In other words, this particular diet invites audiences to wonder how America could be so brainless as to wantonly destroy the natural world. Likewise, these speedy zombies capture the urgency of the crisis, suggesting that environmental decay can no longer be viewed at a distance, as some lumbering thing to worry about at a later date. It is rushing toward us with terminal force, and all aspects of society from punk teenagers to government officials need to make a more concerted effort to protect the earth.

In Ken Weiderhorn's *The Return of the Living Dead Part II*, toxic chemicals again cause zombie-inducing acid rain, but the horrors of this pollution primarily get linked with suburbia. The film opens with a voiceover that recounts the first 2–4–5 Trioxin spill, explaining that the chemical functioned as "a catalyst in genetic reactification. What this means and why Trioxin was useful has never been revealed. But one thing is certain. Trioxin was soon considered too dangerous and volatile even for experimental use. Interest in the lethal compound was abandoned several years ago. The Army will not comment other than to say, 'All Trioxin has since been destroyed.'" This narrative is juxtaposed with images of governmental duplicity as the army transports Trioxin through a suburban neighborhood. One soldier, while smoking pot and listening to loud music through earphones, fails to notice the three canisters that fall off his truck. One rolls into the river, and this moment foreshadows the environmental contamination to come. The next afternoon, several teens come across this container inside a storm drain, and, predictably, they push several buttons that unleash a toxic green gas. The kids cough violently from the fumes, and a thick cloud engulfs the nearby trees, hillside, and stream. This gas soon creeps across the community cemetery and drifts into the atmosphere to produce acid rain.

While this narrative mirrors the plot of the first film, *The Return of the Living Dead Part II* largely uses it as a device for critiquing the environmental harm caused by suburbia. America's love affair with the suburbs began in earnest after the First World War, but when William J. Levitt applied Ford's assembly-line principles to develop Levittown in 1946 (in Hempstead, Long

Island), he transformed the housing crisis of World War II into a booming industry. Nearly 1.7 million single-family startups were built in 1950 alone, and as Kenneth T. Jackson explains in *Crabgrass Frontier*, "Between 1950 and 1970, the suburban population doubled from 36 to 74 million, and 83 percent of the nation's total growth took place in the suburbs" (283). By 1970, more people lived in suburbia than on farms or in cities, and suburbanites outnumbered city dwellers in fourteen of the fifteen largest American cities by 1980 (284). The environmental costs of such massive developments, which historian Adam Rome likens to a "catastrophe on the scale of the Dust Bowl," became increasingly evident in the 1960s and 1970s. In *The Bulldozer in the Countryside*, he examines the damage caused by suburbanization as well as the activism it inspired. Septic tanks, for example, increasingly polluted groundwater, lakes, and streams (91). Urban development between the mid-1950s and 1970s destroyed "almost a million acres of marshes, swamps, bogs, and coastal estuaries" (121). Bulldozers decimated vegetation, ripped out trees, filled streams, flattened hills, silted rivers, and facilitated erosion that increased "the likelihood of flood damages" (168). A number of efforts were launched to curtail this harm, such as the Urban Growth and New Community Development Act of 1970, but the cost of integrating housing developments into the existing landscape discouraged most developers. "In 1981, the Reagan administration decided to eliminate the program, and it was killed in 1984" (261). While the 1980s witnessed efforts to protect against some of these problems, suburban sprawl continued in unprecedented ways. "The nation lost almost 1.4 million acres a year to development from 1982 to 1992" (264). Ultimately, the 1980s consumer found self-interest (trying to get the most house for the money) in conflict with the environmental risks of such desires.

The Return of the Living Dead Part II announces the link between environmental contamination and suburbia in its portrait of the Wilson's housing development. After the toxic container falls into the river, the camera cuts to this active construction site. A large tract of land has been cleared here, and when juxtaposed with the foliage surrounding the storm drain and cemetery, this project clearly required the destruction of countless trees and plants. As the camera pans left, dozens of unfinished houses appear as well, giving a sense for the vastness of this development and its future cost to the environment. Specifically, it extends to the nearest hillside, and various markers (i.e., poles with flags) indicate that this landmass will be bulldozed to make room for more houses. Even the current residents live next to unfinished lots. Scaffolding, a cement mixer, stacks of roofing tiles, and other building equipment surround the structure next to the Wilson's, and prior to the outbreak, construction crews provide a kind of soundtrack for this tireless expansion. In fact, every exterior shot includes a reminder of this development as ongoing to emphasize the extent of suburban sprawl in America.

Cars reflect these environmental costs as well, and this establishing shot shows vehicles on every street, a reminder of the automobile's essential role in these planned communities. In a fitting choice, the survivors rely on a 1959 Cadillac Fleetwood 60 special to escape the zombies. This type of large gas-guzzler defined the 1950s investment in driving and suburban life. Americans purchased approximately 7 million cars annually throughout the 1950s, and a record 7.9 million sold in 1955.[18] As Miller and Nowak explain, "By 1958 over 76.4 million cars and trucks were in use, more than one for every household. (Nearly 12 million families, mostly in the suburbs, had two or more cars.)" (139). Between 1945 and 1960, the annual miles driven by passenger cars jumped an astonishing 194 percent from "200 billion to 587 billion" (McCarthy 152). For *The Return of the Living Dead Part II*, this Cadillac links fifties suburban tastes with the eighties, and this continuity highlights the country's increasing appetite for petroleum. This sequel may have chosen a pristine Cadillac instead of Suicide's junk heap from the first film, but this substitution is sleight of hand only. Both harm the environment. Like the shiny exterior of the Cadillac, these homes, with their manicured lawns and covered garages, obfuscate the labor and resources needed to sustain them.[19] They encourage spending without guilt.

Nevertheless, the porosity of these unfinished houses—whether through walls without sheetrock or missing garage doors—invites audiences to look more closely at suburban life and the consumer impulses driving it. Among the living, this community gets characterized by latchkey kids, bullies with too much free time, pretentious teens, and elderly alcoholics. Yet the film's most powerful indictment comes from the zombies themselves. They still wear suits, neckties, glasses, formal shoes, and dresses indicative of middle-class professional culture. They appear to want nothing more than to return to their previous lives, stumbling through the development as if coming home after a long day at work. Against the backdrop of minimal streetlight and unilluminated houses, the undead initially blend into the landscape. Doc Mandel (Philip Burns), for instance, expresses more concern over the scratches on his car than reanimated corpses, and the cable guy mistakes a zombie for someone looking after a hit-and-run victim. These details reinforce the film's larger portrait of suburbia as a kind of living death. When zombies finally enter the Wilson's they make themselves at home, rummaging through kitchen cabinets, examining boxes of processed foods, and watching an aerobics video on television. Apparently, the routine of working and consuming becomes so ingrained that one can't even escape it in death.

The ecohorror film *Toxic Zombies*, written and directed by Charles McCrann, seems to draw its inspiration from both Rachel Carson's account of pesticides in *Silent Spring* and the crop-dusting sequence in Alfred Hitchcock's *North by Northwest* (1959). After marijuana farmers kill two federal agents during a raid, the government decides to use an experimental herbicide to destroy the drugs. A drunken crop duster, hired by corrupt bureaucrats, not only sprays the crop and most of its farmers, but he also contaminates himself and some nearby farmland in the process. This toxic chemical, Growmax, transforms people and animals into zombie-like creatures that act on violent impulses and eat human flesh. Instead of acid rain, *Toxic Zombies* focuses its environmental critique on pesticides and herbicides, and it follows a similar pattern to the other films. It attributes the poisoning of the planet and people to governmental (and arguably industrial) irresponsibility, making zombies a vehicle for nature's revenge.

The impact of Growmax offers a repudiation of any policy or practice encouraging the use of chemicals on farmland. Early in the film, while discussing the possibility of spraying the herbicide, two federal agents begrudgingly acknowledge its potential side effects: "Research says it might be dangerous. They haven't finished testing it yet." Nevertheless, the men justify its use on the illegal crops, in part, by claiming the area to be uninhabited. (This proves to be untrue as one farmer lives there and a regional agent enjoys fishing nearby.) They also have no qualms about infecting the criminals responsible for killing the agents. As one facetiously concludes, "Remember, we don't know that Growmax is toxic to humans." The marijuana farmers' subsequent transformation, however, warns against the possible dangers of such chemicals. They become violently ill within moments after exposure, vomiting and coughing uncontrollably. By the next morning, they struggle to communicate, rock back and forth nonsensically, develop skin lesions, and lose their balance and coordination. Growmax does not kill the infected, but it does change them into zombie-like creatures that lack coherent speech and develop cannibalistic tastes. The crop duster kills his wife, for instance, and the marijuana farmers murder their healthy companions as well as several bystanders in the woods. This chemical agent does not merely harm people. According to the farmer whose cabin becomes a temporary refuge for survivors, the herbicide destroyed his garden and infected his dog, turning the animal violent. The marijuana farmers even complain about abandoning sixty kilos of harvest for the "fucking rabbits," but these rabbits will presumably experience the same fate as the dog. In this way, *Toxic Zombies* portrays the chemicals associated with the modern food industry as dangerous to plant, animal, and human life.

The film also captures humanity's exploitative relationship with nature through the family of campers. Jerry (Roger Miles) views camping as an important tool for teaching his children to appreciate nature: "I don't want those kids to grow up without ever having known the wilderness. I want Amy to get a taste of nature before her brain is packed up and carted away by Madison Avenue." His comments suggest that modern life, particularly through the temptations of consumer culture, creates a division between urban and rural. The wilderness, for him, must be experienced, but despite this philosophy, he comes across as a relatively inept woodsman. Unlike the protagonist (Tom) who can catch, clean, and cook his own fish, Jerry can't even use a can opener successfully. His children already possess an affinity for the outdoors, walking through the woods, holding frogs, and identifying fungus, but Jerry never strays more than a few feet from his car. While reminiscing about his days as a logger, he explains: "I spent two summers in a lumberjack camp. I had to haul some giant logs through some pretty tough terrain. I remember once when a giant timber got loose from the cable operator. You could hear the screams of agony a mile away. Not really agony, more like surprise. They just couldn't believe what was about to happen to them." This anecdote both foreshadows his fate at the hand of the infected farmers and casts these zombie-like creatures as tools for nature's wrath. The loggers' shock at the accident reveals their unwillingness to believe the dangerous consequences of deforestation for both people and the environment. The threat posed by the zombified farmers inspires Jerry to flee, leaving his wife and children behind, and this act of selfishness represents the broader relationship between most of the characters and nature—viewing it either for exploitation (pot growers, loggers) or with careless disregard.

The latter can be seen through the truck driver whose pickup stalls several times, giving Jerry's wife (Pat Kellis) some hope of being rescued. As the truck tries to navigate the winding dirt road, it appears dwarfed by the surroundings. Greenery overwhelms most of the shots with trees lining both sides of the road and branches stretching overhead like a canopy. At several moments, the vehicle disappears from view as if swallowed up by the woods themselves. Both the setting and the recurring engine trouble highlight the limitations of technology. In fact, the truck proves completely ineffectual as a tool for transport or rescue. The wife cannot start the engine, and her attempt to do so only activates the windshield wipers, which oscillate pointlessly during her murder. Additionally, the death of the trucker is preceded by an act of littering. After the first stall, he finishes a can of beer and throws it out the window. This moment adds another dimension to the revenge of nature motif as zombies lash out against the use of a poisonous herbicide (killing the federal agents and pilot), the exploitation of nature for profit (through loggers and drug dealers), and litter.

Surf II (1984) uses gas-guzzling cars and soda to warn against the dangers of overconsumption. Through its amalgamation of styles such as music videos, surfing documentaries, stoner flicks, parodies (most notably of *Jaws* [1975] and *The Spy Who Loved Me* [1977]), and comedies like *Animal House* (1978), one might generously argue that the film comments on the excesses of popular culture. Even the title, *Surf II*, plays into the popularity of sequels in the 1980s, yet no prequel for the film exists. These details mock the public's hunger for more of something regardless of its artistic, comedic, or cultural value—let alone its cost to the environment.[20] In any case, *Surf II* announces a loose environmental agenda in the epigraph: "Long ago in 'The Good Old Days' surfers ruled. It was bitchin'! That was before the threat of chemical pollution, nuclear waste and the horror of Buzzz Cola." The film's focus on petroleum-infused soda presents zombification as a metaphor for America's addiction to harmful substances, and though this surfing community remains largely oblivious to these problems, its ability to maintain a safe connection with the natural world—to ride the waves and sit on the beach—requires some stance against pollution.

Unlike eighties vampire films that present bloodlust as a metaphor for sugar addiction, no one likes Buzzz Cola. Its vile taste hints at the drink's design to transform teenagers into petroleum- and waste-consuming zombies. When Menlo Schwatzer (Eddie Deezen), a teenage mad scientist, crafts Buzzz as a means to avenge his mistreatment by surfers, he partners with two local businessmen to distribute the product. Their greed and utter indifference about its content satirize corporate America, which encourages excess consumption for profit regardless of the health and environmental consequences. Even their wives refer to the soda as "crap" and complain that it could not pass for fertilizer: It's "a soft drink that unclogs drains and strips the paint off battleships." Despite their husbands' claims that they use "organic glass" and "no preservatives," the drink makes people lose the capacity to speak, moan like zombies, become violent (toward themselves and others), and return from the dead. Jacko (Tom Villard), for example, begins drinking motor oil and antifreeze after his exposure to the beverage, and he later engages in a vile eating contest that involves swallowing seaweed, fish, glass, car parts, and other slimy waste. This contest culminates with a challenge to drink Buzzz Cola, but the surfer passes out from a combination of illness, overeating, and presumably horror at such a prospect.

This connection among soda, petroleum, and oceanic detritus further highlights the harm caused by consumer culture. In addition to having Menlo sell Buzzz while wearing a Ghutrah, the national headdress for Saudi Arabian men, Mr. Beaker (Peter Isacksen) analyzes the soda and determines that its ingredients, petroleum waste and unidentified chemicals, are designed to create "gas guzzling junkies." One post-autopsy zombie even returns to life for another swig! As suggested by the film's emphasis on driving, these gas-guzzling zombies embody the mindless addiction to fuel in Southern California car culture. These surfers constantly rely on cars to go back and forth between their homes and the beach. They might be too high to recognize it, but their automobiles harm the very environment they cherish as surfers. These vehicles not only emit greenhouse gasses, but various auto parts and oil also litter the beach as well as the yard of Johnny Big Head's (Joshua Cadman's) house. It appears that these surfer teens are already gas-guzzling zombies.

As one might suspect from their willingness to support the oil industry (no one considers walking or taking the bus—though admittedly few Los Angelinos associate the city with either), the danger caused by the petroleum sludge of Buzzz inspires only tepid activism at best. The science teacher appeals to a corrupt city council to ban the drink, and several surfers destroy Menlo's underwater lair—a former refinery that still mines enough oil to generate endless quantities of toxic soda. Nevertheless, this beach community's love of surfing, sex, and addictive substances (the adults get drunk and the surfers smoke pot) comes across as too powerful to inspire lasting change. Chuck (Eric Stoltz) wears a T-shirt reading "No Nukes" for most of the film, but it has no meaning for him. His obsession with surfing blinds him to everything else. Mr. Beaker addresses the physiological side effects of the drink—namely, turning the town's children into zombies—but he does not mention the dangerous chemicals in Buzzz to the city council. He also does not address the risk of having an oil refinery so close to shore. In fact, not a single character in *Surf II* cares about the environment.

I certainly don't want to take the film more seriously than it takes itself (which I suspect I've already done), but this careless disregard for nature makes an interesting point from an ecocritical perspective, though not necessarily an intentional one on the part of the filmmaker. The closing scene depicts a return to the status quo with everyone hanging out on the beach, drinking alcohol, sipping sodas, shoving food into their mouths, and getting ready to play volleyball. Menlo has even joined them for a picnic, and Chuck has abandoned his "No Nukes" shirt to go topless. Someone conveniently explains that the effects of Buzzz Cola will wear off, so the crisis in the film has no real consequences. No one has learned a thing. Certainly, this moment undercuts any potential environmental message, which was admittedly convoluted from the start, but this return can be interpreted as more than a mere reflection of B-comedy conventions at the time. *Surf II* portrays American culture as blinded to the environmental costs of consumerism by its own desire for pleasure.

Redneck Zombies (1989) reworks the premise of *The Return of the Living Dead* series to craft a satire about southern stereotypes and to warn against the environmental consequences of toxic contamination. Its epigraph links the dangers of nuclear waste with military malfeasance: "In late 1986, a fifty-five-gallon drum of highly toxic experimental chemical warfare nuclear waste was rumored to be missing from a high security warehouse facility." It goes on to note that the Pentagon acknowledged one missing drum but reassured the public that it posed no threat to "human health." Subsequently, a soldier driving a military jeep, smoking pot, and complaining about the difficulty of finding a place to dump toxic sludge loses control of his vehicle. The crash causes this container of waste to roll onto private property where several moonshiners decide to use it for a new still. None of them can read the "Danger—Radioactive" warning printed on the yellow drum—though their illiteracy comes as no surprise from a film trafficking in every tasteless stereotype about southern life. After some spills into their mash, the green drink, which no one balks at trying, transforms customers into zombies. The corn mash, sugar, and yeast needed for moonshine has, in effect, become contaminated here, so in addition to killing people, toxic chemicals poison the food items necessary for distilling alcohol—a connection that gets reinforced when the first zombie attack happens in a cornfield.

The toxic waste also spills onto the ground by the still, and wherever the zombies go, the landscape dies with them. When the urban campers search for their missing friends, for example, one notices that everything around them—foliage, bushes, grass, and trees—appears dead. Similarly, the final girl's encounter with the zombie family (a sequence that evokes the family dinner in *The Texas Chainsaw Massacre*) gets associated with the dying landscape. Dead crops line both sides of the road that she stumbles along for help, and this image connects the fate of human life with the natural world. The only thing saving her from a zombie is a tree branch, which she lances through its eye. Nature, the very thing being treated so callously in the film, proves central to human survival.

Arguably the most interesting aspect of *Redneck Zombies* (in addition to its tagline, "Tobacco Chewin', Gut Chompin', Cannibal Kinfolk from Hell!") involves the connection between egregious examples of industrial toxic waste and everyday practices in the United States that cause environmental harm. One camper, for instance, uses excessive amounts of aerosol deodorant, and when the group determines that the zombie outbreak can be attributed to toxic contamination, they use aerosol deodorant to defend themselves. Against zombie skin, the spray causes a chemical reaction that melts flesh and kills the creatures. The humor operates on a number of levels. This product for masking body odor mocks the rednecks' poor hygiene in life, which has carried over into death. Even in a reanimated state, they cannot tolerate cleanliness. At the same time, the urban campers use deodorant in excess, urinate in lakes, and care more about drugs than finding a suitable campsite. They pose a danger to themselves and to the wilderness. By pitting one product that damages the ozone layer against nuclear waste, the film places both on a continuum. Individuals—like waste-producing industries—need to make better choices to protect nature.

Finally, *Redneck Zombies* includes the food industry in its critique as well. The moonshiners have dozens of customers, including two serial killers who watch footage of chick culling—the execution of baby chicks at an egg production facility. Male chicks tend to be killed right after hatching (since they don't produce eggs), and one method for this execution—maceration—runs the chicks through a high-speed grinder. This footage plays on a television next to a woman bound with rope and duct tape. Blood covers one killer's apron, as he moves in and out of the kitchen with a large knife, and the other watches her menacingly. Here the cruelty inflicted on these animals gets aligned with the woman's impending death. In the context of the film's environmental message, man's relationship with nature—as exemplified by the careless indifference of consumerism (aerosol deodorants), the cruel practices of the poultry and meat industries, and the dangerous risks of nuclear technology—also proves to be the stuff of horror. Toxic zombies become an image for the most extreme consequences of this abusive relationship with the natural world.

Book of the Dead: Zombie Fiction in the 1980s

John Skipp and Craig Spector's introduction to *Book of the Dead* (1989) describes it as "the most *overt* anthology of original horror fiction ever assembled." These editors not only view the volume as a literary homage to Romero's films, but they also consider such work crucial in a century that witnessed the horrors of chemical warfare, atomic bombs, assassinations, cult murders, drive-by shootings, "day-care rapists, hijackings, [. . .] death squads, and body dumps." Only art that "[goes] too far," Skipp and Spector claim, "will help us come to grips with how far over the edge we've gone" (12). The extreme nature of zombie fiction makes it particularly effective for pushing boundaries and

A book for the dead. "Bub" (Sherman Howard) tries to read in *Day of the Dead* (1985). © United Film Distribution Company.

challenging audiences to make sense of the violence being done to the world. In Romero's foreword to the book, he echoes the importance of this subject matter despite "the denunciations of society" that come with it, and he considers zombie fiction quite brave in the "self-centered, get-rich-and-look-good-at-all-costs eighties" (2). This self-centered consumerism, as Romero demonstrates in his films, has done irrevocable damage to nature, and not surprisingly, environmental catastrophes loom large in *Book of the Dead*. Some stories offer explanations for a zombie outbreak that include an airborne bacterium, chemical warfare, radiation, voodoo, and worm-like creatures from outer space. Others attribute it to the inexplicable ("No one knows how it starts. [. . .] It could have dozens of different forms" [121]). No matter the cause, all of these works depict a society struggling with lifeless landscapes, limited resources, and insatiable corpses. More specifically, the image of flowers in the ecohorror stories framing the collection, Chan McConnell's "Blossom" and Robert McCammon's "Eat Me," the damaged ozone layer and threat of nuclear war in Stephen King's "Home Delivery," and the insulated biosphere of Steven Boyett's "Like Pavlov's Dogs" present a terrifying vision of environmental collapse that challenges Western culture's exploitative relationship with the planet.

Chan McConnell's "Blossom," the opening story of the anthology, uses flowers as an image for the way consumerism robs people of their humanity and respect for nature. Both characters work at a bank, and they view people and nature in terms of economic transactions. Amelia only agrees to a date with Quinn after reading his personnel file and determining his net worth: "He drove a Jaguar XJS and was into condo development" (15). She notes that all of the receptionists in the office approach dating the same way, suggesting that money and status matter more than emotional attachment or sexual desire. Not surprisingly, Amelia calculates the expense of the evening before deciding whether or not to have sex with him: "Dinner had run to ninety-five bucks, not counting the wine or the tip. Dessert had been high-priced [. . .] Cabs had been taken and token gifts dispensed" (15). She has learned to objectify herself long before he ties her up in bed, yet she finds a certain power in performing desire. For instance, she nods just enough to convince him that she is "actually listening" (16), and she hides the truth about her STD, describing the deception as "compensation." Disease, it would seem, is just another cost in the sexual currency of modern dating. Such calculations do little to mitigate her resentment over the social limitations defining women's lives: "She fought hard to keep what she had and had nothing to show for her effort except a stupid airhead bimbo job at Columbia Savings. So much bitterness, there beneath the manner and cosmetics" (16). In many ways, her bloom as a thirty-four-year-old woman has faded under the strain of callous men, sex without emotion, and disease. This dynamic parallels her literal taste for flowers. After Quinn invites her to disclose an "aberration" to him, she reveals her lifelong penchant for eating flowers. The act of chewing and swallowing irises titillates Quinn, and like eating expensive foods and wearing elegant clothes, it becomes just another act of consumerism. This peccadillo also hints at the underlying environmental costs of a society that values acquiring so much stuff. Like the flowers used to make Amelia's perfumes, all of the items they value (and waste) tax natural resources.

In fact, McConnell uses flowers as an image for the dangerous excesses of consumer culture. When Amelia mentions her affection for flowers, Quinn fills his apartment with them: "He and his Gold Card had come through in rainbow colors. All over the penthouse were long-stemmed roses, carnation bouquets, spring bunches, mums, more" (17). While his finances give him access to "more" of everything, this abundance of blooms merely operates as a prop for seduction and erotic stimulation. Their beauty and aroma go unremarked in the story, and they literally become something to consume in Amelia's hands. As such, killing flowers points to the wastefulness of consumerism more broadly. McConnell reinforces this point by linking flowers with other displays of Quinn's affluence: "There was a tall vase of irises on an antique end table, near the fireplace. Firelight mellowed all the glass and Scandinavian chrome in the room, and danced in the floor-to-ceiling wrap-around windows of Quinn's eighth-floor eyrie" (16–17). These details about

Scandinavian chrome and antiques come from Amelia, suggesting a shared value system on her part, but the description of his home as an eyrie, the nest of an eagle or other bird of prey, reveals her vulnerability. She can easily become a victim to his sense of privilege, viewed as prey or chewed up like an iris. Indeed, Quinn's callous response to her death from autoerotic asphyxiation and decision to rape her warm corpse demonstrate as much: "Sometimes it went down that way, he thought. The price of true passion, however aberrant. But she was still moist and posed at the ready, so he opted to have one more go" (18). Similar to the way raptors (from the Latin term *rapere* meaning to seize or acquire by force) feed on small animals and rodents, Quinn has treated her the same way. This bird of prey image also highlights the revenge of nature motif in the story. Amelia's subsequent zombification transforms him into a victim, avenging her degradation and abuse by castrating and eating him. The inversion of gendered power from man to (undead) woman mirrors the power shift between humanity and nature during a zombie apocalypse. Amelia and Quinn, with their shared consumer sensibility, have now become perpetual eaters, turning their hungers on those most responsible for exploiting the planet's resources—humans.

Finally, McConnell's title, "Blossom," foreshadows the tension between consumerism and nature in the story. Amelia's flower-eating fetish offers one example of this: "'Ever since I was a little girl,' she said. 'Perhaps because I saw my cat, Sterling, eating grass. I like the flavor. I don't know. I used to think the flower's life added to mine'" (17). While the cat's name may indicate its outstanding qualities, "sterling" is also a term for British currency, and this detail points to Amelia's lifelong association between money and exceptionalism. She will spend her days chasing wealth at the expense of herself and nature. Yet Sterling, like the people in the story, eats things he shouldn't, so he relies on grass to induce vomiting, to expel indigestible matter from his digestive tract. Flowers do not have the same effect on Amelia, though, and this distinction underscores a fundamental difference between the way animals and humans interact with the environment. Nature provides a system of checks and balances for animals. Amelia, however, approaches nature and dating the same way—with calculated self-interest. Even as an adult, she believes eating flowers can add to her life. When biting "off the delicate chiffon of the iris" (17) to seduce Quinn, she hopes his money might "add" luxury, ease, and contentment to her lifestyle. Interestingly, she consumes flowers one last time as a zombie: "She began eating the flowers in their vases [. . .]. The flowers were alive, but dying every moment. Their life might become hers. When she stopped, all the bouquets had been stripped" (20). Only after zombification, with her appetite shifting from flowers to human flesh, do flower petals get appreciated aesthetically. Amelia becomes truly beautiful in the closing lines of the story: "She blended with the shadows, a striking, cream-skinned nude with flower petals drifting down from her mouth, ochre, mauve, bright red" (20). Described in terms of a painting, her skin accentuates the vibrant colors of the flowers. This moment of authentic beauty, however, only emerges after the abandonment of consumer values and after it is too late to preserve either nature or humanity.

The final story of the anthology, Robert R. McCammon's "Eat Me," also juxtaposes consumerism and flowers (nature) but in the context of zombies struggling with the loss of humanity, love, and the environment. One evening, zombie Jim Crisp meets Brenda at a singles bar for the undead, and after spending hours together, they decide to eat each other as an expression of love. Broadly speaking, these sentient, urban zombies cope with the loneliness of eternity by behaving as they did before the apocalypse. They apply cologne, take baths, wear jewelry, listen to records, consult calendars, own clocks, and go to bars. They also participate in consumer culture. Instead of money, however, zombies use "freshly-killed rats, roaches, spiders, and centipedes" (382) as currency, and "a particularly juicy rat [can buy] two bottles of Miller Lite." These beers do not intoxicate or quench thirst, however. They merely pass through the body, allowing some fleeting connection with one's former identity. For Jim, beer drinking offers another reminder of the hollowness of consumerism, and like the stoplights that continue to regulate phantom traffic, most of the acquisitions acquired in life have no value or meaning in death. They represent a society invested more in things than in human connections. Jim himself admits that he dedicated his time to being an accountant and that he preferred being governed by mathematics, logic, and tallying figures. Like Amelia in "Blossom," these calculations have isolated him, and part of his existential crisis as a zombie comes from wondering if he died long before the outbreak.

Jim's loneliness stems from both a lack of companionship and the absence of nature, and he consistently pairs the two in his memories. In the post-apocalyptic landscape of Dead World, nature has become hostile to most forms of life. Violent winds sweep the undead into the atmosphere. Zombies exist under sunless skies charged with dangerous electrical storms. And no seasons mark the passage of time: "what happened to summer, like it used to be? All the days and nights seemed to bleed together now, and nothing made any of them different" (387). As a result, Jim retreats into the memory of beauty: "a yellow flower, the scent of a woman's perfume" (380). He later tells Brenda about a childhood trip to Lake Michigan, and again he associates joy with nature: the coldness of the water, "the sound of happy laughter, and the smell of flowers" (386). The vibrant color and aroma of these blooms recall some of the natural pleasures of human life such as sexual desire and laughter. Art, too, gets aligned with the natural world. Beethoven's music plays almost harmoniously with the crashing wind outside Brenda's apartment (388), and Jim likens his anxieties about approaching her to the fruit in "The Love Song of J. Alfred Prufrock": "He had dared to eat the peach, as Eliot's Prufrock lamented, and found it rotten" (384). Jim's sexual frustration and fears about missed romantic opportunities prove premature, and he later compares the flavor of Brenda's lips to "slightly overripe peaches" (389). As these examples suggest, the end of nature means the end of the very qualities (desire, laughter, love) and expressions (literature, music) that make us most human. This is one reason Jim finds the past so painful—"The power of memory taunted him unmercifully" (380). As with Romero's *Day of the Dead*, nature in "Eat Me" punishes what remains of humanity by denying access to its beauty and sustenance. The only thing left in a world devoured by consumerism is simulacrum. Brenda continues her hobby of making silk flowers, filling her apartment with "pots of flowers set around the room and out on the fire escape" (387). Even though this display inspires momentary wonder in Jim, he remains aware of its artificiality. Silk flowers do not grow from the earth, require water, or smell. Like himself, they are dead yet will "live" forever, and this state terrifies Jim: "He had a terrible sensation of not belonging in this world, of being suspended in a nightmare that would stretch to the boundaries of eternity" (379). Everlasting life without nature and love, in other words, is something too horrifying to contemplate.

"Blossom" and "Eat Me" offer a chilling frame for *Book of the Dead*. The callous couple that divorces sex from love and considers flowers (nature) as expendable as people do not suggest that much is worth preserving in humanity. The zombies in "Eat Me," by contrast, seek intimacy and love. Jim's recurring question, for instance, is not T. S. Eliot's "Do I dare to eat a peach?" but "When did love die?" He and Brenda think of poetry, listen to Classical music, reminisce about happiness, and long for the beauty of the natural world. I think it is fair to say that McCammon's zombie love story provides the most positive depiction of romance in the anthology, and because of this, it offers the most damning portrait of humanity. Modern life has become so corrosive that only zombification gives people enough perspective to recognize its stagnancy and the dangers of such a destructive relationship with nature. Together, these stories reveal a profound blindness on the part of humankind and express a fear that people may not be able to recognize their failings to society, each other, and the environment before it is too late.

Numerous stories in *Book of the Dead* offer similar environmental critiques, and Stephen King's "Home Delivery"[21] depicts consumerism as both depleting natural resources and damaging the ozone layer—the very thing protecting the planet from an apocalypse. King crafts the experiences of Maddie Pace—an indecisive young woman who must learn to cope with her family history, the sudden death of her husband, pregnancy, and a zombie outbreak—as an urgent call for environmental activism. The community on Jenny Isle relies on nature for survival. Most residents work as fishers or farmers. Maddie's domineering, abusive father, George Sullivan, earns a living as a lobsterman until his death, and her mother manages a roadside stand, selling enough vegetables to get by during hard times. This seemingly innocuous relationship with the environment comes into question when George buys his neighbor's two-acre property in order to chainsaw its trees: "The hardwood was logged off for the two wood stoves that heated the house in three years" (53). For George, trees serve as fuel (he never replants anything, for example), and lobsters and vegetables provide revenue. In fact, everyone on the island participates in consumer culture. Maddie's husband wants an Oldsmobile, not a "friggin' Chevrolet," and a "house on the mainland" (55) to prove that he will be more than a lobsterman one day, and Maddie struggles to choose between the braised veal and the lamb chops at fine restaurants.

These tastes reflect the social value placed on consumer excess. Just as George reduces *all* the trees to firewood, Jack drinks five beers before ordering dinner, and when Maddie discovers his favorite soup to be chicken noodle in a can, she buys an entire case at the grocery store. She even calls an 800 number after a news report about the walking dead. This moment underscores the link between modern American life and consumerism: "When you could no longer call the 800 number and order the Boxcar Willy records that were not available in any store, when there were for the first time in her living memory no Operators Standing By, the end of the world was a foregone conclusion" (60). For King, all of these acts have severe environmental consequences. At one point, Maddie notes that her Christmas gift to Jack, a L.L. Bean black-and-red-checkered shirt, "had cost the earth" (74). This phrase characterizes both its economic and environmental expense, for the marketplace has encouraged all of these islanders to devour too many resources (trees, vegetables, lobsters, oil) for goods such as mainland homes, processed foods, and mail-order clothing. Indeed, these items literally "cost the earth."

King captures the environmental harm of overconsumption most explicitly through the link between ozone depletion and the zombie apocalypse. A living satellite made up of worm-like creatures causes the dead to rise by exploiting "the expanding hole in the earth's ozone layer. It was sending something down from there, and it was not Flowers by Wire" (66). Certainly, this natural disaster offers a moral condemnation of humanity's production of chlorofluorocarbons. Even the official name for the satellite, Star Wormwood, suggests as much by alluding to the Book of Revelations: "The third angel blew his trumpet, and a great star fell from heaven, blazing like a torch, and it fell on a third of the rivers and on the fountains of water. The name of the star is Wormwood. A third of the waters became wormwood, and many men died of the water, because it was made bitter" (8:10–11). The third trumpet constitutes part of the judgment of the seven seals. The first two describe bloody fire burning up a third of the planet's resources, specifically trees and oceans, and the third announces the contamination of fresh water. The apocalypse, in other words, begins with environmental devastation. This biblical allusion not only characterizes the nation's reckless treatment of the atmosphere as apocalyptic, but it also presents the individual as having a moral responsibility to nature, not merely a pragmatic one.[22]

While the hole in the ozone layer occurred gradually, "Home Delivery" presents nuclear and chemical warfare as an extreme example of humanity's willingness to risk the well-being of the planet for political and social ideology: "*Then*, Russia and America came very, very close to blowing the whole world to smithereens, both of them accusing the other of causing the phenomenon of the walking dead" (56). Specifically, each superpower claims to have evidence that the other side used chemical weapons to reanimate the dead: "It was the *Russians* who had committed an act—a *heinous* act—of chemical warfare, bringing loyal Americans back to life with no urge to consume anything but other loyal Americans" (63). Here the Soviet Union appears to have found a way to augment the consumer impulses of its enemy through cannibalism. At the same time, this accusation encapsulates contemporary fears about the impact of chemicals on people and the planet—particularly the ability to transform something healthy (a person, a crop) into something harmful and even deadly. While chemical or nuclear warfare gets averted by the discovery of Star Wormwood, enabling these nations to "[swap] one nightmare for another" (65), the specter of these weapons reinforces King's message about the environmental terrors of the Cold War.

Ultimately, King leaves readers with a call for environmental action through Maddie Pace's shift from indecisive passivity to action. Prior to the outbreak, Maddie cannot decide what to eat, what to buy, and what to do with her time. The zombie outbreak, however, necessitates a radical change. She needs to survive on much less, to deliver her baby at home, and to make her own decisions. When Jack's corpse returns, Maggie knows that he no longer hungers for processed soup. Barnacles and moss have grown onto his body. He drags kelp into the house and reeks of "salt and fathoms" (74). The ocean has imprinted itself onto him, and he becomes a vehicle for nature's wrath here, hungering for flesh the way he hungered for material goods in life. Maddie stabs him in the eye with a sewing needle, cleaves his skull with an ax, and chops up his body before burying the pieces in an unused cistern. In many ways her trajectory as a character can be viewed in environmental terms. The climate challenges of the 1980s demanded widespread action, and for King, America—and arguably the world—needed to "cope" (one of Maddie's favorite terms) with the realities of pollution, toxicity, and waste. It needed to act before the consequences became apocalyptic.

The longest story of the anthology, Steven R. Boyett's "Like Pavlov's Dogs," appears roughly at the midpoint, and while it mocks the frivolity of consumerism prior to the zombie outbreak, it primarily examines the disconnection between everyday life and environmental harm in America. The story focuses on eight scientists who have volunteered to spend two years in an Ecosphere in the Arizona desert. The structure's interior replicates every aspect of the Earth's ecosystem, "including a tropical rain forest, a savanna, a marshland, a desert, and a 50,000-gallon salt-water ocean, complete with fish" (222). It has been designed to test plans for colonizing Mars by the end of the century, but midway through the experiment, a zombie outbreak occurs. Little changes for these "Ecosphereans," however, as they continue to live inside this bubble, far removed from the reality of the crisis. Meanwhile, Sailor and several companions decide to approach them for food. When the Ecosphereans refuse, Sailor breaks into the structure, releases several zombies, and plants explosives to destroy it. Boyett uses the insularity of the Ecosphere as a metaphor for the country's willful blindness to its destructive relationship with nature and its unwillingness to change, seeking other planets to colonize instead of repairing the Earth.

Much like the zombies that stumble through the mall and ride escalators in Romero's *Dawn of the Dead*, Boyett's zombies get used to mock consumerism by wearing an array of ridiculous T-shirts such as "I'M WITH STUPID," "SAVE THE WHALES," and "EAT ME." This clothing, taken from a shop at the Westside Mall, has been placed on several zombies by some of Sailor's companions. It humorously comments both on the zombies' condition as literally dead and unintelligent and on the mindless consumption characterizing American life before the outbreak. The last two shirts, which appear in the final pages of the story, hint at the fundamental conflict between consumerism and environmental activism. Eating, literally and metaphorically, drives the marketplace, and the natural resources required to mass-produce T-shirts such as "SAVE THE WHALES" undermine its message. True activism requires changing behaviors that harm the planet and altering a thoughtless, zombie-like approach to consumerism. Boyett uses Michael Jackson's *Thriller* as another humorous example of the zombifying effects of this culture. Sailor's gang takes a Pavlovian approach to training zombies, and the shiny CD for Jackson's album, whose title video famously features dancing zombies, effectively draws their attention. Like T-shirts, mass-produced CDs, cassette tapes, and records—along with their plastic packaging and paper inserts—produce tons of garbage. *Thriller*, which sold tens of millions of copies in the eighties alone and continues to be one of the best-selling albums in history,[23] illustrates the environmental footprint of popular music. Later, one of Sailor's gang carries a large ghetto blaster on his shoulder, and while listening to Run D.M.C., he dance-walks around the University of Arizona campus. His spasmodic movements and reflective glasses make him resemble a deadhead, and Jimmy shoots him: "'He was walkin' funny an' his eyes was all fucked an' shit'" (251).[24] Zombies and consumers once again get conflated.

For Boyett, the Ecosphere provides an ironic commentary on America's ecological neglect. The station, "a model for our planet" with thousands of fish, plants, animals (including livestock), birds, insects, vegetables, fruit, and soil, primarily functions as a self-sustaining environment (222). One member notes that they do not have watermelon because "it would require far too much water to be ecologically justifiable" (229). They raise pigs for food as well as for their ability to clear and fertilize the land reserved for vegetable crops. Filtration systems operate in garbage-disposal units and sewage facilities. They utilize water-reclamation systems, and even the air gets "cleaned by pumping it beneath the Ecosphere and allowing it to percolate through the soil from several areas" (230). All of this efficiency aligns with the Ecosphere's "Golden Rule" to "waste not, want not" (235) and to maintain balance. When the group decides whether or not to give food to Sailor, most of them consider the risk to the Ecosphere too great: "We can't introduce anything new or take anything away. [. . .] We're a *self-contained* unit. We grew that food ourselves. We live on a day-to-day basis" (240). This balance and environmental responsibility stand in stark contrast with the excesses of modern American culture prior to the outbreak. Although designed ostensibly for the prospect of colonizing Mars, the Ecosphere in a zombie-infested world raises questions about humanity's ongoing relationship with nature. None of the characters ask whether or not their efforts would be better served in implementing a more mindful approach to the Earth's ecosystem. They seem reconciled to the idea that planetary colonization will be necessary for future survival. At one point, Marly wonders about the status of the Land Pavilion and the Living Seas exhibits at Walt Disney's EPCOT Center. With this reference, Boyett takes another jab a country incapable of maintaining a healthy relationship with the planet outside an amusement park—the epitome of consumer culture.

The environmental failings of the Ecosphere, like those of the 1980s, stem from its inhabitants' willful insularity. The marine biologist recalls various romantic pairings during the first few months inside, yet "now everybody is more or less an environment unto his or her self" (232). Marly segregates herself by sleeping in a tent in the downhill desert. Bonnie locks herself in her room during the assault on the Ecosphere. And the only couple, Haiffa and Deke, "have become a unit unto themselves" (218). When Bill, the unofficial leader, argues that "maintaining this station is maintaining civilization," Marly counters, "But not humanity" (244). This moment encapsulates the central theme of the story. The distinction between survival and humanity involves some ethical responsibility outside the self—to people and the planet. Most of these scientists, however, only feel this way about maintaining the Ecosphere. They continue to care for the plants and animals, and Leonard appreciates the ways his duties "[give] him an abundance of opportunity to feel fulfilled" (230). They do not care about each other or the outside world. Their unwillingness to share food with the couple and their baby (which they do not realize is a zombie), for instance, reveals the extent of their emotional disconnectedness. By insulating themselves from the struggles impacting the rest of the world, they have cut off an essential part of their humanity. Sailor blames this selfishness on an attempt to maintain the fantasy of consumer culture: "Nice little ratbox you people have here [. . .]. All the comforts of home. Air conditioning. Barcaloungers. MTV" (269). Marly, conversely, challenges it in terms of a broader responsibility to the planet, and she scoffs at Bill's insistence on maintaining their daily routines in order to pull through: "Pull *through*, Bill? What is this, some *phase* the world's going through? Going to grow out of it, is that it?" (234). The world can change irrevocably, and just as every action within the Ecosphere impacts the whole, the same is true for nature outside of this artificial space. Whether through the public's addiction to cars (Sailor drives an El Camino and the Ecosphere has a Land Rover and a Jeep Cherokee), air conditioning, T-shirts, or CDs, each of these acts has serious environmental consequences.

Finally, both the zombie outbreak and life within the ecosphere encapsulate the revenge of nature motif in the story. To some extent, these zombies get associated with nature. Sailor likens them to "plants that turn to follow the sun. Only they follow live meat" (248). Bonnie echoes a similar sentiment just before her death: "They didn't *ask* to be what they are, and what they are is really not very different from plants. Hungry plants, mobile plants, but plants all the same" (268). And Marly compares them to snakes that wait for their prey, moving only to eat. Like reptiles, killing them requires decapitation or "massive neutral destruction" (259). The zombie attack on Haiffa occurs while she swims in the ocean, making her wonder initially if it could be a tiger shark. Grace gets mauled by both a zombie and the pigs she has cared for, and Marly barely escapes when zombies grab her in the cornfield. All of these details cast zombies as nature's tool for protecting itself against mankind. At the same time, the artificiality of the Ecosphere offers a different vision of the apocalypse. A zombie outbreak, like a nuclear war, tends to reflect an abrupt end to nature. The Ecosphere represents the slow, more gradual consequences of harming the planet. The Ecosphereans fear going outside. They breathe recycled air, and they witness beauty at a distance: "Stars shine in the Arizona sky above glass above desert built in desert" (252). Here, the revenge of nature also comes from denied access to its beauty.

Overpopulation, Environmentalism, and Food in *Motel Hell*

The zombie's insatiable hunger and its perpetual snacking in the 1980s embodied America's unchecked desire for processed foods, gas-guzzling cars, suburban homes, and other material goods. Whether in Romero's trilogy, zombie B-movies, or short fiction, the living dead functioned as a referendum on these appetites. The public had become mindless in its pursuit of more, taxing natural resources to the breaking point, producing vast amounts of trash, and poisoning the environment and each other. Nature's response came in the form of zombies consuming the very consumers destroying the planet and in the way their massive numbers tapped into the country's preoccupation with overpopulation. Fears about not having enough food and water to sustain the human race intensified throughout the decade, and horror explored these concerns. The characters in Romero's films and *The Return of the Living Dead* series get overwhelmed by the scope of the zombie threat. The entire moonshine-drinking town in *Redneck Zombies* attacks the remaining campers, and the zombified marijuana farmers in *Toxic Zombies* outnumber their victims until the final showdown. Likewise, there is enough petroleum-laced soda in *Surf II* to mutate an entire beach community in Southern California, and the scientists in "Like Pavlov's Dogs" prove no match for the T-shirt zombies. In short, the message of eighties zombie fiction is to consume, produce, and procreate less because the planet simply cannot sustain it.

The role of environmentalism, food, and zombie imagery in *Motel Hell* (1980) closely aligns this ecohorror film with the zombie fiction of the period. Farmer Vincent (Rory Calhoun) and his sister Ida (Nancy Parsons) operate a motel, farm, and butchery that produces exquisite meats. For decades these smoked delicacies have been legendary in the county. No one, including

Farmer Vincent (Rory Calhoun) and Ida (Nancy Parsons) tend their secret garden in Kevin Connor's *Motel Hell* (1980). United Artists/Photofest. © United Artists.

Sheriff Bruce (Paul Linke), realizes that these pork products have been mixed with human flesh. Every night, Vincent manufactures automotive accidents near his farm and plants these semiconscious victims in his secret garden, severing their vocal chords and waiting for them to tenderize before harvesting. A perverse activism inspires Vincent: "I'm not trying to play God. [. . .] I'm just helping out. There are too many people in the world and not enough food. This takes care of both problems at the same time." Overpopulation has created a crisis that requires action, and both he and Ida view themselves as environmentalists. "Somebody's gotta take a little responsibility for the planet!" Ida exclaims after working in the garden one evening. Certainly, Vincent exploits Americans' dependency on automobiles by crafting a range of traps that include shooting tires, stretching chains across the highway, and lying Ida "by the side of the road next to that old Chevy we set on fire." Like the violent crashes themselves, the disabled Chevy captures the dangers of car culture for people and the environment. His most humorous ruse—and the one most connected with feeding an overpopulated planet—comes in the form of blocking the road with artificial cows. Americans have no trouble killing millions of cattle each year to feed its appetite for beef, but two young women do not want to drive through these plywood cutouts for fear of damaging their car. The car, in effect, becomes more important than their own safety.

This environmental ideology shapes Vincent's identity as a farmer and his sense of responsibility both for the humane treatment of livestock and for the cultivation of healthy food. Vincent and Ida consistently refer to their human crops as "critters" or "animals," and Vincent insists that "No animal should ever suffer any unnecessary pain." As he explains at the end of the film, "I treat most of my stock better than farmers treat their animals. I don't feed them chemicals or hormones. When you consider the way the world is today, there is no question that I'm doing a lot of them a big favor." This indictment of the meatpacking industry includes both the cruelty inflicted on animals and the poisoning of consumers through toxins. Not surprisingly, he takes great pride in his meat products. He only distributes meats within a hundred-mile radius to ensure quality, and as he tells two customers, "No chemicals or preservatives. Just 100% honest-to-goodness hickory smoked meat." Additionally, thick ivy engulfs the garden's fence, and from a distance, it blends naturally into the surrounding trees, open fields, and shrubs.[25] The lush greenery inside further illustrates the care he invests in cultivating his "crops," which appear in rows of freshly tilled soil and beside stalks of corn and other plants.

During a picnic in which Terry (Nina Axelrod) and Bruce praise the deliciousness of the meat ("It's like I've never really tasted ham before" and "You can't beat the flavor"), the camera focuses on the vibrant green mountains before panning down to the meal. Birds chirp cheerfully in the background and flowers sway in the gentle breeze as the characters discuss food. This camera work and mise-en-scène align with Vincent and Ida's philosophy, presenting the meats as a reflection of nature's abundance. Even Terry, who appears radiant, has been compared to a flower, and natural remedies are used to help her recover from one of Vincent's accidents. After bringing her home, he tells Ida that "The good Lord has chosen to pluck this flower away from the Grim Reaper, and I want to make good and sure he keeps his hands off her." Ida agrees on the condition that they use herbal remedies: "I'll fix your little flower for you . . . but first you got to go out and pick me some goldenseal, comfrey, valerian, and plantain." All of these roots facilitate the natural healing process, and they reflect her efforts to maintain a balanced relationship with the planet's resources. The flower imagery also highlights Terry's vulnerability, for her beauty can wither, be plucked (killed), or eaten, which Vincent intends to do.

The zombie imagery in *Motel Hell* underscores Vincent's environmental fears about overpopulation as well. In many respects, Vincent and Ida transform their victims into figurative zombies. Buried in the ground like vegetables and rendered speechless by severed vocal chords, they take on the characteristics of the living dead. When Vincent's zombies finally free themselves from

Complimenting Farmer Vincent's delicious meats in *Motel Hell* (1980). United Artists/Photofest. © United Artists.

captivity, they stagger toward the farm, making guttural noises. Their mud-streaked faces and clothes, disheveled hair, erratic movements, and moaning liken them to zombies. Mist obscures their individual identities when they first appear as a group, and they eventually overwhelm Ida with numbers. These sequences could come from any zombie film, and they evoke a similar message about overpopulation. The planet simply cannot provide enough resources to feed so many people. Of course, these zombie figures are motivated by a hunger for revenge here, not meat, but this aligns them with other examples of nature's vengeance in the film. Bruce and Terry, for example, watch *The Monster That Challenged the World* (1957) at the town drive-in—a film about giant prehistoric mollusks that devour unsuspecting sailors, swimmers, and livestock. Likewise, Vincent attacks Bruce with a chainsaw while wearing a hog's head. At this moment, he assumes the identity of an animal that people have been mistreating in order to eat in great quantities.

Even though this vengeance motif reinforces Vincent's environmental ideology, it also gets directed at him and his sister. Ida's fatness, for instance, represents her excesses. While making a breakfast of eggs and toast with peanut butter, she complains to Vincent about being hungry, and she eats unhealthy foods throughout the film, including bowls of ice cream covered with whipped cream and chicken legs with barbeque sauce. At one point, Vincent attributes her absence in the butchery to "stuffing her face again," and this detail helps explains his underlying concerns about her commitment to their work. His reservations stem from her eating habits. She consumes too much and, in this way, embodies the problem Vincent has been trying to combat. A certain environmental hypocrisy runs in the family, though. Vincent, Ida, and Bruce gleefully embrace their grandmother's mantra, "Meat's meat, and a man's gotta eat," never considering a vegetarian diet. Over a half dozen empty beer cans have been tossed on the ground behind the picnickers. Vincent obsessively uses an aerosol disinfectant to sanitize his hand after touching people, and this product, like the exhaust from his tractor, harms the atmosphere. In his final moments, he even confesses that "My whole life has been a lie. I'm the biggest hypocrite of them all. My meats . . . I used preservatives." Vincent and his siblings prove to be guilty of the same offenses as their victims, and accordingly they suffer the same fate.

Motel Hell, in keeping with zombie fiction throughout the decade, raises provocative environmental questions. It does not invite audiences to be like Vincent or the insulated Ecosphereans in Boyett's "Like Pavlov's Dogs"—all of whom sacrifice their humanity in the name of ecological responsibility. Instead, it highlights the horrors of overpopulation in a consumer culture, and in doing so, it challenges audiences to think about their own impact on the environment. High demand for Vincent's meats spurred his actions, and similar demands for "stuff" led to the shopping culture satirized in *Dawn of the Dead* and King's "Home Delivery." All of this consumption captures the dangerous extent of America's appetite. There are too many mouths to feed literally and metaphorically, and as suggested by the limited space of Vincent's garden, the defunct mine in *Day of the Dead*, and the toxic contaminants in *The Return of the Living Dead* series, *Toxic Zombies*, and *Redneck Zombies*, the planet can only sustain so much damage. Thus, 1980s zombie fiction becomes a cautionary tale about the nation's environmental irresponsibility and the need for change.

CONCLUSION

"Enough Is Never Enough": Junk Food, Dieting, and Environmental Harm in *The Stuff*

The Stuff

Larry Cohen, whose wonderfully campy horror films in the 1970s and 1980s included *It's Alive* (1974), *It Lives Again* (1978), and *Q* (1982), turned his attention to America's sugar addiction in *The Stuff* (1985). The film explores the tension between the country's sweet tooth and diet culture, while offering an ecohorror narrative about the environmental harm of mindless consumption. In the opening scene, an employee at an industrial refinery discovers (and tastes!) a pulsating white substance in the snow. The delicious flavor inspires him to sell it, and once in the hands of greedy distributors and unwitting marketers, this organic material becomes "The Stuff," a low-calorie dessert that resembles yogurt and tastes better than ice cream. Soon, millions of Americans find themselves addicted. Street vendors peddle it. Roadside parlors remain open twenty-four hours a day to accommodate customers, and Stuff restaurants appear alongside prominent fast-food giants such as McDonald's and Kentucky Fried Chicken. Fearful of The Stuff's extraordinary success, unscrupulous ice cream executives hope to steal its formula ("I wish the hell we knew how they made it. Yeah, we could copy it. What I meant to say is we could . . . uh . . . improve on it"), and they hire an industrial spy, David "Mo" Rutherford (Michael Moriarty), to do so. His investigation, however, uncovers the strange truth about this mysterious goo. It can control a person's thoughts and actions while gradually devouring them from within. In short, it transforms people into zombified "stuffies."

Eventually, Mo tracks down the spring-like source of the goo, enlists the help of a private militia, destroys its primary distribution center, and helps

The Stuff muscles its way into American food culture in Larry Cohen's *The Stuff* (1985). © New World Pictures.

broadcast a nationwide warning about the product. In the closing moments of the film, the corporation responsible for distributing The Stuff has combined forces with the same ice cream executives that hired Mo. They intend to launch a new product called "The Taste," which contains only 12 percent Stuff. Such scurrilous forces are only part of the problem, though. The Stuff can still be purchased like illicit drugs in crime-ridden neighborhoods, and this shift from over-the-counter dessert to black market narcotic reinforces the film's message about the dangers of America's addictive impulses and of processed foods more broadly. In discussing the inspiration for the film, Larry Cohen has noted that

> dangerous products were, and still are, deeply embedded into our way of life. I mean, look at the sheer volume of junk food we consume every day. We continue to eat these foods despite the fact that some of them are killing us. That's when I started thinking that *The Stuff* could be an imaginary product—in this case an ice cream dessert—that is being consumed by millions and is doing irreparable damage to humanity. Everybody is gobbling down this yummy food, so how can it possibly be wrong for us? (qtd. in Doyle 326)

These consumer addictions also exposed the country's exploitative relationship with nature. Whether through food, suburban homes, cars, yachts, or private planes, America in the 1980s had fully embraced the ideology of The Stuff's marketing campaign: "Enough is never enough." The consequences of unchecked consumerism threatened to create a zombified public with a bottomless appetite for more, and this hunger risked destroying the planet. Ultimately, *The Stuff* warns viewers against sacrificing the self and the environment for so much stuff.

Ice Cream, Frozen Yogurt, and The Stuff:
Junk Food and the Diet Craze in America

To understand Cohen's satire of modern food culture, it is helpful to view The Stuff alongside the history of ice cream and frozen yogurt. Americans loved ice cream long before the twentieth century (George Washington even purchased a "cream machine for ice" and an ice cream serving spoon by 1796[1]), but when the 1904 Saint Louis World's Fair popularized the ice cream cone, this dazzling treat became a staple in the nation's diet. Average per capita consumption rose from one quart to a gallon between 1900 and 1915 alone. Put another way, the national production of ice cream went from twenty-nine million gallons in 1909 to seventy-two million in 1914. The Temperance movement and Prohibition inspired an even greater surge in sales as Americans sought to replace one addiction for another. As Jeri Quinzio has noted, many bars became ice cream parlors in the twenties, and "brewers, including Anheuser-Busch, became ice cream manufacturers. A Brooklyn brewery sold ice cream at Coney Island during the summer of 1920 in the hopes that it would replace beer sales" (161). When Howard Dearing Johnson opened a pharmacy in 1925, his soda fountain quickly became the most profitable part of the business. He opened several beachfront concession stands in Massachusetts a few years later, and he eventually unveiled twenty-eight ice cream flavors. This frozen treat proved to be the biggest seller for his 1929 business venture, the Howard Johnson Restaurant ("HoJo's") (Weiss 103).

Ice cream became too expensive for many people during the Great Depression, and as sales slowed, ice cream bootleggers began offering low-quality imitations in brand-name containers. Soft-serve, however, would help save the day, revolutionizing the marketplace by the end of the decade. On August 4, 1938, "Grandpa" McCullough and his son, H. A. "Alex," the founders of Dairy Queen, got their start by offering "All the Ice Cream You Can Eat for 10 Cents." They sold over 1,600 servings of the semi-frozen cream in two hours, and soft ice cream became a hit—both for the taste and the price. Likewise, Tom Carvel, who began operating his first ice cream truck in 1929, "pioneered such concepts as 'Buy one, get one free' promotions, gift certificates, round ice cream sandwiches called Flying Saucers, kosher ice cream products, and, in 1939, soft-serve" (Quinzio 192). Ice cream continued to captivate the nation in the late 1940s and 1950s. The US government even considered it an important morale booster during World War II. "In 1945, the navy built a barge that was a floating ice cream parlor, at a cost of one million dollars" (194). This dessert soon shifted from bolstering the troops to ushering in a new era of peace. The end of rationing, particularly for rubber and gasoline, allowed America to reembrace the automobile, and according to Anne Funderburg, ice cream stands became a favorite destination for the family drive: "They were informal, family places. Children did not have to sit still, and no one cared if they made a little noise" (151).

The popularity of these roadside stores can partially be attributed to the bland, unappealing taste of most grocery store ice cream. Supermarkets needed to use various additives to enhance shelf life and to prevent the formation of ice crystals. Some of these ingredients included cane or beet sugars, corn syrup, artificial flavors, emulsifiers, and stabilizers such as gelatin, guar gum, and ethyl cellulose (CMC). The result, as Laura Weiss explains, "was inexpensive and long-lasting—but one whose texture was much thinner and fluffier than that found in traditional ice creams" (97). It did not take long for companies like Häagen-Dazs and Ben and Jerry's to transform this aspect of the market. In 1960, entrepreneurs Reuben and Rose Mattus created a "superpremium ice cream" for high-end customers willing to pay for quality. Their gourmet dessert boasted no additives, preservatives, or stabilizers. They also sold it in pints, instead of quarts, made up a Danish-sounding name, and charged twice the price of supermarket brands. "Superpremium, status-symbol ice cream," Funderburg observes, "fit neatly into the Reagan era of conspicuous consumption. It was a deliciously sinful treat for yuppies who wanted aerobics-toned hard bodies but felt they had the right to indulge themselves, too. After all, everyone needed occasional relief from the fad diets hyped by the professional dieters on TV talk shows" (156). By 1981, Häagen-Dazs was selling over 6 million gallons a year.

Likewise, high school buddies Ben Cohen and Jerry Greenfield found similar success with their homemade ice cream the following decade. Their first store opened in Vermont in 1978, featuring twelve "orgasmic flavors" a day. Because of Cohen's sinus problems, the friends enhanced the flavorings and added cookies and other chunky treats to their recipes. This approach proved tremendously successful, making Oreo mint ice cream their first best-seller. By the 1980s, scoop shops (also called dipping stores) could be found in almost every college town across the country. They often charged seven dollars for a hand-packed quart, but customers stood in long lines for more. *Time* magazine declared ice cream "America's drug of choice" in 1981, and the magazine reported that "America produced 829,798,000 gallons of ice cream in 1980, the equivalent of 'ten single-scoop cones for every human being on earth'" (qtd. in Quinzio 206).

Yogurt tried to tap into the popularity of ice cream—particularly soft-serve—by presenting itself as a healthy alternative to its more decadent cousin. I Can't Believe It's Yogurt launched in 1977, and TCBY (originally This Can't Be Yogurt and subsequently The Country's Best Yogurt) opened its first soft-serve store in 1981. The product proved highly successful for both companies. The impressive sales of TCBY, for instance, inspired the owners to take the firm public in 1983. Within the year, the company had forty-one stores earning a revenue of $1.7 million, and annual sales reached $33.3 million in 1986. As founder and CEO Frank Hickingbotham explains, "it tastes like premium ice cream, but has 80 percent less fat and half the calories" (Gorman).[2] This feature resonated powerfully with consumers struggling to navigate a culture that encouraged indulgence alongside weight control. I Can't Believe It's Yogurt capitalized on this trend further when it became the first company to offer nonfat frozen yogurt in 1988 and sugar-free, nonfat frozen yogurt in 1989. Sweetened with aspartame, the latter promised no sugar, fat, or cholesterol. As cofounder Julie Brice put it, "With all the interest in healthy eating and having a lean body, there's only one direction that frozen yogurt sales can go" (Stube 62).[3]

With the fictional product The Stuff, Larry Cohen alludes both to the popularity of junk food (particularly soft-serve ice cream) and the health consciousness driving the frozen yogurt market. One evening in search of a late-night snack, Jason (Scott Bloom), a Long Island suburban kid, opens the refrigerator to discover The Stuff moving in and out of its container. This animate dessert appears alongside an array of processed food including Pillsbury's Best Cinnamon Rolls, Kraft's Grated Parmesan Cheese, a quart of Hershey's Chocolate Milk, a six-pack of Olympia Beer, and margarine spread. Nothing healthy—no fruits or vegetables—takes up space in this refrigerator; instead, nearly all of the products contain fats, sugars, artificial flavors, and preservatives. With this snapshot of the family's eating habits, one can safely assume that the orange juice served the following morning is not freshly squeezed either. This home represents the average American family and its addiction to such foods. Jason's brother demonstrates as much when he quickly scarfs down cereal only to ask for some Stuff before school.

Later, as Jason tries to destroy the local grocery store's supply of the product, he notices crowds of people buying junk food (sodas, ketchup, crackers, juice) and consuming The Stuff as if they cannot resist the urge to eat before leaving the store. From babies and young kids to fat women and heavyset moms, these shoppers depict America as a country constantly eating and indoctrinating its children to do the same. Fatness gets linked implicitly with both unhealthy foods and excess consumption here, making The Stuff shorthand for all the harmful, addictive junk food being produced and consumed in the country. Stuff restaurants appear alongside fast-food chains. Its secret formula gets compared to Coca-Cola's. And vendors tend to carry The Stuff alongside other sugary treats. Jason's rampage at the supermarket, for example, topples displays of The Stuff as well as Chew-On Cookies and Whoppers candy. A Virginian postmaster and convenience store manager sells Tangy Taffy, Snickers, Mars Bars, M&Ms, and 7-Up. He even replaces the sodas in a Pepsi refrigeration unit with The Stuff. It comes as little surprise that Jason screams in the supermarket: "It's going to kill you. It's going to kill you all!" The pronoun "it" refers to The Stuff at this moment, but the film clearly implicates junk food in general.

While The Stuff's association with sugary treats highlights its addictive quality, the product's claims to be a natural, low-calorie snack and its advertising campaign align it with 1980s weight-loss and exercise imperatives. Stuff containers boast "No Artificial Ingredients," and when Jason tosses one against the kitchen cabinet, his mother responds, "Look at that. Not a spot. Low in calories, good tasting, and it doesn't even spot." She echoes something similar when the family replaces everything in the refrigerator with The Stuff: "We're dieting. I've lost five pounds already this week, and I've never felt better." These moments capture some of the more destructive impulses of diet culture. Jason's family did not purchase much healthy food to begin with (though the kitchen contains eggs and a bowl of fruit), but any hope of eating well has been abandoned for a diet no one needs. Everyone in the family appears quite fit, which makes the mother's comments indicative of a weight-loss ethos divorced from personal health. Additionally, when Jason's brother observes that he does not get tired anymore, his father replies, "We don't get tired now that we're eating properly." He does not use terms like "healthy" or "nutritious," just "properly," and this echoes other aspects of The Stuff's marketing campaign that imply the illusion of healthiness. One television commercial, for example, alludes to contemporary exercise fads by showing young people in an array of casual sportswear as they play street basketball and perform aerobics-style dancing. This athletic imagery gets undercut, however, by the jingle: "Enough is never enough. The Stuff . . . the taste that makes you hungry for more!" One radio advertisement sings, "One big, exciting, sweet surprise. One lick is never enough of The Stuff." These lyrics reduce exercise and diet products to just another consumer item. The point is not a healthier body or weight loss, but tireless consumerism. As Bowdoin Van Riper has argued, "The faux ads for The Stuff are subtly devoid of the pro forma nods to moderation familiar from real-world ads for alcoholic beverages ("drink responsibly") and sugar-laden cereals ("part of the balanced breakfast"); instead they enthusiastically seek to normalize mindless consumption—chanting, purring, and whispering to the audience that 'enough is never enough'" (90). This consumer drive involves more than junk foods, though. It has been fueled by the diet and exercise programs being sold in the same marketplace.

Poisoning America: Zombies and Ecohorror in The Stuff

Cohen presents "Stuffies" (people who have devoured enough Stuff to fall victim to its control) as figurative zombies, and these mindless eaters represent the impact of consumerism on both the individual and the environment. In *Larry Cohen: The Radical Allegories of an Independent Filmmaker*, Tony Williams views the mimicking of commercial jingles among Stuff devotees as a sign of zombification: "the family audience become consumerist zombies that television sponsors ideally hope their present-day counterparts will also turn into" (136). Yet the film's exploration of this theme draws much more heavily on zombie conventions than has previously been noted. Stuffies eat ravenously. They move fast, like the zombies in *The Return of the Living Dead* series, and their bodies fall apart easily. They no longer have functional internal organs or bodily fluids. All of this interiority has been eaten away and replaced by Stuff, transforming them quite literally into the living dead. Stuffies and zombies also get defined by their appetite for one thing. As various advertisements promise, The Stuff makes one "hungry for more," but consumers gradually acquire an insatiable taste for only this item. One commercial shows an elderly couple discussing the cuisine at an elegant restaurant when the wife throws down her utensils in disgust, demanding angrily, "Where's the Stuff?" The flavor of steak and potatoes simply cannot compete with Stuff. In fact, the product makes consumers lose the desire for natural foods. It alters human taste buds, just like the products produced by the processed food industry. Furthermore, this parody of Wendy's famous 1984 slogan "Where's the beef?" emphasizes the connection between Stuff and meat. Zombies eat flesh, in part, as an extension of their meat-eating sensibilities before death, but as suggested by the substitution of Stuff here, the undead of the 1980s would likely prefer sugar to flesh.

This zombie imagery also helps establish its ecohorror narrative about the environmental costs of consumerism. Like other 1980s zombies, Stuffies function as a metaphor for consumerism, and Jason's suburban family offers one example of this. Their home has all the trappings of middle-class material culture—television sets, video games, furniture, toys, appliances, and a fully stocked refrigerator. As his parents pressure Jason to eat The Stuff, they discuss food as an extension of the marketplace: "We thought you loved this

With a font akin to Reddi-Whip and Cool Whip and three simple colors resembling Neapolitan ice cream, The Stuff associates itself with the decadence and fun of ice cream sundaes. This innocuous packaging masks the hidden risks of the product, and Cohen uses The Stuff to represent the more troubling aspects of the processed food industry in the United States. *The Stuff* (1985). © New World Pictures.

house, Jason. That's why we bought it. What about your new room? We got you everything you asked for. Are we asking you for so much?" Their attempts to force-feed Jason typify the relentless pressure in America to have more of something. All of this consumption, however, leads to wastefulness. The family's desire to fill their refrigerator with Stuff, for example, necessitates throwing away the other food in the house. A jar of peanut butter, a salted pretzel, an unopened can of Planter's Peanuts, hard taco shells in plastic wrapping, eggs in a Styrofoam carton, and a peach fill the kitchen waste bin. This moment offers a snapshot of the kind of garbage produced by the average suburban home—with containers that will not degrade in landfills for decades at the very least.

Likewise, the recurring images of bleak, rocky quarries in the film establish a parallel between devouring The Stuff and the planet. The conglomerate that distributes the product owns mining companies throughout Georgia, and Stuff is consistently associated with the extraction of geological materials. It gets discovered near a refinery. The same tanker trucks used for gasoline ship Stuff. And when Mo and Chocolate Chip Charlie defend themselves from a group of Stuffies in Virginia, they escape using a boat next to a natural gas refinery. These details provide a way for interpreting the image of The Stuff hovering over planet Earth in its faux television commercials. Consumerism literally gets privileged over the planet in modern America. As Mo remarks, "That stuff comes right out of the center of the earth and straight into our supermarkets." The American marketplace viewed nature in exactly these terms—as something to exploit, package, and sell. When considered together, this rampant consumerism—from private planes to suburban homes with junk food—depicts a nation devouring the planet from the inside out.

Other examples of environmental harm reinforce the film's ecological message. Mo solicits the Colonel's help by tapping into Cold War fears: "You were worried about the Commies putting fluoride in our water system. You know there's a thing going around now that's a lot worse. Americans are being poisoned faster and quicker than you can imagine." The Colonel will echo similar sentiments in his radio broadcast to the nation exposing the dangers of The Stuff. Other news reports subsequently reveal that "the product was toxic" and that the company introduced poisonous substances to the public. Such a narrative seemed plausible in the wake of Love Canal, and contemporary distrust of greedy corporations and ineffectual government agencies helps explain the public's readiness to accept the Colonel's warning. Not a single listener questions the legitimacy of his claims. Instead, the nation lashes out at the product and its vendors—detonating franchises and burning Stuff in bonfires. On a smaller scale, the film offers a microcosm of humanity's wanton disregard for the environment through Mr. Vickers (Daniel Aiello), a former veteran of the FDA who helped approve The Stuff. His entire home has been decorated with dead butterflies in glass frames, and they appear prominently on the fireplace mantle as well as the walls. This effort to celebrate the beauty of nature—much like the large vase with flowers—comes at the cost of killing these insects. Though the butterflies function as an image for the transformation he and his dog have been undergoing by eating The Stuff, it is also a reminder of the country's destructive relationship with the natural world.[4]

Lastly, a revenge of nature motif emerges in *The Stuff* that can be attributed to fears about overpopulation. A significant part of the threat posed by Stuffies, like zombies, comes from their numbers. The executive overseeing distribution notes his efforts to "market it to tens of millions." Mo and Charlie can only defend themselves against a town of Stuffies for so long before needing to flee, and Jason nearly succumbs to his family's aggressive efforts to make him eat Stuff. The prospect of "tens of millions" of Stuffies alludes to the overwhelming consumer demands on the planet. Like oil, minerals, ores, wood, and other natural resources, Stuff comes directly from the earth, and its emergence from the core is a response to this human threat. Through the sound system at the main refinery, employees under the control of The Stuff communicate its message: "Soon the hunger in the world will be a thing of the past. The Earth is giving off the food that will nourish all and guide us all to a new order of life." Despite depleting so many natural resources to produce junk food and consumer goods, millions continued to starve globally in the 1980s (as they do today), and in the film the planet responded to the specter of overpopulation by striking back. After filling the body completely, Stuff leaves by stretching open the victim's mouth to the point of tearing apart the skull. The stretched mouth, an obvious image for overconsumption, highlights the unnatural quantities Americans eat. It also helps explain the Stuff's message to create a "new order of life." Nature, in effect, is calling for humanity to reorder its approach to living and to create a more balanced relationship between human life and the world.

Still Hungry after All These Years: The Legacy of 1980s Horror

The Stuff ends with Mo's rhetorical question—"Are you eating it or is it eating you?"—and this seems a fitting way to reflect on the works discussed in this book. Nineteen-eighties horror located the frightening and unnerving in American consumerism. Whatever pleasures this consumption promised seemed as short lived as ice cream on a warm summer's day. The slogan "enough is never enough" typified American life by capturing the way horror could be found in both the longing for more and the dangers of consuming too much. Images of fatness in works such as *Thinner* or *The Silence of the Lambs* reflected profound anxieties about using the body as a tool for measuring self-worth. The punishing standards that pressured men and women to reshape their bodies and to privilege muscular thinness over bodily diversity stalked the country like a serial killer. They situated the horror not in deviant bodies but in an American culture that often facilitated cruelty, indifference, and greed.

The humans in eighties vampire fiction often appear vampiric in their quest for junk food—from combination meals at McDonald's to candy. Much like the gradual transformation of humans into vampires in *The Hunger*, *The Lost Boys*, *Near Dark*, *Once Bitten*, and *Fright Night Part 2*, a change was happening in the public as well. Processed food companies used technology to instill a vampire-like hunger for their products, and people began consuming more and more sugar, salt, and fat. They did so without much knowledge about what they were eating and about the health consequences of these choices. At the same time, just as the addictive impulses of vampires could represent the country's relationship with junk food and consumer excess, vampires choosing a natural diet offered an additional condemnation of contemporary eating practices. Many vampires eat only what they need to survive, and these organic, measured meals—particularly as half-vampires begin rejecting the junk from their former diet—reveal a desire for healthier eating in America.

Zombie fiction continued this examination of excess consumption, in part, by considering its environmental consequences. The zombie's tireless and irresponsible eating habits (consuming only a small percentage of its victims) certainly functioned as a metaphor for consumerism. Americans, as many of these works from Romero's trilogy to the anthology *Book of the Dead* suggest, had become zombies, consuming natural resources in order to drive cars, build suburban homes, and buy stuff. In the process, they generated too much garbage and poisoned the air, water, plant life, and animals. The severity of humanity's impact on the world stemmed both from recklessness and overpopulation. According to zombie fiction, too many people were demanding too much from the planet, and the consequences from ozone depletion to acid rain were already proving horrific. The suddenness of zombie outbreaks, which resulted from either natural phenomenon or toxic waste, offered a glimpse of abrupt environmental collapse and suggested an urgency for developing more ecofriendly practices.

Horror can provide a powerful lens for examining cultural moments. This genre has consistently responded to and commented on some of the more troubling aspects of American life. It can scare us out of complacency and break us free from the status quo. It can raise important questions about practices that have harmful consequences for the individual, society, and the planet. Eighties horror thrived at a time when technology changed the nation's relationship with the genre. The development and proliferation of VCRs brought horror films out of the theater and into our living rooms—just as it brought celebrities into our homes to help us exercise and lift weights. Video cassettes and sequels ensured a steady diet of horror, inviting audiences to reflect on their own consumer patterns in a more personal way than ever before.

Nevertheless, the cultural lessons offered in 1980s horror would remain largely unheeded. This might explain the incredible popularity of the genre today. Its messages about fatness and thinness, about excess and restraint, about the dangers of addiction, and about environmental responsibility are more pressing than ever. They demand attention and activism just as they did in the 1980s. Perhaps, when placed in dialogue with these works, contemporary horror might be most frightening in its revelation about how little has changed or at least about how far we still need to go to combat issues such as fat bias, processed food addiction, and ecological harm. Fat shaming continues everywhere from playgrounds to the White House.[5] Fast-food restaurants have added healthier options to their menus, but McDonald's still offers salads with more calories than a double cheeseburger. Deforestation continues at alarming rates, and global warming has worsened. According to NASA, the sixteen warmest years on record occurred in the twenty-first century with the hottest being 2016: "Not only was 2016 the warmest year on record, but eight of the 12 months that make up the year—from January through September, with the exception of June—were the warmest on record for those respective months."[6] Nevertheless, in August 2017, President Donald Trump announced his intention to withdraw the United States from the Paris Climate Accord, and his 2018 budget proposed severe cuts to the Environmental Protection Agency, including a 25 percent reduction of funds for cleaning up hazardous waste (Davenport).

To be fair, most of the works discussed in this book did not view themselves primarily as vehicles for social and cultural change. They did, however, exploit contemporary anxieties to comment on some of the more horrific aspects of American life. They invited audiences to question consumer ideology. They crafted unsettling portraits of diet, exercise, and food culture. And they presented pollution and waste as moving the country toward an apocalypse of its own making. When considered collectively, the message of 1980s horror is much more severe and more politicized than Freddy Krueger's glib humor would suggest. The country spent the decade dining with—and like—madmen. It invited the danger inside, consuming foods and a weight-loss ideology that punished the body, and it depleted and poisoned the environment to feed a reckless addiction for more.

NOTES

Introduction

1. This song, which played during the closing credits of *A Nightmare on Elm Street 4: The Dream Master*, did not prove to be as popular as "A Nightmare on My Street" by DJ Jazzy Jeff and the Fresh Prince (Will Smith) in the same year. The Fat Boys, however, had acquired the legal right to use Krueger in the lyrics and video; whereas, DJ Jazzy Jeff and the Fresh Prince considered their song a parody and released it without permission. A lawsuit eventually forced the video of "A Nightmare on My Street" to be destroyed. See Andy Greene's "Flashback: Will Smith and Freddy Krueger Battle in Court."

2. In the Canadian film *Happy Birthday to Me* (1981), one teenager is killed in the middle of a workout session.

3. For more on the slasher film, see works such as Carol Clover's seminal study *Men, Women, and Chainsaws: Gender in the Modern Horror Film*, Mark Whitehead's *Slasher Movies*, Richard Nowell's *Blood Money: A History of the First Teen Slasher Film Cycle*, Adam Rockoff's *Going to Pieces: The Rise and Fall of the Slasher Film, 1978–1986*, and Jessica Robinson's *Life Lessons from Slasher Films*.

4. "Other things equal, wages of people with below-average looks are lower than those of average-looking workers; and there is a premium in wages for good-looking people that is slightly smaller than this penalty" (Hamermesh and Biddle 1192).

5. Bill Fabrey and Lew Louderback formed the National Association to Aid Fat Americans in 1969; the NAAF changed its name in the mid-1980s to the National Association to Advance Fat Acceptance. See Wann.

6. Anthropology continues to guide Food Studies, and its roots can be traced back to scholars such as Claude Lévi-Strauss and Mary Douglas. In *The Raw and the Cooked* (1964), for example, a study of the Bororo Indians of central Brazil and South American cooking myths, Lévi-Strauss argues that food preparation is central to the development of society. The act of cooking functions as a mediator between "the raw product and the human consumer," and social convention—not instinct—determines the food people eat (336). This social process is eventually shaped by cultural practices such as table manners and religious beliefs. In "Deciphering a Meal," British anthropologist Mary Douglas uses her family's eating habits to elaborate on her work in *Purity and Danger* (1966). Her analysis of Hebrew dietary laws fits into a broader argument about meals as "structured social events" and as expressions of shared identity and kinship (44).

7. More specifically, Mintz argues that the processes of "extensification" (the reduction of its status as a luxury item) and "intensification" (its association with rituals such as weddings and other celebrations) help explain this product's important place in the Western diet (122).

8. As Rozin explains in "The Selection of Foods by Rats, Humans, and Other Animals," omnivores have always faced "the danger of eating something harmful or too much of a good thing" (23), but the versatility and flexibility in "[considering] anything of potential nutritional value as a possible food" has been crucial for the species' ability to adapt to environmental change (23, 27).

Chapter 1

1. The actor playing Chubby (Mark Holton) plays a similar role in *Leprechaun* (1993) as the heavyset, clumsy, and developmentally disabled Ozzie.

2. See Bob Batchelor and Scott Stoddart, 95–96.

3. In the closing moments of "Physical," this shift from fat to thin coincides with a shift from heterosexual to homosexual as the men pair off together. While this change is presented humorously, an unintended irony emerged shortly after the video's release: the thin gay body's association with AIDS. By the time "Physical" won a Grammy for Video of the Year in 1983, televangelist Jerry Falwell was pleading with blood banks to reject gay donors as a way of preventing the spread of HIV, helping to fuel widespread misconceptions that the virus predominantly afflicted gay men. The American public grew steadily more anxious about the disease, and they had reason to be. By June of 1984, approximately 2,300 Americans in forty-six states had died from AIDS, and on the evening of Reagan's reelection, AIDS cases in the United States exceeded 7,000 (Shilts 465 and 495). This disease transformed the body as well. The AIDS wasting syndrome—losing 10 percent or more of one's weight, particularly muscle—was a visible sign of the illness's horrifying and tragic progression. As Susan Sontag remarks in *AIDS and Its Metaphors*, diseases that physically deform a person inspire the greatest dread: "The marks on the face of a leper, a syphilitic, someone with AIDS are the signs of a progressive mutation, decomposition. [. . .] The most feared diseases [. . .] are not simply fatal but transform the body into something alienating" (41, 45). In a culture obsessed with weight loss, the epidemic of AIDS in the 1980s was a sobering reminder of the terrifying possibilities of bodily changes caused by indulgence or illness, excess or restraint. Just as the thin body could signal a healthy diet and regular exercise regimen, it could also indicate an eating disorder or illness. Such contradictory meanings would characterize the country's relationship with body size in the eighties.

4. These latter efforts were inspired, in part, by her own experiences with breast cancer in the 1990s and her desire to raise money and awareness for the disease. See the introduction to Olivia Newton-John's *Livwise: Easy Recipes for a Healthy, Happy Life*.

5. She details these experiences in the "A Body Abused" section of *Jane Fonda's Workout Book*, 13–16.

6. Amy Erdman Farrell addresses the supposed health-care crisis and costs of obesity in the first chapter of *Fat Shame: Stigma and the Fat Body in American Culture*: "According to the National Institutes of Health, two-thirds of the U.S. population are currently medically defined as 'overweight' or 'obese,' constituting what has become popularly known as an 'obesity epidemic.' With its connotations of disease, contagion, and proliferation, the choice of the term 'epidemic' is deliberately alarmist, suggesting imminent danger and sure catastrophe if not addressed" (9).

7. For more on the way economic forces within the health industrial complex shaped the NIH's findings, see Oliver, 28–34.

8. Farrell also discusses the patriotic implications of fatness in twenty-first-century America, citing Surgeon General David Satcher's declaration of "war on obesity" on December 13, 2001, and Human Services secretary Tommy G. Thompson's statement at the same press conference that "all Americans—as their patriotic duty—[should] lose 10 pounds" (7). In *Weighing In: Obesity, Food Justice, and the Limits of Capitalism*, Julie Guthman, who examines obesity as an ecological condition that must be understood in a socioeconomic and culture context, cites a 2009 London study that "linked obesity to global warming, harming the environment, and depleting resources by assuming that fat people drive and eat more than thin people. 'The main message,' the study concluded, 'is staying thin. It's good for you, and it's good for the planet'" (7).

9. King published five novels under the pseudonym Richard Bachman—*Rage* (1977), *The Long Walk* (1979), *Roadwork* (1981), *The Running Man* (1982), and *Thinner* (1984). King intended to publish *Misery* (1987) under Bachman's name, but the truth about his identity was revealed before King had the chance. See chapter 3 of Tony Magistrale's *Stephen King: The Second Decade*, Danse Macabre *to* The Dark Half.

10. For a detailed discussion of Schwarzenegger's anti-obesity initiatives and his plan "Vision for California: 10 Steps Toward Healthy Living," see Susan Greenhalgh's *Fat-Talk Nation: The Human Costs of America's War on Fat*, 45–48.

11. For the track featuring Journey's "Don't Stop Believin,'" Schwarzenegger begins: "Let's start our special program of resistance training without weights: push-ups. My method of doing push-ups between two chairs will give your chest the ultimate workout."

12. In their study of twenty-first-century fitness magazines, Dworkin and Wachs found a similar pattern, arguing that the emphasis on size reduction for women tended to cast women as passive. Men, however, were most often presented as active, allowing them to retain a greater degree of subjecthood. See chapter 3, "Size Matters: Male Body Panic and the Third Wave 'Crisis of Masculinity.'"

13. For more on these types of ploys in sideshows, see Bogdan, 210.

14. Furthermore, these chapter titles instill an obsessive quality in the reader. We want to monitor Billy's weight loss (we want to know the next number), and this curiosity mirrors our own cultural and personal obsession with weight. In this way, the novel keeps our focus on the body, not the interior. This is part of the problem with American weight-loss culture, and it is part of Billy's problem as a character.

15. See the Guinness Book of World Records: http://www.guinnessworldrecords.com/world-records/heaviest-man/.

16. See *Oxford Companion to the Body*, 682.

17. Controversy erupted more recently over thalidomide when the German drug company, the Grünenthal Group, issued an official apology for the drug in 2012, just over fifty years after it had been withdrawn from the market. See "Thalidomide Apology Insulting, Campaigners Say."

18. For more on its publication history and cult status, see Caitlin Roper and Michael LaPointe.

19. This interview was reprinted in Carolyn Kellog's article about Dunn's death in 2016. See Kellog.

20. For examples of these readings, see Kathryn Weese and Nell Sullivan.

21. Anna Mae Duane focuses on women's rights more generally in her analysis of the way the marketplace during the Reagan era utterly transformed domestic life and helped establish terms that prevented the ratification of the Equal Rights Amendment in 1981.

22. Early in his career, Mack went by the stage names "Giant Baby" and the "Infant Lambert"—a reference to Daniel Lambert, the 700-pound British man with the largest recorded weight in Western culture at the time.

23. See Frank McElroy, *The Life of Vantile Mack, the Infant Lambert; or Giant Baby, Together with the Causes Assigned for His Extraordinary Growth*, 26.

24. See Bogdan, 13.

25. See also Henig.

26. See Morgan, 29.

27. Lean Cuisine earned $120 million in its first year. See Belasco's *Appetite for Change*, 226.

28. In 1896, long after Thanksgiving had been celebrated in various ways throughout the United States, Abraham Lincoln proclaimed the last Thursday of November as the national holiday of Thanksgiving. Roosevelt changed it to the second to last week. See James W. Baker's *Thanksgiving: The Biography of an American Holiday*, 41.

29. In her reading of class tensions in the novel, Nell Sullivan has argued that Miss Lick disfigures these women only to train them "for managerial positions safely within the middle class" (418). In this way *Geek Love* captures profound class resentments and portrays the severe cost of social mobility in America.

30. Among those receiving Lick's "fatness treatment," however, one proves to be a "failure." Vita gets reduced to "a round of dark flesh [. . .] on a pillow. Thin hair straggling in greasy tangles suggests that it is a human head" (162–63). As a seventeen-year-old girl on her high-school track and field team, Vita possesses an athletic body and youthful vigor, but Lick's thyroid treatments rob Vita of the ability to define herself in terms of athletic skill. She cannot be the school's star hurdle jumper, for instance. Only after Vita (the Latin word for "life") attempts suicide does Miss Lick reluctantly admit some failing on her part: "She'd been an athlete and this was the wrong route for her. [. . .] Acid would have been O.K., but not this. Made me realize I had to tailor the treatments" (163). Lick assumes that the girl's athletic ability makes a sedentary life of extreme fatness too much for her, but the girl's failed recovery suggests something more: "I've been working on bringing her back. Her body is close, now. But her head is . . . And she was sharp" (163). Vita's body can recover, but the real

damage is psychological. Miss Lick presents bodily transformation as a freedom from objectification, but she has reduced this girl to nothing more than a pile of flesh.

31. As Deborah Sullivan shows in *Cosmetic Surgery: The Cutting Edge of Commercial Medicine in America*, the use of cosmetic surgery continued to skyrocket throughout the rest of the century. In 1999, the American Society of Plastic and Reconstructive Surgeons released a report stating that "cosmetic surgery procedures by members increased 50 percent between 1996 and 1998 and 153 percent since 1992. Liposuction was the most frequently performed cosmetic procedure by plastic surgeons in 1998, followed by breast augmentation, eyelid surgery, facelift, and chemical face peel. [. . .] The organization estimates that members did more than 1 million cosmetic procedures in 1998, only 10 percent less than the estimated number of reconstructive procedures they did" (15).

32. For the details on this listing, see http://www.realtor.com/realestateandhomes-detail/8-Circle-St_Perryopolis_PA_15473_M47256-72384. Date of access: September 15, 2015. The realtor not only reduced the price several times throughout 2015 and 2016, but she also modified the description.

33. Quoted in Ryan Reed's "Buffalo Bill's 'Silence of the Lambs' House for Sale."

34. In the novel, Catherine would be Gumb's seventh female victim.

35. In his essay "Tortured Objects: Patriarchy and Eroticism in *The Silence of the Lambs*," Philip C. DiMare has noted some compelling similarities between Gumb and Dali. "Like Dali, Gumb has no interest in the individualities or inner worlds of the women who are joined together in his masterpiece. They are anonymous, faceless, confirmed by his use of 'it,' rather than 'you,' or even 'she' as he addresses them" (179).

36. In her monograph on the film, Yvonne Tasker notes the intimacy created by Demme's close-up shots and adds another important point: "Though *Silence*'s emotional intensity stems most obviously from its use of close-ups, the design of the production is absolutely central to its effect as horror. The film employs a resolutely muted palette. Browns, greys, and blues dominate, with occasional glimpses of green. [. . .] Both Quantico and the world of the film's two serial killers are typically bland in color. [. . .] Catherine Martin's lurid blouse is discarded at the scene of her abduction in favor of a grey jump suit" (60–61). The muted colors of the poster are in keeping with the film's evocation of horror.

37. Throughout the film, the latter gets reinforced with various images of gender inequity, such as the elevator packed with male FBI agents, the male trainees ogling at Clarice and her roommate during a run, and the male, West Virginia police officers crowding around Fredrica Bimel's body at the funeral home.

38. More specifically, in *Manhood in Hollywood from Bush to Bush*, Greven argues that *The Silence of the Lamb*'s "homophobic tendencies" are offset by its broader commentary about the construction of manhood throughout the Bush era. However, numerous critics have taken issue with the depiction of sexuality in this adaptation. Diana Fuss, for instance, notes the troubling link between homosexuality and "perversion and death" (95) in the film. Douglas Crimp considers Demme's film a homophobic text that contributes to the tendency in Hollywood to stereotype "gay men as psychopathic killers" (10). Adrienne Donald situates the homophobia in "the film's overarching treatment of class. Buffalo Bill is dirty, inarticulate, artisanal (as opposed to artistic), vulgar, faggy, misogynistic, violent, perverted, tattooed,

and mutilated; he listens to heavy metal, he drives a van, he lives in the suburbs, he owns a toy poodle named Precious, he is a Vietnam veteran. In short, he is an unformed, shadowy, vaguely working-class, gay composite non-character, a study in suburban Gothic, an appalling stereotype of class and erotic loathsomeness" (354). And Christina Hodel describes Buffalo Bill as "the quintessential queer-as-monster, horrific not just due to his unspeakable acts of murder, but also because of the gender dysmorphia that is his motivation to kill—and the cause of a backlash from LGBTQ audiences" (160). She also notes that "Demme completely exploited the Otherness of gay and transgendered people" in his depiction of Buffalo Bill (164).

39. For more data on sexual reassignment surgeries, see Lynn Conway's "How Frequently Does Transsexualism Occur?"

40. Of course, Gumb's approach to achieving a new skin does not come from transforming the self through healthy food and exercise—no evidence of workout videos or Lean Cuisine dinners appear in his home. His response is surgical in that he intends to achieve a different, more beautiful, more idealized body by stealing the skin of others.

41. The death's-head moth comes from the genus *Acherontia*, which was named after Acheron, the River of Pain in Greek mythology.

42. Prior to his incarceration, "Lecter was known for the excellence of his table and had contributed numerous articles to gourmet magazines" (28). The tabloid magazine *National Tattler* offered him $50,000 for some recipes (6), and he keeps a copy of the *Joy of Cooking* in his cell (195). (The film shows an issue of *Bon Appétit* [with phrase "Winter Fun" beneath the title] in his temporary cell in Tennessee.)

43. *New York* magazine food critic first used the term *foodie* on June 2, 1980, and at the same time, it was also being popularized by Ann Barr and Paul Levy in their book *The Official Foodie Handbook* (1984).

44. According to David Greven, "Lecter is associated throughout with conventional markers of queerness. Taste, cultivation, heightened aesthetic propensities: all these qualities mark Lecter as stereotypically gay (at least for an older generation; queer life of the present does not as readily conform to these signifiers)" (100). Donald also discusses Lecter as "a gay dandy" (355), and Hodel considers him the "quintessential queer" (160).

45. See Fahy, "Classical Music in *Silence* and *Seven*."

46. Robert H. Waugh has noted several links between Lecter and butterflies, including "his trick of wearing Pembry's face in the ambulance, [which suggests] that he is molting into a new form" (75).

47. For the full text of this speech, see http://www.pbs.org/wgbh/americanexperience/features/primary-resources/carter-crisis/.

48. Quoted in Farris, *Kennedy and Reagan*, 332.

49. Nancy Reagan spent an estimated $46,000 for the second inaugural (Mills 22).

50. Trump launched Trump Ice (bottled water) in 2005, Trump Vodka in 2006, and Trump Steaks in 2007. For more on his relationship with the food industry, see Natasha Geiling's "A Definitive History of Trump Steaks."

51. See Murphet, 24.

52. Murphet, 17.

53. Hitchcock changed her first name to Marion in the film.

54. For more on this, see Levenstein's *Paradox of Plenty*, 138–39.

55. In this way, Bateman's relationship with dining is no different than his assessment of popular music. As Carl F. Miller has persuasively argued in "'Where the Beat Sounds the Same': *American Psycho* and the Cultural Capital of Pop Music," Bateman's discussions of popular music icons such as Huey Lewis, Whitney Houston, and Phil Collins read much like album reviews in the *Times* (though punctuated with occasional inaccuracies), and his interest in these artists stems from their commercial and popular success. "Bateman," as Miller demonstrates, "does not actually know anything about music; he simply repeats what he has read and heard elsewhere" (62); "[he] is, consequently, a critical reactionary who can only reproduce random—and often incomplete or inaccurate—sound bites" (57). Miller also briefly notes Bateman's equally superficial relationship with food. Instead of reading the menu, Bateman regurgitates "elitist mainstream reviews in the most prominent culinary publications of the day" (57), and Miller goes on to point out that "Bateman rarely enjoys eating any of the restaurant dishes, but instead simply feels compelled to order them for the cultural prestige they offer" (58).

56. See Gael Greene's "Westward, Haute!"

57. Even Bateman's rant about red snapper pizza proves to be manufactured. When McDermott subsequently shows Bateman an article from the *Times* about Donald Trump referring to Pastels as having the best pizza in Manhattan, Bateman has to admit that he needs to "retaste" the food. If it's "okay with Donny [. . .] it's okay with me" (110). Even though Trump's opinion probably ran counter to one of the reviews that Bateman read, he cannot deviate from the opinion of his cultural and financial hero.

58. Patrick's recommendation of Diet Pepsi horrifies his friends, and Colby offers a compelling reading of this moment in terms of Republican censoring of Madonna's *Like a Prayer* video. In 1989, the company used the artist and song in a commercial, and several organizations, including the American Family Association, called "for the boycott of all Pepsi products on April 4, 1989, in response to blasphemous imagery in Madonna's video" (69). She concludes that "Ellis here shows the effect of the reactionary politics of the Reagan administration on the consumer choices of the public, and points to the influence that the measures taken in the culture war period had on American society" (70).

59. Quoted in Levenstein, 239.

60. For more on the publication history of the novel and the response of the media, see chapter 3 of Murphet.

61. In the summer of 2013, when a movie theater in Williamsburg, Brooklyn, hosted a screening of *American Psycho* with a six-course meal based on dishes in the film, their menu did not include the swordfish, rare roasted partridge breast, or free-range rabbit. See Jen Carlson's "Dine Like Patrick Bateman at This *American Psycho* Screening."

Chapter 2

1. See "Crack Cocaine: A Short History." http://www.drugfreeworld.org/drugfacts/crackcocaine/a-short-history.html.

2. See *Alcohol and Temperance in Modern History: An International Encyclopedia: Volume 1*, 30.

3. See N. R. Kleinfield's "Hershey Bites Off New Markets." Candy consumption was actually higher in the 1960s, and he attributes this dip in the 1980s to rising candy prices and growing concerns about weight gain. However, this article does not include data about the overall consumption of sugar in the American diet, which was skyrocketing.

4. Poole examines the way food functions "as a code, a sign, a system, a leitmotif of fascinating complexity, to expand the possible repertoire of readings of a play, performance, or film" (4). She also briefly discusses the cannibal motif in horror films (75–82). Dunn views kitchens in literature and film as a crucial space for "[providing] the setting and structure for a drama of pain and redemption, sorrow and joy" (33). And Cynthia Baron considers the connection between foodstuffs and the emotional development of male and female characters in *Bagdad Café*.

5. More specifically, Davis notes that "Creators of 1930s horror movies used food scenes in part for their power to show the monsters' potential for becoming civilized. At the same time, since eating is such a common activity, these same scenes, while showing monsters hoping to become accepted by humans, to become human even, could expose the hidden appetites within audience members and cause them to wonder if within their own civilized beings there lurked some share of monster-like appetites" (295).

6. The Sugar Research Foundation, for example, began funding research in the late 1960s to downplay the link between sugar and coronary heart disease in order to increase profits and to shape public policy. As Cristin E. Kearns, Laura A. Schmidt, and Stanton A. Glantz note in "Sugar Industry and Coronary Heart Disease Research: A Historical Analysis of Internal Industry Documents," Sugar Research Foundation paid three Harvard scientists nearly $50,000 (in today's money) to publish a paper on sugar, fat, and heart disease in the *New England Journal of Medicine* that shifted the focus from sugar's role in coronary heart disease to saturated fat. The two-part literature review in 1967 concluded that "there was 'no doubt' that the only dietary intervention required to prevent CHD (Coronary Heart Disease) was to reduce dietary cholesterol and substitute polyunsaturated fat for saturated fat in the American diet." The authors also point out that the sugar industry continued to fund similar research that directly influenced public policy, including the 1976 Food and Drug Administration's evaluation of sugar safety.

7. In *For God, Country, and Coca-Cola: The Definitive History of the Great American Soft Drink and the Company That Makes It*, Mark Pendergrast argues that Pemberton himself was likely a morphine addict after his experiences in the war.

8. See "Revisiting Buffett—Coca-Cola in 1988" (January 19, 2013). http://www.gurufocus.com/news/205476/revisiting-buffett—cocacola-in-1988.

9. 7-Eleven launched the Super Big Gulp (a forty-four-ounce drink) in 1986. For more on the history of 7-Eleven and supersized drinks, see Robert Klara's "The Tall, Cold Tale of the Big Gulp."

10. See "What Americans Are Drinking."

11. Controversy erupted, however, when it was revealed that some of the flavoring still involved beef tallow. This news inspired protests in India and a lawsuit by vegetarians in the United States. For more, see Andrew F. Smith's *Encyclopedia of Junk Food and Fast Food*, 111.

12. In her examination of the fragmentation of urban landscapes in *Celluloid Vampires*, Abbott notes that "the young vampires ride motorcycles with attitudes like Marlon Brando, challenge Michael to a game of chicken on a cliff like the similar challenge in *Rebel without a Cause*, and to further make the point, they decorate their underground lair with a poster of the Los Angeles-identified rock 'n' roll rebel Jim Morrison" (188).

13. Of course, this is not Grandpa's only addiction, but food gets implicated in his other obsessive behaviors as well. Immediately following the tour of the refrigerator, for instance, Michael notices a marijuana plant on the kitchen windowsill, and both boys chuckle over his recreational drug use. Grandpa never admonishes them about his pot plants, though. One deleted scene shows Sam trying to burn a pot leaf with a match, but when Grandpa catches him, he doesn't press the issue. These moments remind the audience once again that junk food is Grandpa's primary preoccupation. The placement of marijuana in the kitchen—so close to his sacrosanct second shelf—further suggests sugar as a drug. It also probably functions as a humorous nod to the idea of snacking or "having the munchies" after getting high, which again links these addictions.

14. Numerous critics have discussed Bigelow's hybridization of the horror and Western genres in *Near Dark*. In making a case for Bigelow as an auteur, for example, Leo Braudy highlights her investment in genre revisionism, and he considers *Near Dark* "a genre landmark." For Braudy, the fusion of horror and Western—through her world-weary vampires and bored young cowboys in dead-end towns—expose "the old heroic myth of the West long vanished" (31). Likewise, Cynthia J. Miller argues that *Near Dark*, "while easily 'readable' as either contemporary Western or horror, is, in fact, something different—a true hybrid, with genre elements that do not merely coexist, but intertwine with and inform each other" (273).

15. They eventually worry that Jeremy's strange behavior indicates homosexuality, and the homophobic humor in the film suggests that nothing could be worse than having a gay son, not even a vampire.

16. See Tim Sullivan's "Mr. Holland's Opus."

17. According to Box Office Mojo, *Fright Night* ranks thirty-five on the list of top grossing films in the United States in 1985, and it only underperformed two other horror films that year—*Teen Wolf* and *A Nightmare on Elm Street 2: Freddy's Revenge*.

18. Rice, working mostly at night, composed the novel in just five weeks (19). See Katherine Ramsland's "The Lived World of Anne Rice's Novels."

19. Janice Doane and Devon Hodges make note of this in "Undoing Feminism: From the Preoedipal to Postfeminism in Anne Rice's *Vampire Chronicles*," 433.

20. As Haggerty explains in *Queer Gothic*, "For all the homoerotics of these volumes, Rice seems unable to create a bond between two men that is more than the symptom of corrupt and corrupting culture. Even in creating moments of the most intense intimacy or of unbridled sexual attraction, Rice insists on the repulsion that homosexuality regularly breeds in the minds of fundamentalist politicians and other members of the extreme right" (195).

21. In a deft touch, Rice presents Louis, a white plantation owner, as recognizing the humanity of blacks only after his death to underscore the dehumanizing impact of slavery on slave owners. For more on the link between sugar and colonialism, see chapter 2 of Sidney Mintz's *Sweetness and Power: The Place of Sugar in Modern History*.

22. Robert Albritton even considers sugar addiction potentially more dangerous than smoking: "Tobacco often kills after the age of sixty, while sugar attacks the teeth of the young and may in many cases be the main cause of obesity and all of its related chronic illness throughout life" (344).

23. I am using contemporary measurements even though the calorie count and fat content of the fries would have been much higher in 1981 since McDonald's primarily cooked their fries in beef tallow until 1990 (Schlosser 120). Current information about the content of McDonald's food items can be found through the McDonald's Nutrition Calculator at www.mcdonalds.com.

24. This detail also points to one of the more problematic aspects of *The Hunger*. In the world of this novel, all transformation that deviates from white, heterosexual norms and Western standards of beauty gets presented as horrific. The shift from human to vampire, in other words, gets aligned with any deviation from heterosexuality, patriarchy, and thinness.

25. Bram Stoker was certainly familiar with the vampire fiction that preceded his novel, most notably John Polidori's *The Vampyre* (1819), Jameste Malcom Rymer's *Varney the Vampire* (1847), which first appeared serially in penny dreadfuls beginning in 1845, and fellow Irish writer Sheridan Le Fanu's *Carmilla* (1872). Yet his novel has resonated more powerfully than these other works in large part because of the highly successful Hollywood adaptation in 1931. This is not a value judgment on the merits on these other works per se, but a statement about the unprecedented impact of film in the early twentieth century.

26. As Rebecca Housel has noted in "Suckers for Blood: Vampire Pop Culture," the 1948 film *Abbot and Costello Meet Frankenstein* "is counted amongst one of the most historically significant in American cinema for not only its comedy, but for marking the end of the Gold Age of the monster mash. The film features three classic 'monsters': Dracula, Frankenstein, and the Wolf Man. The evil aspects of the monsters are made parody, a hallmark of the social shift to postmodernism" (111–12).

27. See William Hughes's "Fictional Vampires in the Nineteenth and Twentieth Centuries," 198.

Chapter 3

1. According to Riki Ott, "The active ingredient, 2-butoxyethanol, [in Simple Green] is a known human health hazard, which the EPA recognizes as a 'fetal-toxin.' Corexit 9527 and Inipol were sprayed on beaches despite safety warnings to prevent product from entering sewers, low areas, and watercourses. Cleanup workers had used Simple Green by the gallon to wash skiffs, skin, rain gear, and personal clothing" (218).

2. See the website for the *Exxon Valdez* Oil Spill Trustee Council website: http://www.evostc.state.ak.us/%3FFA=facts.QA.

3. Additionally, a court acquitted Captain Joseph Hazelwood of being intoxicated since he was sleeping off a night of heavy drinking below deck at the time of the accident. The third mate actually grounded the tanker, but according to investigative journalist Greg

Palast, he could have easily avoided the accident had the radar on the ship been functional. Exxon knew about the damaged equipment for over a year, but considered it too costly to repair. See Greg Palast, "Court Rewards Exxon for Valdez Oil Spill."

4. Bernice M. Murphy admits that popular horror in the seventies took its cue from *Silent Spring*, but she traces this "threat of environmental catastrophe" trope back to seventeenth-century American writings (179).

5. More specifically, the NOAA National Centers for Environmental Information cites N. Lott and T. Ross's "Tracking and Evaluating U.S. Billion Dollar Weather Disasters, 1980–2005."

6. For more about the book and its reception, see the author's webpage: http://www.billmckibben.com/.

7. See the website for the United States Census Bureau: https://www.census.gov/programs-surveys/decennial-census/decade.1990.html.

8. According to Roberts, "In 1885, more than half of the U.S. population was engaged in farming; in 1985, that share had fallen to less than 3 percent," even though the country produced 40 percent of the global supply (23).

9. Since garbage disposal remained relatively inexpensive in the 1970s and early 1980s, local and state governments did not seek alternatives such as recycling. Gradually, throughout the eighties, environmental activism, government policy, and the waste industry started to view recycling as the most sensible alternative to building more landfills and incinerators. See chapter 3 of Pellow's *Garbage Wars*.

10. See Jamie Russell's *The Book of the Dead: The Complete History of Zombie Cinema* (64–65) and Peter Dendel's *The Zombie Movie Encyclopedia* (3–7).

11. *Dead and Buried* attributes Dobb's power to reanimate the town of Potter's Bluff to voodoo, black magic, and witchcraft.

12. I will reference a range of criticism regarding consumerism throughout the chapter, but here are some examples of scholarship that address these other issues in Romero's films. According to Wood, for example, *Night of the Living Dead* offers an analysis of a "typical American nuclear family" (103) at the farmhouse. The destruction of the Coopers "at the hands of their zombie daughter represents the film's judgment on them and the norm they embody" (103). Tony Williams in *Hearths of Darkness: The Family in the American Horror* extends this reading to include Romero's desire to "define a new society without patriarchal family structures. His future groups reject Western sexist and racist formations and move toward a future postcapitalist world where hierarchical barriers no longer exist." He concludes that "Both *Dawn* and *Day* strongly suggest patriarchal structures contaminate white males" (149). Barbara Bruce examines the ambivalent portrait of race in *Night of the Living Dead*, with a particular emphasis on the "conflicting racial expectations" surrounding Ben's interactions with Barbra: "Ben's aggressive entrance [to the farmhouse] evokes the racist stereotype of the black man as (sexual) threat and the more contemporary image of the black militant, but his clean-cut good looks evoke the non-violent, non-threatening icons of the Civil Rights Movement and integrationism: Martin Luther King and, particularly [Sidney] Poitier" (64–65). For a discussion of feminism in the film, see Barry Keith Grant's "Taking Back the *Night of the Living Dead*: George Romero, Feminism, and the Horror Film." It is my

intention in this chapter to add Romero's environmental critique of overpopulation to these discussions.

13. Even though Pretty Things is a British Rock Band, this song is clearly indebted to some of the conventions of country music.

14. Inadvertently, the illnesses that cast and crew experienced while shooting in this location reinforced Romero's environmental message in the film. "An equally insidious problem throughout production was the mine's damp, 55-degree chill, which resulted in a cold and flu epidemic among the cast and crew who barely saw sunlight for seven weeks. 'At the end, we were all pretty sick,' recalls Lori Cardille. 'The last day of filming, George, Terry Alexander, and I all had 103–104 temperatures. It was terrible!'" (Gagne 159).

15. To offer a twenty-first-century example, the United States discarded most of the 1.9 billion pounds of pumpkin purchased in 2014. The Department of Energy also announced that Americans added 254 million tons of municipal waste to landfills as a result of Halloween pumpkins in 2016, and this waste, it reminded the public, generates additional greenhouse gas emissions. See Alastair Bland, "Do We Waste a Lot of Pumpkins We Could Be Eating?" and Alex Swerdloff's "The Government Says Our Halloween Pumpkins Are Destroying the Environment."

16. Some recent works that examine the racial and class politics of pollution in America include Rob Nixon's *Slow Violent and the Environmentalism of the Poor*, Dorceta Taylor's *Toxic Communities: Environmental Racism, Industrial Pollution, and Residential Mobility*, and Carl A. Zimring's *Clean and White: A History of Environmental Racism in the United States*. As Sarah Jaquette Ray notes in *The Ecological Other: Environmental Exclusion in American Culture*, "Environmental justice ecocritics increasingly address the ways in which disenfranchised groups—communities of color, women, and children, for instance—are disproportionately burdened with the costs of environmental degradation and may even be blamed for it" (23).

17. Russo coauthored the script for *Night of the Living Dead*.

18. McCarthy, 100.

19. As Timothy Morton has argued in *Ecology without Nature: Rethinking Environmental Aesthetics*, "The suburban lawn's flat, almost opaque surface [. . .] obscures in plain view the work that goes into it. [. . .] The lawn expresses the disappearing of the worker that resulted in picturesque landscape [. . .]. Thomas Jefferson's design for Monticello was for a seamless 'vista flowing from the mansion through the lawned garden fringed by trees to the foothills of the Blue Ridge Mountains.' [. . .] Monticello's open lawn, however, also hid a plantation full of slaves, and was designed explicitly to exclude the sight of slaves from the front view. Side paths prevented them from being seen in their traffic to and from the house" (90).

20. For more on the waste produced by filmmaking, see Robin L. Murray and Joseph K. Heumann's *Ecology and Popular Film: Cinema on the Edge*.

21. King revised this story slightly before including it in *Nightmares and Dreamscapes* (1993).

22. As a side note, some of the other uses of wormwood include producing vermouth and absinthe as well as a medicine for digestive disorders and upset stomachs. This may be another joke on King's part. Star Wormwood reduces the president of the United States and

his wife to a "Zombie Blue Plate Special," leaving them to roam the streets of Washington "gnawing on human arms and legs like people eating chicken legs at a picnic" (67). This new diet might necessitate wormwood to mitigate stomach problems.

23. See Bill Wyman's "Did 'Thriller' Really Sell a Hundred Million Copies?"

24. Certainly, racism plays a role in this murder. The hip-hop music sounds alien to white men in the group, and Jimmy, who views African Americans as "niggers," has been looking for an excuse to hurt Cheesecake. Marly is aware of the racial stereotypes used to categorize her as the "Chinese gardener" (233) and a "Chink bitch" (259). Both of these examples reflect the story's attempt to depict racism as something that isolates and dehumanizes people.

25. Most characters seem unaware of the garden. Sheriff Bruce has no idea of its existence until Vincent tells him about it. Likewise, the garden has presumably gone unnoticed for years by the government official who does monthly inspections of the livestock. Only a momentary glance and Vincent's strange behavior inspire him to investigate further.

Conclusion

1. See Funderburg, 6.
2. See Gorman.
3. See Stube, 62.
4. Williams has noted another example of this in one of the television commercials for The Stuff: "The models wear beautiful fur coats taken from the bodies of animals murdered for consumer satisfaction. They offer the Stuff to audiences, a substance whose addictive properties eventually lead to grotesque deaths" (*Larry Cohen* 136).
5. White House chief strategist Steve Bannon told reporters in 2017 that press secretary Sean Spicer would no longer be holding televised briefings because he "got fatter." For more, see Jeet Heer.
6. See "Climate Change: How Do We Know?" at https://climate.nasa.gov/evidence/.

WORKS CITED

Abbott, Stacey. *Celluloid Vampires: Live after Death in the Modern World.* Austin: U of Texas P, 2007.
Adams, Rachel. *Sideshow U.S.A.: Freaks and the American Cultural Imagination.* Chicago: U of Chicago P, 2001.
Albritton, Robert. "Between Obesity and Hunger: The Capitalist Food Industry." *Food and Culture: A Reader.* Ed. Carole Counihan and Penny Van Esterik. 3rd ed. New York: Routledge, 2012. 342–54.
Alcohol and Temperance in Modern History: An International Encyclopedia: Volume 1. Ed. Jack S. Blocker, David M. Fahey, and Ian R. Tyrrell. Santa Barbara, CA: ABC-CLIO, 2003.
Allué, Sonia Baelo. "Serial Murder, Serial Consumerism: Bret Easton Ellis's *American Psycho*." *Miscelanea: A Journal of English and American Studies* 26 (2002): 71–90.
Aoyama, Tomoko. *Reading Food in Modern Japanese Literature.* Honolulu: U of Hawaii P, 2008.
Appelbaum, Robert. *Aguecheek's Beef, Belch's Hiccup, and Other Gastronomic Interjections: Literature, Culture, and Food among the Early Moderns.* Chicago: U of Chicago P, 2006.
Archer, Jayne Elizabeth. *Food and the Literary Imagination.* New York: Palgrave Macmillan, 2014.
Asava, Zélie. "'You're Nothing to Me But Another . . . [White] Vampire': A Study of the Representation of the Black Vampire in American Mainstream Cinema." *Images of the Modern Vampire: The Hip and the Atavistic.* Ed. Barbara Brodman and James E. Doan. Madison, NJ: Farleigh Dickinson UP, 2013. 99–112.
Auerbach, Nina. *Our Vampires, Ourselves.* Chicago: U of Chicago P, 1995.
Bacon, Simon. "Eat Me! The Morality of Hunger in Vampiric Cuisine." *Images of the Modern Vampire: The Hip and the Atavistic.* Ed. Barbara Brodman and James E. Doan. Madison, NJ: Farleigh Dickinson UP, 2013. 41–54.
Bailey, Matthew. "Memory, Place, and the Mall: George Romero and Consumerism." *Studies in Popular Culture* 35.2 (Spring 2013): 95–110.
Baker, James W. *Thanksgiving: The Biography of an American Holiday.* Lebanon: U of New Hampshire P, 2009.
Barnum, P. T. *Struggles and Triumphs; or, Forty Years' Recollections of P. T. Barnum, Written by Himself.* Buffalo, NY: Warren, Johnson, and Company, 1872.
Baron, Cynthia. "Food and Gender in *Bagdad Café*." *Food and Foodways* 11.1 (2003): 49–74.

Baron, Cynthia, Diane Carson, and Mark Bernard. *Appetites and Anxieties: Food, Film, and the Politics of Representation*. Detroit: Wayne State UP, 2014.

Barr, Ann, and Paul Levy. *The Official Foodie Handbook*. Westminster, MD: Arbor House, 1984.

Batchelor, Bob, and Scott Stoddart. *The 1980s (Popular Culture through History)*. Westport, CT: Greenwood, 2007.

Belasco, Warren. *Food: Key Concepts*. New York: Bloomsbury, 2008.

Belasco, Warren. *Appetite for Change: How the Counterculture Took on the Food Industry, 1966–1988*. New York: Pantheon Books, 1989.

Bishop, Kyle William. *American Zombie Gothic: The Rise and Fall (and Rise) of the Walking Dead in Popular Culture*. Jefferson, NC: McFarland, 2010.

Bland, Alastair. "Do We Waste a Lot of Pumpkins We Could Be Eating?" NPR, October 30, 2015. http://www.npr.org/sections/thesalt/2015/10/30/452856477/are-we-wasting-millions-of-jack-o-lanterns-that-we-could-be-eating.

Bloch, Robert. *Psycho*. 1959. New York: Overlook Press, 2010.

Bogdan, Robert. *Freak Show: Presenting Human Oddities for Amusement and Profit*. Chicago: U of Chicago P, 1988.

Bordo, Susan. *Unbearable Weight: Feminism, Western Culture, and the Body*. Berkeley: U of California P, 1993.

Bosky, Bernadette Lynn. "Playing the Heavy: Weight, Appetite, and Embodiment in Three Novels by Stephen King." *The Dark Descent: Essays Defining Stephen King's Horrorscape*. Ed. Tony Magistrale. Westport, CT: Praeger, 1992. 137–56.

Bower, Anne L. "Watching Food: The Production of Food, Film, and Values." *Reel Food: Essays on Food and Film*. Ed. Anne L. Bower. New York: Routledge, 2004. 1–16.

Boyett, Steven R. "Like Pavlov's Dogs." *Book of the Dead*. Ed. John Skipp and Craig Spector. New York: Bantam, 1989. 216–79.

Braudy, Leo. "*Near Dark*: An Appreciation." *Film Quarterly* 64.2 (Winter 2010): 29–32.

Braziel, Jana Evans, and Kathleen LeBesco. "Editors' Introduction." *Bodies Out of Bounds: Fatness and Transgression*. Ed. Jana Evans Braziel and Kathleen LeBesco. Berkeley: U of California P, 2001. 1–18.

Brown, Jennifer. *Cannibalism in Literature and Film*. New York: Palgrave Macmillan, 2013.

Brown, Michael. *Laying Waste: The Poisoning of America by Toxic Chemicals*. New York: Pantheon, 1980.

Bruce, Barbara. "Guess Who's Going to Be Dinner: Sidney Poitier, Black Militancy, and the Ambivalence of Race in Romero's *Night of the Living Dead*." *Race, Oppression, and the Zombie: Essays on Cross-Cultural Appropriations of the Caribbean Tradition*. Ed. Christopher M. Moreman and Cory James Rushton. Jefferson, NC: McFarland, 2011. 60–73.

Buell, Lawrence. *The Future of Environmental Criticism: Environmental Crisis and Literary Imagination*. Hoboken, NJ: Blackwell, 2005.

Buell, Lawrence. *Writing for an Endangered World: Literature, Culture, and the Environment in the U.S. and Beyond*. Boston, MA: Harvard UP, 2001.

Buell, Lawrence. *The Environmental Imagination: Thoreau, Nature Writing, and the Formation of American Culture*. Boston, MA: Harvard UP, 1995.

Calavita, Kitty, Henry N. Pontell, and Robert Tillman. *Big Money Crime: Fraud and Politics in the Savings and Loan Crisis*. Berkeley: U of California P, 1997.

Carlson, Jen. "Dine Like Patrick Bateman at this *American Psycho* Screening." *Gothamist*, January 15, 2013. http://gothamist.com/2013/01/15/dine_like_patrick_bateman_at_this_a.php.

Carroll, Noël. *The Philosophy of Horror or Paradoxes of the Heart*. New York: Routledge, 1990.

Carruth, Allison. *Global Appetites: American Power and the Literature of Food*. New York: Cambridge UP, 2013.

Carson, Rachel. *Silent Spring*. New York: Houghton Mifflin, 1962.

Christou, Maria. *Eating Otherwise: The Philosophy of Food in Twentieth-Century Literature*. New York: Cambridge UP, 2017.

"Climate Change: How Do We Know?" NASA. https://climate.nasa.gov/evidence/.

Clover, Carol J. *Men, Women, and Chainsaws: Gender in the Modern Horror Film*. Princeton, NJ: Princeton UP, 1992.

Colby, Georgina. *Bret Easton Ellis: Underwriting the Contemporary*. New York: Palgrave Macmillan, 2011.

Collings, Michael R. *Stephen King Is Richard Bachman*. Mercer Island, WA: Starmont House, 1985.

Conway, Lynn. "How Frequently Does Transsexualism Occur?" http://ai.eecs.umich.edu/people/conway/TS/TSprevalence.html.

Counihan, Carole M. "Introduction: Food and the Nation." *Food in the USA: A Reader*. New York: Routledge, 2002.

Counihan, Carole M., and Penny Van Esterik. "Why Food? Why Culture? Why Now? Introduction to the Third Edition." *Food and Culture: A Reader*. Ed. Carole M. Counihan and Penny Van Esterik. New York: Routledge, 2013. 1–18.

"Crack Cocaine: A Short History." Drug Free World. http://www.drugfreeworld.org/drugfacts/crackcocaine/a-short-history.html.

Creed, Barbara. *The Monstrous-Feminine: Film, Feminism, Psychoanalysis*. New York: Routledge, 1993.

Crimp, Douglas. "Right On, Girlfriend!" *Social Text* 33 (1992): 2–18.

Crowther, Gillian. *Eating Culture: An Anthropological Guide to Food*. Toronto: U of Toronto P, 2013.

Davenport, Coral. "Trump Budget Would Cut E.P.A. Science Programs and Slash Cleanups." *New York Times*, May 18, 2017. https://www.nytimes.com/2017/05/19/climate/trump-epa-budget-superfund.html.

David, Richard. "Orso Bucko: Backstage at Joe Allen's Smash Hit." *New York Magazine*, July 29, 1991: 40–44.

Davis, Blair. "Banquet and the Beast: The Civilizing Role of Food in 1930s Horror Films." *Reel Food: Essays on Food and Film*. Ed. Anne L. Bower. New York: Routledge, 2004. 281–96.

Delville, Michel, and Andrew Norris. *The Politics and Aesthetics of Hunger and Disgust: Perspectives on the Dark Grotesque*. New York: Routledge, 2017.

Dendel, Peter. *The Zombie Movie Encyclopedia*. Jefferson, NC: McFarland, 2000.

Dillard, R. H. W. "*Night of the Living Dead*: It's Not Like Just a Wind That's Passing Through." *American Horrors: Essays on the Modern American Horror Film*. Ed. Gregory A. Waller. Champaign: U of Illinois P, 1987. 14–29.

DiMare, Philip C. "Tortured Objects: Patriarchy and Eroticism in *The Silence of the Lambs*." *The Silence of the Lambs: Critical Essays on Cannibal, Clarice, and a Nice Chianti*. Ed. Cynthia J. Miller. New York: Rowman & Littlefield, 2016. 171–84.

Doane, Janice, and Devon Hodges. "Undoing Feminism: From the Preoedipal to Postfeminism in Anne Rice's *Vampire Chronicles*." *American Literary History* 2.3 (1990): 422–42.

Dolan, Kathryn Cornell. *Beyond the Fruited Plain: Food and Agriculture in U.S. Literature, 1850–1905*. Lincoln: U of Nebraska P, 2014.

Donald, Adrienne. "Working for Oneself: Labor and Love in *The Silence of the Lambs*." *Michigan Quarterly Review* 31.3 (1992): 347–60.

Douglas, Mary. "Deciphering a Meal." *Myth, Symbol, and Culture* 101.1 (Winter 1972): 61–81. Rpt. in *Food and Culture: A Reader*. Ed. Carole M. Counihan and Penny Van Esterik. New York: Routledge, 2013. 36–54.

Doyle, Michael. *Larry Cohen: The Stuff of Gods and Monsters*. Albany, GA: BearManor Media, 2015.

Drug Free World. "Crack Cocaine: A Short History." http://www.drugfreeworld.org/drugfacts/crackcocaine/a-short-history.html.

Duane, Anna Mae. "The Angel and the Freak: The Value of Childhood and Disability in Katherine Dunn's *Geek Love*." *Studies in American Fiction* 39.1 (2012): 103–22.

Dunn, Katherine. *Geek Love*. 1989. New York: Vintage, 2002.

Dunn, Maggie. "Licking the Pots in Sorrow's Kitchen: Food as Metaphor in Fiction and Film." *Journal of the Association for the Interdisciplinary Study of the Arts* 5.1 (1999): 33–41.

Dworkin, Shari L., and Faye Linda Wachs. *Body Panic: Gender, Health, and the Selling of Fitness*. New York: New York UP, 2009.

Ellis, Bret Easton. *American Psycho*. New York: Vintage, 1991.

Exxon Valdez Oil Spill Trustee Council. http://www.evostc.state.ak.us/%3FFA=facts.QA.

Fahy, Thomas. *Freak Shows and the Modern American Imagination: Constructing the Damaged Body from Willa Cather to Truman Capote*. New York: Palgrave, 2006.

Fahy, Thomas. "Killer Culture: Classical Music and the Art of Killing in *Silence of the Lambs* and *Se7en*." *Journal of Popular Culture* 37.1 (August 2003): 28–42.

Farrell, Amy Erdman. *Fat Shame: Stigma and the Fat Body in American Culture*. New York: New York UP, 2011.

Farris, Scott. *Kennedy and Reagan: Why Their Legacies Endure*. New York: Lyons Press, 2013.

Fitzpatrick, Joan. *Food in Shakespeare: Early Modern Dietaries and the Plays*. Burlington, VT: Ashgate, 2007.

Fo, M. "Interview with Robert Englund." *Thrasher* (February 1988): 72–77.

Fonda, Jane. *Jane Fonda's Workout Book*. New York: Simon and Schuster, 1981.

Fonesca, Tony. "Bela Lugosi's Dead, but Vampire Music Stalks the Airwaves." *The Fantastic Vampire: Studies in the Children of the Night—Selected Essays from the Eighteenth*

International Conference on the Fantastic in the Arts. Ed. James C. Holte. New York: Praeger, 2002. 59–68.

Frank, Alexandra C. "All-Consuming Passions: Vampire Foodways in Contemporary Film and Television." *What's Eating You: Food and Horror on Screen*. Ed. Cynthia J. Miller and A. Bowdoin Van Riper. New York: Bloomsbury, 2017. 339–54.

Freedman, Paul. *Food in Time and Place: The American Historical Association Companion to Food History*. Berkeley: U of California P, 2014.

Funderburg, Anne Cooper. *Chocolate, Strawberry, and Vanilla: A History of American Ice Cream*. New York: Popular Press, 1996.

Fuss, Diana. *Identification Papers: Readings on Psychoanalysis, Sexuality, and Culture*. New York: Routledge, 1995.

Gagne, Paul R. *The Zombies That Ate Pittsburgh: The Films of George A. Romero*. New York: Dodd, Mead, and Company, 1987.

Gambin, Lee. *Massacred by Mother Nature: Exploring the Natural Horror Film*. Baltimore, MD: Midnight Marquee Press, 2012.

Garrard, Greg. *Ecocriticism*. 2nd ed. New York: Routledge, 2012.

Geiling, Natasha. "A Definitive History of Trump Steaks." thinkprogress.org, March 4, 2016. http://thinkprogress.org/politics/2016/03/04/3756135/trump-steaks-a-definitive-history/.

Gelder, Ken. *New Vampire Cinema*. London: British Film Institute, 2012.

Gigante, Denise. *Taste: A Literary History*. New Haven, CT: Yale UP, 2005.

Glotfelty, Cheryll. "Introduction: Literary Studies in an Age of Environmental Crisis." *The Ecocriticism Reader: Landmarks in Literary Ecology*. Ed. Cheryll Glotfelty and Harold Fromm. Athens: U of Georgia P, 1996. xv–xxxvii.

Gomel, Elana. "'The Soul of this Man is his Clothes': Violence and Fashion in *American Psycho*." *Bret Easton Ellis: American Psycho, Glamorama, Lunar Park*. Ed. Naomi Mandel. New York: Bloomsbury, 2011. 50–63.

Gorman, John. "This Can't Be Success (but It Is): Frozen Yogurt Business Even Sweeter Than Retirement." *Chicago Tribune*, October 12, 1987. http://articles.chicagotribune.com/1987-10-12/business/8703170182_1_tcby-americana-foods-frank-hickingbotham.

Grant, Barry Keith. "Taking Back the *Night of the Living Dead*: George Romero, Feminism, and the Horror Film." *The Dread of Difference: Gender and Horror Film*. 2nd ed. Ed. Barry Keith Grant. Austin: U of Texas P, 2015. 228–40.

Greene, Andy. "Flashback: Will Smith and Freddy Krueger Battle in Court." *Rolling Stone*, June 7, 2016. http://www.rollingstone.com/music/videos/flashback-will-smith-and-freddy-krueger-battle-in-court-20160607.

Greene, Gael. "Westward, Haute!" *New York Magazine*, November 25, 1985: 100–104.

Greenhalgh, Susan. *Fat-Talk Nation: The Human Costs of America's War on Fat*. Ithaca, NY: Cornell UP, 2015.

Greven, David. *Manhood in Hollywood from Bush to Bush*. Austin: U of Texas P, 2009.

Guthman, Julie. *Weighing In: Obesity, Food Justice, and the Limits of Capitalism*. Berkeley: U of California P, 2011.

Haggerty, George E. *Queer Gothic*. Champaign: U of Illinois P, 2006.

Halberstam, Judith. *Skin Shows: Gothic Horror and the Technology of Monsters*. Durham, NC: Duke UP, 1995.

Hallab, Mary. "Humor in Vampire Films." *The Laughing Dead: The Horror-Comedy Film from Bride of Frankenstein to Zombieland*. Ed. Cynthia J. Miller and A. Bowdoin Van Riper. New York: Rowman & Littlefield, 2016. 138–53.

Hamermesh, Daniel S., and Jeff E. Biddle. "Beauty and the Labor Market." *American Economic Review* 84.5 (December 1994): 1174–94.

Hardin, Michael. "Fundamentally Freaky: Collapsing the Freak/Norm Binary in *Geek Love*." *Critique: Studies in Contemporary Fiction* 45.4 (2004): 337–46.

Harris, Thomas. *The Silence of the Lambs*. New York: St. Martin's Press, 1988.

Hartzman, Marc. *American Sideshow: An Encyclopedia of History's Most Wondrous and Curiously Strange Performers*. New York: Tarcher, 2005.

"Heaviest Man Ever." *Guinness World Records*. June 30, 2017. http://www.guinnessworldrecords.com/world-records/heaviest-man.

Heller, Tamar, and Patricia Moran. *Scenes of the Apple: Food and the Female Body in Nineteenth- and Twentieth-Century Women's Writing*. Albany: State U of New York P, 2003.

Henig, Robin Marantz. "Body and Mind: The High Cost of Thinness." *New York Times Magazine*, February 28, 1988. http://www.nytimes.com/1988/02/28/magazine/body-and-mind-the-high-cost-of-thinness.html?pagewanted=all.

Herndon, April Michelle. *Fat Blame: How the War on Obesity Victimizes Women and Children*. Lawrence: UP of Kansas, 2014.

Hertweck, Tom. *Food on Film: Bringing Something New to the Table*. New York: Rowman & Littlefield, 2014.

Hiltner, Ken. "General Introduction." *Ecocriticism: The Essential Reader*. Ed. Ken Hiltner. New York: Routledge, 2014. xii–xvi.

Hodel, Christina H. "The Filleting of Gender and Sexuality in *The Silence of the Lambs*." *The Silence of the Lambs: Critical Essays on a Cannibal, Clarice, and a Nice Chianti*. Ed. Cynthia Miller. New York: Rowman & Littlefield, 2016. 159–70.

Housel, Rebecca. "Suckers for Blood: Vampire Pop Culture." *A History of Evil in Popular Culture: What Hannibal Lecter, Stephen King, and Vampires Reveal about America*. Ed. Sharon Packer and Jody Pennington. Westport, CT: Praeger, 2014. 107–24.

Hughes, William. "Fictional Vampires in the Nineteenth and Twentieth Centuries." *A New Companion to the Gothic*. Ed. David Punter. Hoboken, NJ: Blackwell, 2012. 197–210.

Jackson, Kenneth T. *Crabgrass Frontier: The Suburbanization of the United States*. New York: Oxford UP, 1985.

Jeffords, Susan. *Hard Bodies: Hollywood Masculinity in the Reagan Era*. New Brunswick, NJ: Rutgers UP, 1994.

Kearns, Cristin E., Laura A. Schmidt, and Stanton A. Glantz. "Sugar Industry and Coronary Heart Disease Research: A Historical Analysis of Internal Industry Documents." *JAMA Internal Medicine*, September 12, 2016. http://archinte.jamanetwork.com/article.aspx?articleid=2548255.

Keller, James R. *Food, Film, and Culture: A Genre Study*. Jefferson, NC: McFarland, 2006.

Kellog, Carolyn. "Katherine Dunn Has Died; The *Geek Love* Author Once Took the World by Storm." *Los Angeles Times*, May 12, 2016. http://www.latimes.com/books/jacketcopy/la-et-jc-katherine-dunn-geek-love-20160512-snap-story.html.

Kimber, Shaun. "'Meat's meat, and a man's gotta eat.' (*Motel Hell*, 1980): Food and Eating within Contemporary Horror Cultures." *Food, Media, and Contemporary Culture: The Edible Image*. Ed. Peri Bradley. New York: Palgrave Macmillan, 2015. 125–43.

King, Stephen. *On Writing: A Memoir of the Craft*. New York: Scribner, 2000.

King, Stephen "Home Delivery." *Book of the Dead*. Ed. John Skipp and Craig Spector. New York: Bantam, 1989. 51–79.

King, Stephen *Thinner*. New York: Signet, 1985.

King, Stephen *Danse Macabre*. New York: Everest House, 1981.

Klara, Robert. "The Tall, Cold Tale of the Big Gulp." *Adweek*, February 16, 2015. http://www.adweek.com/news/advertising-branding/tall-cold-tale-big-gulp-162960.

Kleinfield, N. R. "Hershey Bites Off New Markets." *New York Times*, July 22, 1984. http://www.nytimes.com/1984/07/22/business/hershey-bites-off-new-markets.html?pagewanted=all.

Kleinknecht, William. *The Man Who Sold the World: Ronald Reagan and the Betrayal of Main Street America*. New York: Nation Books, 2009.

Koç, Mustafa, Jennifer Sumner, and Tony Winson. "Introduction: The Significance of Food and Food Studies." *Critical Perspectives in Food Studies*. Ed. Mustafa Koç, Jennifer Sumner, and Tony Winson. New York: Oxford UP, 2012. xi–xiv.

La Berge, Leigh Claire. *Scandals and Abstractions: Financial Fictions of the Long 1980s*. New York: Oxford UP, 2014.

LaPointe, Michael. "A Portrait of the Artist as a Young Convict." *The Atlantic*, October 2017: https://www.theatlantic.com/magazine/archive/2017/10/katherine-dunn-geek-love-attic/537879/.

Larkin, Judith Candib, and Harvey A. Pines. "No Fat Persons Need Apply: Experimental Studies of the Overweight Stereotype and Hiring Preference." *Sociology of Work and Occupations* 6.3 (August 1979): 312–27.

Lauro, Sarah Juliet. *The Transatlantic Zombie: Slavery, Rebellion, and Living Death*. New Brunswick, NJ: Rutgers UP, 2015.

Leiss, William, and Douglass Powell. *Mad Cows and Mother's Milk: The Perils of Poor Risk Communication*. 2nd ed. Kingston, Ontario: McGill-Queen's UP, 2004.

Levenstein, Harvey. *Paradox of Plenty: A Social History of Eating in Modern America*. Rev. ed. Berkeley: U of California P, 2003.

Lévi-Strauss, Claude. *The Raw and the Cooked: Introduction to a Science of Mythology, Volume 1*. 1964. Trans. John and Doreen Weightman. Chicago: U of Chicago P, 1983.

Lindenfeld, Laura, and Fabio Parasecoli. *Feasting Our Eyes: Food Films and Cultural Identity in the United States*. New York: Columbia UP, 2016.

Lott, N., and T. Ross. "Tracking and Evaluating U.S. Billion Dollar Weather Disasters, 1980–2005." *AMS Forum: Environmental Risk and Impacts on Society: Success and Challenges* (2006). https://www.ncdc.noaa.gov/billions/.

Loudermilk, Andrew. "Eating *Dawn* in the Dark: Zombie Desire and Commodified Identity in George Romero's *Dawn of the Dead*." *Journal of Consumer Culture* 3 (March 2003): 83–108.

Love, John F. *McDonald's: Behind the Arches*. New York: Bantam, 1986.
Lutts, Ralph H. "Rachel Carson's *Silent Spring*, Radioactive Fallout, and the Environmental Movement." *Environmental Review* 9.3 (Autumn 1985): 210–25.
Lyons, Pat. "Prescription for Harm: Diet Industry Influence, Public Health Policy, and the 'Obesity' Epidemic." *The Fat Studies Reader*. Ed. Esther Rothblum and Sondra Solovay. New York: New York UP, 2009. 75–87.
Magistrale, Tony. "Transmogrified Gothic: The Novels of Thomas Harris." *A Dark Night's Dreaming: Contemporary American Horror Fiction*. Ed. Tony Magistrale and Michael A. Morrison. Columbia: U of South Carolina P, 1996. 27–41.
Magistrale, Tony. *Stephen King, The Second Decade: Danse Macabre to The Dark Half*. Woodbridge, CT: Twayne, 1992.
Maguire, Joseph, and Louise Mansfiend. "'No-Body's Perfect': Women, Aerobics, and the Body Beautiful." *Sociology of Sport Journal* 15 (1998): 109–37.
McCammon, Robert R. "Eat Me." *Book of the Dead*. Ed. John Skipp and Craig Spector. New York: Bantam, 1989. 379–90.
McCammon, Robert R. *They Thirst*. 1981. Burton, MI: Subterranean Press, 2013.
McCarthy, Tom. *Auto Mania: Cars, Consumers, and the Environment*. New Haven, CT: Yale UP, 2009.
McConnell, Chan. "Blossom." *Book of the Dead*. Ed. John Skipp and Craig Spector. New York: Bantam, 1989. 15–20.
McElroy, Frank. *The Life of Vantile Mack, the Infant Lambert; or Giant Baby, Together with Causes Assigned for His Extraordinary Growth*. New York: Frank McElroy, 1860.
McKibben, William. *The End of Nature*. New York: Random House, 1989.
McKittrick, Casey. *Hitchcock's Appetites: The Corpulent Plots of Desire and Dread*. New York: Bloomsbury, 2017.
Miller, Carl F. "'Where the Beat Sounds the Same': *American Psycho* and the Cultural Capital of Pop Music." *Write in Tune: Contemporary Music in Fiction*. Ed. Erich Hertz and Jeffrey Roessner. London: Bloomsbury, 2014. 55–67.
Miller, Cynthia J. "Liberating the Vampire, but not the Woman: Kathryn Bigelow's *Near Dark* (1987)." *Dracula's Daughters: The Female Vampire on Film*. Ed. Douglas Brode and Leah Deyneka. New York: Scarecrow Press, 2014. 267–84.
Miller, Cynthia J., and A. Bowdoin Van Riper. "Introduction." *What's Eating You? Food and Horror on Screen*. New York: Bloomsbury, 2017. 1–12.
Miller, Douglas T., and Marion Nowak. *The Fifties: The Way We Really Were*. New York: Doubleday, 1977.
Miller, Jeff, and Jonathan Deutsch. *Food Studies: An Introduction to Research Methods*. New York: Bloomsbury, 2010.
Mills, Nicolaus. "The Culture of Triumph and the Spirit of the Times." *Culture in an Age of Money: The Legacy of the 1980s in America*. Ed. Nicolaus Mills. Chicago: Ivan R. Dee, 1990. 11–26.
Mintz, Sidney. *Sweetness and Power: The Place of Sugar in Modern History*. New York: Penguin, 1985.
Mitchell, David T. and Sharon L. Snyder. *Narrative Prosthesis: Disability and the Dependencies of Discourse*. Ann Arbor: U of Michigan P, 2000.

Morgan, Kathryn Pauly. "Women and the Knife: Cosmetic Surgery and the Colonization of Women's Bodies." *Hypatia* 6.3 (Autumn 1991): 25–53.

Morton, Timothy. *Ecology without Nature: Rethinking Environmental Aesthetics*. Boston, MA: Harvard UP, 2007.

Moss, Michael. *Salt Sugar Fat: How the Food Giants Hooked Us*. New York: Random House, 2013.

Murphet, Julian. *Bret Easton Ellis's* American Psycho: *A Reader's Guide*. New York: Bloomsbury, 2002.

Murphy, Bernice M. *The Rural Gothic in American Popular Culture: Backwoods Horror and Terror in the Wilderness*. New York: Palgrave, 2013.

Murray, Robin L., and Joseph K. Heumann. *Ecology and Popular Film: Cinema on the Edge*. New York: State U of New York P, 2009.

Murray, Robin L., and Joseph K. Heumann. *Monstrous Nature: Environment and Horror on the Big Screen*. Lincoln: U of Nebraska P, 2016.

Newbury, Michael. "Fast Zombie/Slow Zombie: Food Writing, Horror Movies, and Agribusiness Apocalypse." *American Literary History* 24.1 (2012): 87–114.

Newman, Richard S. *Love Canal: A Toxic History from Colonial Times to the Present*. New York: Oxford UP, 2016.

Newman, Tony. "Nancy Reagan's Role in the Disastrous War on Drugs." *Drug Policy Alliance*, March 6, 2016. http://www.drugpolicy.org/blog/nancy-reagans-role-disastrous-war-drugs.

Newton-John, Olivia. *Livwise: Easy Recipes for a Healthy, Happy Life*. Guilford, CT: Lyons Press, 2012.

Newton-John, Olivia. "Physical." *Physical*. MCA, 1991.

Nixon, Nicola. "When Hollywood Sucks: Or Young Girls, Lost Boys, and Vampirism in the Age of Reagan." *Blood Read: The Vampire as Metaphor in Contemporary Culture*. Philadelphia: U of Pennsylvania P, 1997. 115–28.

Nixon, Rob. *Slow Violent and the Environmentalism of the Poor*. Boston, MA: Harvard UP, 2013.

Nowell, Richard. *Blood Money: A History of the First Teen Slasher Film Cycle*. New York: Bloomsbury, 2010.

Oliver, Eric. *Fat Politics: The Real Story behind America's Obesity Epidemic*. New York: Oxford UP, 2006.

Ott, Riki. *Not One Drop: Betrayal and Courage in the Wake of the Exxon Valdez Oil Spill*. White River Junction, VT: Chelsea Green Publishing, 2008.

The Oxford Companion to the Body. Ed. Colin Blakemore and Shelia Jennett. New York: Oxford UP, 2002.

Palast, Greg. "Court Rewards Exxon for Valdez Oil Spill." *Chicago Tribute* (revised), June 25, 2008. Rpt: http://www.gregpalast.com/court-rewards-exxon-for-valdez-oil-spill/.

Pellow, David Naguib. *Garbage Wars: The Struggle for Environmental Justice in Chicago*. Cambridge, MA: MIT Press, 2004.

Pendergrast, Mark. *For God, Country, and Coca-Cola: The Definitive History of the Great American Soft Drink and the Company That Makes It*. New York: Basic Books, 1993.

Pharr, Mary. "Vampiric Appetite in *I Am Legend, Salem's Lot,* and *The Hunger*." *The Blood Is the Life: Vampires in Literature*. Ed. Leonard G. Heldreth and Mary Pharr. Bowling Green, OH: Popular Press, 1999. 93–103.

Phillips, Kendall R. "'You Said Forever': Postmodern Temporality in Tony Scott's *The Hunger.*" *Dracula's Daughters: The Female Vampire on Film*. Ed. Douglas Brode and Leah Deyneka. New York: Scarecrow Press, 2014. 253–66.

Phillips, Kendall R. *Projected Fears: Horror Films and American Culture*. Westport, CT: Praeger, 2005.

Pollan, Michael. *The Omnivore's Dilemma: A Natural History of Four Meals*. New York: Penguin Press, 2006.

Poole, Gaye. *Reel Meals, Set Meals: Food in Film and Theatre*. Sydney, Australia: Currency Press, 1999.

Prince, Stephen. *A New Pot of Gold: Hollywood under the Electronic Rainbow, 1980–1989*. New York: Scribner's, 2000.

Quinzio, Jeri. *Of Sugar and Snow: A History of Ice Cream Making*. Berkeley: U of California P, 2009.

Ramsland, Katherine. "The Lived World of Anne Rice's Novels." *The Gothic World of Anne Rice*. Ed. Gary Hoppenstand and Ray B. Browne. Bowling Green, OH: Bowling Green UP, 1996. 13–34.

Ray, Sarah Jaquette. *The Ecological Other: Environmental Exclusion in American Culture*. Tucson: U of Arizona P, 2013.

Reed, Ryan. "Buffalo Bill's *Silence of the Lambs* House for Sale." *Rolling Stone*, August 19, 2015. http://www.rollingstone.com/tv/news/buffalo-bills-silence-of-the-lambs-house-for-sale-20150819.

"Revisiting Buffett—Coca-Cola in 1988." *Gurufocus,* January 19, 2013. http://www.gurufocus.com/news/205476/revisiting-buffett—cocacola-in-1988.

Rice, Anne. *Interview with the Vampire*. 1976. New York: Ballantine, 2014.

Rice, Anne. *The Vampire Lestat*. 1985. New York: Ballantine, 2014.

Rice, Anne. *The Queen of the Damned*. 1988. New York: Ballantine, 2010.

Richardson, Niall. "*Feed*: A Representation of Feederism or Fatsploitation?" *Transgression in Anglo-American Cinema: Gender, Sex, and the Deviant Body*. Ed. Joel Gwynne. New York: Wallflower Press, 2016. 43–56.

Ritzer, George. *The McDonaldization of Society*. 1993. 8th ed. Thousand Oaks, CA: Sage, 2014.

Roberts, Paul. *The End of Food*. New York: Mariner Books, 2009.

Robinson, Jessica. *Life Lessons from Slasher Films*. Lanham, MD: Scarecrow Press, 2012.

Rockoff, Adam. *Going to Pieces: The Rise and Fall of the Slasher Film, 1978 to 1986*. Jefferson, NC: McFarland, 2002.

Rome, Adam. *The Bulldozer in the Countryside: Suburban Sprawl and the Rise of American Environmentalism*. New York: Cambridge UP, 2001.

Roper, Caitlin. "*Geek Love* at 25: How a Freak Family Inspired Your Pop Culture Heroes." *Wired*, March 7, 2014. http://www.wired.com/2014/03/geek-love/.

Roy, Parama. *Alimentary Tracts: Appetites, Aversions, and the Postcolonial*. Durham, NC: Duke UP, 2010.

Rozin, Paul. "The Selection of Foods by Rats, Humans, and Other Animals." *Advances in the Study of Behavior*. Ed. Jay S. Rosenblatt, Robert A. Hinde, Evelyn Shaw, and Colin Beer. New York: Academic Press, 1976. 21–76.

Rueckert, William. "Literature and Ecology: An Experiment in Ecocriticism." *Iowa Review* 91 (Winter 1978): 71–86.
Russell, Emily. *Reading Embodied Citizenship: Disability, Narrative, and the Body Politic*. New Brunswick, NJ: Rutgers UP, 2011.
Russell, Jamie. *The Book of the Dead: The Complete History of Zombie Cinema*. London: Titan Books, 2014.
Rust, Stephen A., and Carter Soles. "Living in Fear, Living in Dread, Pretty Soon We'll All Be Dead." *Interdisciplinary Studies in Literature and Environment* 21.3 (Summer 2014): 509–12.
Saguy, Abigail C. *What's Wrong with Fat?* New York: Oxford UP, 2013.
Sancton, Thomas A. "Planet of the Year: What on Earth Are We Doing?" *Time*, January 2, 1989: 26–30.
Sceats, Sarah. *Food, Consumption, and the Body in Contemporary Women's Fiction*. New York: Cambridge UP, 2000.
Schlosser, Eric. *Fast Food Nation: The Dark Side of the All-American Meal*. New York: Mariner Books, 2001.
Schneider, Steven Jay. "'Suck . . . don't suck': Framing Ideology in Kathryn Bigelow's *Near Dark*." *The Cinema of Kathryn Bigelow: Hollywood Transgressor* Ed. Deborah Jermyn and Sean Redmond. New York: Wallflower Press, 2003. 72–90.
Schwartz, Hillel. *Never Satisfied: A Cultural History of Diets, Fantasies and Fat*. New York: Free Press, 1986.
Schwarzenegger, Arnold. *Shape Up with Arnold*. Charlotte, NC: United American Video, 1982.
Seid, Roberta Pollack. *Never Too Thin: Why Women Are at War with Their Bodies*. New York: Prentice Hall, 1989.
Shabecoff, Philip. "With No Room at the Dump, U.S. Faces Garbage Crisis." *New York Times*, June 29, 1987. http://www.nytimes.com/1987/06/29/us/with-no-room-at-the-dump-us-faces-a-garbage-crisis.html.
Shaviro, Steven. *The Cinematic Body*. Minneapolis: U of Minnesota P, 1993.
Sheraton, Mimi. "Restaurants: In the Village, Creole Charm." *New York Times*, February 18, 1983. http://events.nytimes.com/mem/nycreview.html?res=9501E4D7153BF93BA25751 C0A965948260.
Shilts, Randy. *And the Band Played On: Politics, People, and the AIDS Epidemic*. New York: St. Martin's Press, 1987.
Smith, Andrew F. *Encyclopedia of Junk and Fast Food*. Westport, CT: Greenwood Press, 2006.
Soles, Carter. "'And No Birds Sing': Discourses of Environmental Apocalypse in *The Birds* and *Night of the Living Dead*." *ISLE: Interdisciplinary Studies in Literature and Environment* 21.3 (Summer 2014): 526–37.
Soles, Carter. "Sympathy for the Devil: The Cannibalistic Hillbilly in 1970s Rural Slasher Films." *Ecocinema: Theory and Practice*. Ed. Stephen Rust, Salma Monani, and Sean Cubitt. New York: Routledge, 2012. 233–50.
Solier, Isabelle de. *Food and the Self: Consumption, Production, and Material Culture*. New York: Bloomsbury, 2013.

Sontag, Susan. *AIDS and Its Metaphors*. New York: Farrar, Straus, and Giroux, 1989.

Staats, Hans. "Let Them Eat Steak: Food and the Family Horror Film Cycle." *What's Eating You: Food and Horror on Screen*. Ed. Cynthia J. Miller and A. Bowdoin Van Riper. New York: Bloomsbury, 2017. 31–47.

Striber, Whitley. *The Hunger*. New York: Pocket Books, 1981.

Stuart, Tessa. "Pop-Culture Legacy of Nancy Reagan's 'Just Say No' Campaign." *Rolling Stone*, March 7, 2016. https://www.rollingstone.com/politics/news/pop-culture-legacy-of-nancy-reagans-just-say-no-campaign-20160307.

Stube, Christine. "I Can't Believe It's Yogurt! Dallas." *Dairy Foods* 91.2 (February 1990): 62.

Stutzman, Rene. "Cops Mistook Krispy Kreme Doughnut Glaze for Meth, Orlando Man Says." *Orlando Sentinel*, July 30, 2016. http://www.orlandosentinel.com/news/breaking-news/os-cop-mistook-doughnut-glaze-for-meth-20160727-story.html.

Sullivan, Deborah. *Cosmetic Surgery: The Cutting Edge of Commercial Medicine in America*. New Brunswick, NJ: Rutgers UP, 2000.

Sullivan, Nell. "Katherine Dunn's *Geek Love* and the Vicissitudes of Class." *Critique: Studies in Contemporary Fiction* 54.4 (2013): 410–21.

Sullivan, Tim. "Mr. Holland's Opus." *Shock and Roll* (Issue 2), September 1, 2008. http://www.iconsoffright.com/SHOCK_02.htm.

Swerdloff, Alex. "The Government Says Our Halloween Pumpkins Are Destroying the Environment." *Munchies Vice*, October 28, 2016. https://munchies.vice.com/en_us/article/the-government-says-our-halloween-pumpkins-are-destroying-the-environment.

Tasker, Yvonne. *The Silence of the Lambs*. London: BFI/Palgrave, 2002.

Tasker, Yvonne. *Working Girls: Gender and Sexuality in Popular Culture*. New York: Routledge, 1998.

Taylor, Dorceta. *Toxic Communities: Environmental Racism, Industrial Pollution, and Residential Mobility*. New York: New York UP, 2014.

"Thalidomide Apology Insulting, Campaigners Say." *BBC News*, September 1, 2012. http://www.bbc.com/news/health-19448046. Web, June 30, 2017.

Thomson, Rosemarie Garland. *Extraordinary Bodies: Figuring Physical Disability in American Culture and Literature*. New York: Columbia UP, 1997.

Tordoff, Michael G. "How Do Non-Nutritive Sweeteners Increase Food Intake?" *Appetite* 11 (1988): 5–11.

Toufexis, Anastasia. "Overpopulation: Too Many Mouths to Feed." *Time*, January 2, 1989: 47–49.

Van Riper, Bowdoin. "The Goo in You: Food as Invader in *The Stuff*." *What's Eating You? Food and Horror on Screen*. Ed. Cynthia J. Miller and A. Bowdoin Van Riper. New York: Bloomsbury, 2017. 81–95.

Wann, Marilyn. "Fat Studies: An Invitation to Revolution." *The Fat Studies Reader*. Ed. Esther Rothblum and Sondra Solovay. New York: New York UP, 2009. ix–xxv.

Waugh, Robert H. "The Butterfly and the Beast: The Imprisoned Soul in Thomas Harris's Lecter Trilogy." *Dissecting Hannibal Lecter: Essays on the Novels of Thomas Harris*. Ed. Benjamin Szumskyj. Jefferson, NC: McFarland, 2008. 68–86.

Weese, Katherine. "Normalizing Freakery: Katherine Dunn's *Geek Love* and the Female Grotesque." *Critique* 41.4 (Summer 2000): 349–64.

Weiss, Laura B. *Ice Cream: A Global History*. London: Reaktion Books, 2011.
Westling, Louise. *Cambridge Companion to Literature and the Environment*. New York: Cambridge UP, 2013. 1–16.
"What Americans Are Drinking." *Chicago Tribune*, December 20, 1992. http://articles.chicagotribune.com/1992-12-20/entertainment/9204250625_1_soft-drinks-breakfast-beverage-juice.
"What Is Acid Rain?" United States Environmental Protection Agency. https://www.epa.gov/acidrain/what-acid-rain.
Whitehead, Mark. *Slasher Movies*. Harpenden, England: Pocket Essentials, 2000.
Williams, Tony. *The Cinema of George Romeo: Knight of the Living Dead*. New York: Columbia UP, 2003.
Williams, Tony. *Larry Cohen: The Radical Allegories of an Independent Filmmaker*. Jefferson, NC: McFarland, 1997.
Williams, Tony. *Hearths of Darkness: The Family in the American Horror Film*. Madison, NJ: Fairleigh Dickinson UP, 1996.
Wood, Robin. *Hollywood from Vietnam to Reagan . . . and Beyond*. New York: Columbia UP, 2003.
Wyman, Bill. "Did 'Thriller' Really Sell a Hundred Million Copies?" *New Yorker*, January 4, 2013. http://www.newyorker.com/culture/culture-desk/did-thriller-really-sell-a-hundred-million-copies.
Xu, Wenying. *Eating Identities: Reading Food in Asian American Literature*. Honolulu: U of Hawaii P, 2007.
Zimring, Carl A. *Clean and White: A History of Environmental Racism in the United States*. New York: New York UP, 2016.
Zinoman, Jason. *Shock Value: How a Few Eccentric Outsiders Gave Us Nightmares, Conquered Hollywood, and Invented Modern Horror*. New York: Penguin, 2012.

FILMOGRAPHY

American Psycho. Screenplay by Mary Harron and Guinevere Turner. Dir. Mary Harron. Perf. Christian Bale. Lionsgate, 2000.
American Werewolf in London. Screenplay by John Landis. Dir. John Landis. Perf. David Naughton and Jenny Agutter. Universal Pictures, 1981.
C.H.U.D. Screenplay by Parnell Hall. Dir. Douglas Cheek. Perf. John Heard and Daniel Stern. New World Pictures, 1984.
Dawn of the Dead. Screenplay by George A. Romero. Dir. George A. Romero. Perf. David Emge, Ken Foree, and Scott Reiniger. United Film Distribution Company, 1979.
Day of the Dead. Screenplay by George A. Romero. Dir. George A. Romero. Perf. Lori Cardille, Terry Alexander, and Joe Pilato. United Film Distribution Company, 1985.
Death Spa. Dir. Michael Fischa. Screenplay by James Bartruff and Mitch Paradise. Perf. William Bumiller and Brenda Bakke. MPI Home Video, 1989.
The Fly. Screenplay by Charles Edward Logue and David Cronenberg. Dir. David Cronenberg. Perf. Jeff Goldblum and Geena Davis. 20th Century Fox, 1986.
Fright Night. Screenplay by Tom Holland. Dir. Tom Holland. Perf. William Ragsdale, Roddy McDowall, and Chris Sarandon. Columbia Pictures, 1985.
Fright Night Part 2. Screenplay by Tommy Lee Wallace. Dir. Tommy Lee Wallace. Perf. William Ragsdale and Roddy McDowall. New Century/Vista TriStar Pictures, 1988.
Ghostbusters. Screenplay by Dan Akroyd and Harold Ramis. Dir. Ivan Reitman. Perf. Bill Murray, Sigourney Weaver, and Rick Moranis. Columbia Pictures, 1984.
The Goonies. Screenplay by Chris Columbus. Dir. Richard Donner. Perf. Sean Astin, Josh Brolin, and Jeff Cohen. Warner Brothers, 1985.
Happy Birthday to Me. Screenplay by Timothy Bond, Peter Jobin, and John Saxton. Dir. J. Lee Thompson. Perf. Melissa Sue Anderson, Glenn Ford, and Lawrence Dane. Columbia Pictures, 1981.
The Hunger. Screenplay by Ivan Davis and Michael Thomas. Dir. Tony Scott. Perf. Catherine Deneuve, David Bowie, and Susan Sarandon. MGM/UA Entertainment Company, 1983.
Killer Workout. Screenplay by David A. Prior. Dir. David A. Prior. Perf. Marcia Karr and David James Campbell. Academy Home Entertainment, 1987.
The Lost Boys. Screenplay by Janice Fischer, James Jeremias, and Jeffrey Boam. Dir. Joel Schumacher. Perf. Jason Patric, Kiefer Sutherland, and Dianne Wiest. Warner Brothers, 1987.
Monster Squad. Screenplay by Shane Black and Fred Dekker. Dir. Fred Dekker. Perf. Andre Gower and Brent Chalem. TriStar Pictures, 1987.

Motel Hell. Screenplay by Robert Jaffe and Steven-Charles Jaffe. Dir. Kevin Connor. Perf. Rory Calhoun and Nancy Parsons. United Artists, 1980.

My Best Friend Is a Vampire. Screenplay by Ted Murphy. Dir. Jimmy Huston. Perf. Robert Sean Leonard and Cheryl Pollak. Kings Road Entertainment, 1987.

Near Dark. Screenplay by Kathryn Bigelow and Eric Red. Dir. Kathryn Bigelow. Perf. Adrian Pasdar, Jenny Wright, and Bill Paxton. DeLaurentiis Entertainment Group, 1987.

A Nightmare on Elm Street. Screenplay by Wes Craven. Dir. Wes Craven. Perf. Robert Englund, Heather Langenkamp, and Johnny Depp. New Line Cinema, 1984.

A Nightmare on Elm Street 2: Freddy's Revenge. Screenplay by David Chaskin. Dir. Jack Sholder. Perf. Robert Englund. New Line Cinema, 1985.

A Nightmare on Elm Street 4: The Dream Master. Screenplay by Brian Helgeland and Scott Pierce. Dir. Renny Harlin. Perf. Robert Englund and Lisa Wilcox. New Line Cinema, 1988.

A Nightmare on Elm Street 5: The Dream Child. Screenplay by Leslie Bohem. Dir. Stephen Hopkins. Perf. Robert Englund and Lisa Wilcox. New Line Cinema, 1989.

Night of the Living Dead. Screenplay by George A. Romero and John Russo. Dir. George A. Romero. Perf. Duane Jones and Judith O'Dea. Walter Reade Organization and Continental Distributing, 1968.

Once Bitten. Screenplay by Jonathan Roberts, David Hines, Jeffrey Hause, and Terence Marsh. Dir. Howard Storm. Perf. Jim Carrey and Lauren Hutton. The Samuel Goldwyn Company, 1985.

Poltergeist. Screenplay by Steven Spielberg, Michael Grais, and Mark Victor. Dir. Tobe Hooper. Perf. JoBeth Williams and Craig T. Nelson. MGM/UA Entertainment, 1982.

The Queen of the Damned. Screenplay by Scott Abbott and Michael Petroni. Dir. Michael Rymer. Per. Aaliyah and Stuart Townsend. Warner Brothers, 2002.

Redneck Zombies. Screenplay by Fester Smellman. Dir. Pericles Lewnes. Perf. Lisa de Haven and W. E. Benson. Troma Entertainment, 1987.

The Return of the Living Dead. Screenplay by Dan O'Bannon. Dir. Dan O'Bannon. Perf. Clu Galuger and James Karen. Orion Pictures, 1985.

The Return of the Living Dead Part II. Screenplay by Ken Wiederhorn. Dir. Ken Wiederhorn. Perf. James Karen and Thom Matthews. Lorimar Motion Pictures, 1988.

A Return to Salem's Lot. Screenplay by Larry Cohen and James Dixon. Dir. Larry Cohen. Perf. Michael Moriarty. Warner Brothers, 1987.

The Secret of My Success. Screenplay by Jim Cash, Jack Epps, and A. J. Carothers. Dir. Herbert Ross. Perf. Michael J. Fox and Helen Slater. Universal Pictures, 1987.

The Silence of the Lambs. Screenplay by Ted Tally. Dir. Jonathan Demme. Perf. Jodie Foster, Anthony Hopkins, and Ted Levine. Orion Pictures, 1991.

The Stuff. Screenplay by Larry Cohen. Dir. Larry Cohen. Perf. Michael Moriarty and Andrea Marcovicci. New World Pictures, 1985.

Surf II. Screenplay by Randall M. Badat. Dir. Randall M. Badat. Perf. Eric Stoltz and Peter Isacksen. Media Home Entertainment, 1984.

Teen Wolf. Screenplay by Jeph Loeb and Matthew Weisman. Dir. Rod Daniel. Perf. Michael J. Fox and Mark Holton. Atlantic Releasing Corporation, 1985.

Teen Wolf Too. Screenplay by R. Timothy Kring. Dir. Christopher Leitch. Perf. Jason Bateman and Mark Holton. Atlantic Releasing Corporation, 1987.

Thinner. Screenplay by Michael McDowell and Tom Holland. Dir. Tom Holland. Perf. Robert John Burke and Joe Mantegna. Paramount Pictures, 1996.

Toxic Zombies. Screenplay by Charles McCrann. Dir. Charles McCrann. Perf. Charles McCrann and Beverly Shapiro. Parker National Distributing, 1980.

INDEX

Abbott, Stacy, 98
Acid rain. *See* Toxic contamination
Adams, Rachel, 38
Addiction, 135, 168, 181, 188–89, 198; alcohol, 21, 78, 87, 94, 96, 104–5, 109, 114, 124–25, 127, 132, 134, 136; drug, 19, 21, 78, 87, 94, 103, 114; to natural resources, 139, 169, 188; processed food, 4, 8, 10, 12, 15, 25, 27, 30, 34–35, 87–88, 91–93, 96, 99–100, 103–4, 106, 108, 111, 114, 125, 130–33, 135–36, 191, 197; sugar, 23, 78, 105, 114, 124–25, 133, 136, 138, 187–92, 208n22; tobacco/nicotine, 78, 83, 105, 114, 118, 132, 135–36
Aerobics. *See* Exercise
Agriculture, 12, 75, 89, 106, 144
Al Binewski (*Geek Love*), 37–38
Albritton, Robert, 93
Alcoholism. *See* Addiction
Alex (*Fright Night Part 2*), 120
Alice (*The Hunger*), 134
Allué, Sonia Baelo, 67
Alma Witherspoon (*Geek Love*), 40–43, 45
Amelia ("Blossom"), 172–75
American Psycho (film), 10, 64, 71, 80–82
American Psycho (novel), 7, 10, 17, 63, 66–68, 73–74, 76, 80–81, 84
Aoyama, Tomoko, 89
Appearance. *See* Fatness
Appelbaum, Robert, 89
Appetite. *See* Consumerism
Archer, Jayne, 89
"Are You Ready for Freddy?," 4

Armand (*The Queen of the Damned*), 126–27
Arturo "Arty" Binewski (*Geek Love*), 37–43, 46, 48
Asava, Zélie, 129
Auerbach, Nina, 88

Baby Jenks (*The Queen of the Damned*), 125–26
Bachman, Richard. *See* King, Stephen
Bacon, Simon, 122
Bailey, Matthew, 152
Barbra (*Night of the Living Dead*), 149–50
Barnum, P. T., 32, 39–40
Baron, Cynthia, 89–91
Belasco, Warren, 11, 43, 90
Ben (*Night of the Living Dead*), 149–50
Benjamin Raspail (*The Silence of the Lambs*), 54, 62
Bennett, William, 10
Berent, Stanislaus "Stanley," 36–37
Bernard, Mark, 90–91
Biddle, Jeff, 9
Bigelow, Kathryn, 92, 104–7
Bill ("Like Pavlov's Dogs"), 181
Billy Halleck (*Thinner*), 24–36
Bishop, Kyle William, 151
Bloch, Robert, 68
"Blossom," 141, 172, 174–76
Bodily alteration: through diet, 23–24, 60, 53, 132–33; through exercise, 20, 29, 53, 60, 69–70, 74–75; through surgery, 39, 42, 45–46, 53–55, 60

231

Bogdan, Robert, 40
Bonnie ("Like Pavlov's Dogs"), 181
Book of the Dead, 141, 171–72, 176, 197
Bordo, Susan, 21
Bosch, Carl, 143
Bosky, Bernadette, 25
Bower, Anne L., 89
Boyett, Stephen, 14, 141, 172, 179–80, 186
Braziel, Jana Evans, 9
Brenda ("Eat Me"), 175–76
Brown, Jennifer, 68, 79
Brown, Michael, 145
Browning, Tod, 40, 88, 137
Bryce (*American Psycho*), 84
Bub (*Day of the Dead*), 172
Buell, Lawrence, 13, 139
Buffalo Bill (*The Silence of the Lambs*), 10, 17, 49–62
Bulimia. *See* Fatness
Bundy, Ted, 67
Burt (*The Return of the Living Dead*), 161–62
Bush, George H. W., 65–67, 85

Caleb Colton (*Near Dark*), 92, 104–9
Candy (*My Best Friend Is a Vampire*), 115
Cannibalism: and class, 50, 62, 66, 75, 79, 85; and consumerism, 14, 68, 78–79, 83–84, 91, 123–24, 128, 135, 178–79, 183; and ritual, 127–29; and zombies, 7, 155, 166, 170, 174, 178–79
Carina (*Geek Love*), 45
Carroll, Noël, 17
Carruth, Allison, 89
Cars, 26, 30, 33, 103; and consumerism, 5, 24, 27, 76, 112, 126, 157, 168, 182, 188, 190; dependency on, 108, 165, 169, 181, 183; environmental harm of, 81, 111, 142, 153, 156, 161–62, 165, 169, 181; proliferation of, 142, 165, 188
Carson, Diane, 90–91
Carson, Rachel, 12–13, 148, 166
Carter, Jimmy, 28, 63

Catherine Martin (*The Silence of the Lambs*), 55, 57, 61
Charley Brewster (*Fright Night*), 91, 118–21
Chernin, Kim, 10
Chlorofluorocarbons. *See* Pollution
Chocolate Chip Charlie (*The Stuff*), 194–95
Christie (*American Psycho*), 79, 82–83
Christou, Maria, 88
Chrystal Lil Binewski (*Geek Love*), 37
Chuck (*Surf II*), 169
C.H.U.D., 160
Chunk (*The Goonies*), 15–16
Clarice Starling (*The Silence of the Lambs*), 49–59, 61–62
Climate change/global warming, 5, 23, 89, 141–43, 145, 198
Coca-Cola. *See* Soda
Cohen, Larry, 117, 187–89, 191, 193–94
Colby, Georgina, 67
Collings, Michael, 27
Connor, Kevin, 183
Cooper, Kenneth, 20
Counihan, Carole, 11, 90
Count Chocula, 88
Countess (*Once Bitten*), 110, 112–14
Courtney (*American Psycho*), 81, 83–84
Craven, Wes, 3–4
Craving. *See* Addiction
Creed, Barbara, 62

Dana (*Ghostbusters*), 23
Daniel Molloy (*Interview with the Vampire; The Queen of the Damned*), 126–27
Darla (*My Best Friend Is a Vampire*), 114–17
David (*The Lost Boys*), 99, 102
David "Mo" Rutherford (*The Stuff*), 187–88, 194–95
Davis, Blair, 91
Dawn of the Dead, 148–49, 151–53, 158, 179, 186
Day of the Dead, 14, 141, 147–49, 155–58, 172, 176, 186
Deke ("Like Pavlov's Dogs"), 181

Dekker, Fred, 15
Delville, Michel, 91
Demme, Jonathan, 49, 51–52, 55, 84
Detective Kimball (*American Psycho*), 83
Diet culture: and consumerism, 5, 10, 17; failure of, 8, 22–23, 30, 41, 50, 57; propagation of, 15, 42, 57; as self-destructive, 9, 26–27, 30–31, 33–34, 41–42, 44, 50, 56, 58, 60, 192; and self-restraint, 5, 19, 24, 34, 44–45, 93, 187, 190
Diet food. *See* Processed food
Dillard, R. H. W., 150
Doane, Janice, 128
Doc Mandel (*The Return of the Living Dead Part II*), 165
Dolan, Kathryn, 89
Donald, Adrienne, 61
Donner, Richard, 15–16
Dr. Chilton (*The Silence of the Lambs*), 63
Dr. Logan (*Day of the Dead*), 156, 158–59
Dr. Houston (*Thinner*), 30
Dracula (character), 15, 137
Dracula (film), 88, 136–37
Dracula (novel), 109, 119, 136–37
Dragoti, Stan, 137
Dunn, Katherine, 10, 16, 36–39, 41, 43–44, 48, 84
Dunn, Maggie, 89

"Eat Me," 141, 172, 175–76
Eating disorders. *See* Fatness
Ecocriticism, 12–13, 139–40, 152, 169
Ecohorror, 140–41, 148, 150, 160, 166, 172, 182, 187, 193
Ecojustice, 14
Ecosphereans ("Like Pavlov's Dogs"), 179, 182, 186
Elizabeth (*American Psycho*), 79
Ellis, Bret Easton, 7, 17, 66–73, 78–80, 84
Elly and Iphy Binewski (*Geek Love*), 41
Englund, Robert, 3–5
Evelyn (*American Psycho*), 69, 71–73, 84
"Evil" Ed (*Fright Night*), 118

Exercise: and aging, 19, 54–55, 70–71, 92, 114; anxieties surrounding, 23, 32, 41, 44, 57, 68–70, 72; and consumerism, 5–7, 10, 15, 20, 24, 28, 30, 41, 57, 60, 70, 192–93, 192, 197; and femininity, 19–20, 29–30, 53, 57; and masculinity, 18–20, 28–29, 69; and masochism, 9, 18–20, 56, 69; and self-discipline, 12, 15, 17, 20–21, 24, 26–28, 35–36, 69–70, 83; as supplemental to dieting, 20, 190; and vanity, 33, 69–70, 113. *See also* Bodily alteration

Fad diets. *See* Diet culture
Fang Gang, the (*The Queen of the Damned*), 125–26
Farmer Vincent (*Motel Hell*), 182–86
Fast food. *See* Processed food
Fat Boys, 4, 199n1
Fatness: and consumerism, 24, 42, 92–94; dangers of, 9–10 12, 17, 25–26, 58, 96; and desirability/discrimination, 4–5, 8–10, 15–26, 28–35, 41–46, 50–60, 68–74, 132, 196; and self-restraint, 4–5, 9, 15–16, 19–28, 31, 34–36, 40–45, 57, 70, 87, 124, 185, 191; and self-worth, 7, 15–16, 19, 21, 31–35, 41–60, 63, 69, 72–74, 84, 132, 196; as a spectacle, 15–16, 24, 31–33, 35–41, 47, 56–57, 72, 132; vilification of, 4–5, 10, 15, 17–19, 22–36, 39–45, 50, 53, 56, 58, 68, 74, 196
Fat studies, 9, 16
Fattest Family Exhibit, 37
Fine cuisine. *See* Haute cuisine
Fitness. *See* Exercise
Fitzpatrick, Joan, 89
Fonda, Jane, 18–21, 28, 30, 54, 113
Fonesca, Tony, 92
Food shortages, 14, 90, 141, 143, 145, 146, 155, 182–83
Food studies, 10–11, 89–90, 199n6
Ford, Henry, 142, 163
Fran (*Dawn of the Dead*), 154–55
Frank, Alexandra, 91

Frank (*The Return of the Living Dead*), 161–62
Freddy Krueger (*A Nightmare on Elm Street*), 3–6, 8, 198, 199n1
Fredrica Bimmel (*The Silence of the Lambs*), 53–54, 57–60
Freedman, Paul, 75
Fright Night, 91, 110, 118–19, 121
Fright Night Part 2, 12, 92, 110, 118–21, 196
Frog brothers (*The Lost Boys*), 98–99, 101–2
Funderburg, Anne, 190

Gagne, Paul R., 158
Gambin, Lee, 140
Garbage: consequences of, 144–45, 160, 197; and consumerism, 5, 99, 115, 134, 156, 180, 194, 197; proliferation of, 144, 156–58, 160, 162, 182, 194, 197
Garrard, Greg, 140
Gasoline. *See* Natural resources
Gastrocriticism, 88
Geek Love, 10, 16, 36–38, 40, 46, 48
Gein, Ed, 67
Gelder, Ken, 129
George Cooper (*C.H.U.D.*), 160
George Sullivan ("Home Delivery"), 177
Ghostbusters, 23
Gigante, Denise, 89
Glotfelty, Cheryll, 13
Gomel, Elana, 74
Goonies, The, 15–16
Grace ("Like Pavlov's Dogs"), 182
Grandpa (*The Lost Boys*), 98, 100–103
Greene, Gayle, 77
Greven, David, 54
Grimsdyke (*My Best Friend Is a Vampire*), 116
Gumb, Jame. *See* Buffalo Bill

Haggerty, George, 122
Haiffa ("Like Pavlov's Dogs"), 181
Halberstam, Judith, 54
Hallab, Mary, 109

Halsman, Philippe, 51–52
Hamermesh, Daniel, 9
Hannibal Lecter (*The Silence of the Lambs*), 14, 27, 49–54, 56, 61–63, 79
Hardin, Michael, 38
Harris, Thomas, 16, 50, 52, 56, 60, 84
Harron, Mary, 64, 80–84
Haute cuisine: and change, 50; and consumer excess, 61, 75–78, 82, 127, 173; overindulgence in, 68, 83, 136; and processed food, 127, 193; and refinement, 62, 79–80
Heidi Halleck (*Thinner*), 29–31, 33–34, 36
Heller, Tamar, 89
Herbicides. *See* Toxic contamination
Herndon, April Michelle, 9
Hertweck, Tom, 90
Heumann, Joseph K., 140
High-fructose corn syrup. *See* Sugar
Hitchcock, Alfred, 68, 98, 103, 166
Hodges, Devon, 128
Holland, Tom, 25, 91, 118–19
Home cooking. *See* Natural food
"Home Delivery," 14, 141, 172, 176, 178, 186
Homer (*Near Dark*), 107
Horror, 5, 8–10, 14–17, 24, 62, 82–83, 90, 92, 98, 104, 118–21, 128, 140, 197
Horror fiction, 16, 121, 171
Horror films, 7–8, 92, 119–20, 187
Hunger. *See* Addiction
Hunger, The (film), 130, 135–36
Hunger, The (novel), 92, 129, 136, 196
Huston, Jimmy, 116

Ida (*Motel Hell*), 182–86
In Voluptas Mors, 51–52
Interview with the Vampire, 122, 124, 126, 128

Jack ("Home Delivery"), 177–78
Jack Crawford (*The Silence of the Lambs*), 50, 54, 56, 62
Jacko (*Surf II*), 168
Jackson, Kenneth T., 164

Jackson, Michael, 141, 179–80
Jamie (*Once Bitten*), 111–12
Jason (*The Stuff*), 191–95
Jean (*American Psycho*), 83
Jeffords, Susan, 28
Jeremy (*A Return to Salem's Lot*), 117–18
Jeremy Capello (*My Best Friend Is a Vampire*), 114, 115, 116, 117–18
Jerry (*Toxic Zombies*), 167
Jesse (*Near Dark*), 109
Jesse (*The Queen of the Damned*), 128
Jim Crisp ("Eat Me"), 175–76
Jimmy ("Like Pavlov's Dogs"), 180
Joe Weber (*A Return to Salem's Lot*), 117–18
John (*Day of the Dead*), 156, 158–59
John (*The Hunger*), 130–31, 134–35
Johnny (*Night of the Living Dead*), 149–50
Johnny Big Head (*Surf II*), 169
Judge Rossington (*Thinner*), 32
Judy (*Night of the Living Dead*), 149
Junk food. *See* Processed food
"Just Say No" campaign, 87, 138

Keller, James R., 89
Khayman (*The Queen of the Damned*), 128
King, Stephen, 10, 14, 16, 24–27, 29–36, 84, 141, 172, 176–79, 186
King Enkil of Kemet (*The Queen of the Damned*), 127
Kleinknecht, William, 65
Koç, Mustafa, 11

La Berge, Leigh Claire, 67
Landfills. *See* Garbage
Lauro, Sarah Juliet, 147
LeBesco, Kathleen, 9
Leonard ("Like Pavlov's Dogs"), 181
Lestat de Lioncourt (*Vampire Chronicles*), 122–26, 128–29, 137
Lieutenant Boyle (*The Silence of the Lambs*), 62
"Like Pavlov's Dogs," 14, 141, 172, 179, 182, 186

Lindenfeld, Laura, 90
Lost Boys, The, 12, 92, 98–100, 102–3, 196
Loudermilk, Andrew, 151
Louis (*Ghostbusters*), 23
Louis de Pointe du Lac (*Interview with the Vampire*), 122, 124–26
Love at First Bite, 109–10, 137
Loy Colton (*Near Dark*), 106–7
Lucy (*The Lost Boys*), 98–99, 101–2
Lugosi, Bela, 88, 137
Lutts, Ralph H., 13

Mack, Vantile, 40, 202n22
Maddie Pace ("Home Delivery"), 177–79
Madonna, 19, 58, 59, 205n58
Mae (*Near Dark*), 92, 104–6, 108–9
Magistrale, Tony, 53
Maguire, Joseph, 19
Maharet (*The Queen of the Damned*), 127
Mansfiend, Louise, 20
Marion Crane (*Psycho*), 98
Mark Kendall (*Once Bitten*), 91, 110–14
Marly ("Like Pavlov's Dogs"), 180–82
Mary Crane (*Psycho*), 68, 204n53
Mary Lick (*Geek Love*), 38–39, 43, 44, 45–46, 48
Max (*The Lost Boys*), 98, 102–3
McCammon, Robert R., 91, 141, 172, 175–76
McConnell, Chan, 141, 172–74
McCrann, Charles, 166
McDermott (*American Psycho*), 78
McDermott (*Day of the Dead*), 156
McDonald's, 96–97, 112, 187–88; and class, 78, 84, 133; cravings for, 26, 34, 92, 124, 130, 133, 196; and illness, 97; menu changes, 8, 15, 95, 197; and nutrition, 98, 113; reliance on, 92, 135
McKibben, William, 142–44
McKittrick, Casey, 16
Meat/poultry industry, 96, 106, 155, 171, 184
Mekare (*The Queen of the Damned*), 127
Menlo Schwatzer (*Surf II*), 168–69
Methane gas. *See* Pollution

Michael (*The Lost Boys*), 98–100, 103
Miller, Cynthia J., 91, 92, 104
Miller, Douglas, 165
Mills, Nicolaus, 65
Minnoch, Jon Brower, 35
Mintz, Sydney M., 11
Miranda (*Geek Love*), 38, 41
Miriam Blaylock (*The Hunger*), 129–32, 134–36
Mitchell, David T., 38
Morgan, Kathryn Pauly, 46–48
Moss, Michael, 93, 95
Motel Hell, 182–86
Mr. Beaker (*Surf II*), 169
Mr. Cooper (*Night of the Living Dead*), 149–50
Mr. Vickers (*The Stuff*), 195
Murphet, Julian, 67, 82
Murray, Robin L., 140
My Best Friend Is a Vampire, 12, 93, 110, 114, 116

Natural food: and morality, 114–16, 118; versus processed foods, 90, 121; and vampirism, 92, 131, 134; virtues of, 102, 104, 107
Natural resources: competition for, 63, 141–42, 145, 172, 185; and consumerism, 109, 144, 196–97; squandering of, 5, 14, 109, 139, 142, 145, 148–50, 153–54, 158–60, 165, 167–69, 173, 177, 179, 182, 195–96, 198; and transportation, 104, 108, 150, 197
Near Dark, 12, 92, 104–8, 196
Newbury, Michael, 91, 146
Newman, Richard S., 145
Newton-John, Olivia, 17–19, 21, 26, 28, 30, 60
Night of the Living Dead, 140, 146, 148–50, 152, 161
Nightmare on Elm Street, A, 4, 6
Nightmare on Elm Street 2: Freddy's Revenge, A, 5
Nightmare on Elm Street 4: The Dream Master, A, 3–4

Nightmare on Elm Street 5: The Dream Child, A, 4
Nixon, Nicola, 102
Nixon, Rob, 14
Nora (*My Best Friend Is a Vampire*), 115
Norma Bates (*Psycho*), 68
Norman Bates (*Psycho*), 68–69
Norris, Andrew, 91
Nowak, Marion, 165

O'Bannon, Dan, 161
Obesity. *See* Fatness
Officer Hopley (*Thinner*), 33
Officer Wooley (*Dawn of the Dead*), 152
Oil. *See* Natural resources
Oliver, Eric, 19
Olympia "Oly" Binewski (*Geek Love*), 38, 40–41, 43, 45
Once Bitten, 12, 91–92, 109–11, 196
Organic food. *See* Natural Food
Overpopulation. *See* Zombies

Parasecoli, Fabio, 90
Patrick Bateman (*American Psycho*), 7, 10, 64, 66–74, 76–85
Paul Allen (*American Psycho*), 81
Pellow, David, 144
Pemberton, John, 94
Pembry (*The Silence of the Lambs*), 54
Pesticides. *See* Toxic contamination
Peter (*Dawn of the Dead*), 153–54
Peter Venkman, Dr. (*Ghostbusters*), 24
Peter Vincent (*Fright Night*), 119
Petroleum. *See* Natural resources
Pharr, Mary, 130
Phillips, Kendall R., 8, 92
"Physical," 17–20, 26, 60
Physical fitness. *See* Exercise
Pollan, Michael, 12, 144
Pollution: as atomic weapons, 13, 166, 168, 171; fears about, 8, 12, 14, 139, 141, 179; of groundwater, 144–45, 164; and industrial agriculture, 13, 89, 144, 160, 170;

as a threat to the planet, 5, 8–9, 14, 89, 141–46, 159–60, 162–63, 170, 172, 177–78, 197–98
Poole, Gaye, 89
Processed food: and aging, 19, 68, 110, 118, 120, 130; consequences of, 8, 30, 68; and diet, 22–23, 43–44, 107, 113, 191–92; health risks of, 93–94, 100, 112, 133–34, 196; as a line of defense, 3, 12, 34, 92; proliferation of, 8, 11–12, 15, 24, 43–44, 87–88, 90, 93, 133, 188, 191; reliance on, 12, 24, 26, 61, 78, 87, 92, 99, 106, 115, 119, 121, 128, 130–31, 135, 182; as self-destructive, 4, 12, 34, 98, 101, 125, 185–86; and sex, 105, 110–15, 119–20; standardized production of, 11, 43–44, 96; as waste, 99, 134
Professor McCarthy (*My Best Friend Is a Vampire*), 117
Psycho (film), 68, 98
Psycho (novel), 68

Queen Akasha (*The Queen of the Damned*), 123, 127–29
Queen of the Damned, The (film), 122–23, 128–29
Queen of the Damned, The (novel), 122–23, 125–27
Quinn ("Blossom"), 173–74
Quinzio, Jeri, 189

Ralph (*My Best Friend Is a Vampire*), 115
Reagan, Nancy, 64, 87, 138
Reagan, Ronald: and consumerism, 64–66, 75, 84, 156, 164, 190; political efforts of, 6, 28, 66–67, 84–85; and the war on drugs, 87, 92
Redneck Zombies, 14, 141, 160, 170–71, 182, 186
Reitman, Ivan, 23
Return of the Living Dead, The, 14, 160–62
Return of the Living Dead, The (series), 14, 141, 160, 170, 182, 186, 193
Return of the Living Dead Part II, The, 8, 160, 163–65

Return to Salem's Lot, A, 93, 110, 117
Rice, Anne, 12, 91–92, 122–29, 137
Richardson, Niall, 16
Richie "The Hammer" Ginelli (*Thinner*), 26, 33
Ringling Brothers, 40
Ritzer, George, 11
Roberts, Paul, 143
Robin (*Once Bitten*), 111–14
Robinson, Peter, 40
Rome, Adam, 164
Romero, George A., 14, 140–41, 146–61, 171–72, 176, 179, 182, 197
Roy, Parama, 89
Rozin, Paul, 11
Rueckert, William, 13
Russ (*Once Bitten*), 111–12
Russell, Emily, 38
Russo, John, 148, 161
Rust, Stephen A., 140
Rymer, Michael, 128

Sabrina (*American Psycho*), 82
Saguy, Abigail C., 10
Sailor ("Like Pavlov's Dogs"), 179–81
Sam (*The Lost Boys*), 98–102
Sancton, Thomas A., 141–42
Sarah (*Day of the Dead*), 156, 158–60
Sarah (*Near Dark*), 106–8
Sarah Roberts (*The Hunger*), 129–36
Sceats, Sarah, 89
Schlosser, Eric, 96–97
Schneider, Steven Jay, 105
Schumacher, Joel, 98–99, 102–3
Schwartz, Hillel, 32
Schwarzenegger, Arnold, 20, 28–29, 201n10
Scott, Tony, 92, 130, 135
Sealo the Seal Boy. *See* Berent, Stanislaus "Stanley"
Seid, Roberta Pollack, 20
Severen (*Near Dark*), 107, 109
Shaviro, Steven, 147, 151
Sheraton, Mimi, 78

Sheriff Bruce (*Motel Hell*), 183–86
Silence of the Lambs, The (film), 49–53, 55–56, 58–61
Silence of the Lambs, The (novel), 10, 16–17, 49–51, 53, 56, 60–62, 196
Silent Spring, 12, 140, 148, 166
Skipp, John, 171
Snyder, Sharon L., 38
Soda: and diet, 3, 24, 91, 100, 115–16, 119, 121, 136; as a drug, 78, 92–95, 99, 103–4, 107, 118, 126, 128, 133, 191; health consequences of, 8, 22, 94, 116, 118, 168–69, 182; profitability of, 189, 192; proliferation of, 8, 12, 22, 87, 95, 115, 121, 127
Soles, Carter, 7, 140, 148
Spector, Craig, 171
Stallone, Sylvester, 9, 28–29
Stay Puft Marshmallow Man, 23–24
Stephen (*Dawn of the Dead*), 151, 153–55
Stoker, Bram, 109, 121–22, 136, 208n25
Storm, Howard, 110
Strieber, Whitley, 12, 92, 129–32, 134
Stuff, The, 187–89, 193–96
Suburbia: and class, 26, 113; and consumerism, 5–8, 26, 152, 155, 165, 182, 188, 193, 195, 197; environmental taxation of, 14, 145, 155, 163–65, 194–95; sprawl of, 164–65
Sugar: or artificial sweeteners, 78, 93, 124, 190–91; as a food additive, 11–12, 24, 34–35, 44, 90, 93–96, 101, 113, 115–16, 125, 133–34, 192; and health, 3–4, 19, 95, 107, 113, 121, 191, 206n6; presented as drugs, 78, 94–95, 105, 125, 133, 155, 187, 192, 196
Suicide (*The Return of the Living Dead*), 161–62, 165
Sumner, Jennifer, 11
Surf II, 14, 141, 160, 168–70, 182

Taduz Lemke (*Thinner*), 26, 34
Tally, Ted, 50, 56
Tasker, Yvonne, 53, 61
Terry (*Motel Hell*), 184–85

Thinner (film), 25, 30
Thinner (novel), 10, 16–17, 24, 26–27, 29–30, 35, 196
Thinness. *See* Fatness
Thirst. *See* Addiction
Thomson, Rosemarie Garland, 39
Thriller, 141, 180
Tim Price (*American Psycho*), 71–72
Tom (*The Hunger*), 130–36
Tom (*Night of the Living Dead*), 149–50
Tom (*Toxic Zombies*), 167
Tordoff, Michael, 94
Toufexis, Anastasia, 143
Toxic contamination: and consumerism, 14, 145, 162–63, 171; ecological threat of, 8–9, 141, 144, 150, 161–62, 166, 170, 197; health risks of, 12–13, 37, 109, 144, 151, 161–62, 166–67, 195
Toxic Zombies, 14, 141, 160, 166, 182, 186
Trash. *See* Garbage

US Environmental Protection Agency, 12, 144, 198

Vampire Chronicles, 122, 128
Vampire fiction, 10, 88, 92, 122, 138, 196
Vampire films, 92, 109–10, 168
Vampire Lestat, The, 122–24
Vampires: and addiction, 8, 14, 87, 91, 98–100, 105–6, 126, 135–36; and consumerism, 9, 12, 14, 92, 100, 196; and diet, 10, 12, 91–92, 99, 102, 107, 110, 113, 116–17, 134, 196–97; and excess, 80, 92, 98, 107, 127–32, 136, 138; and the processed food industry, 12, 88, 91–92, 101, 103, 109, 113, 116
Vampire television, 137
Van Esterik, Penny, 11, 90
Van Patten (*American Psycho*), 72
Van Riper, A. Bowdoin, 91, 192
Vincent (*Motel Hell*), 182–86

Wann, Marilyn, 9
Waste. *See* Garbage

Weiderhorn, Ken, 163
Weight. *See* Fatness
Weight loss. *See* Diet culture
Weight Watchers, 15, 22, 30, 58
Weiss, Laura, 190
Williams, Tony, 151, 153, 156, 193
Winson, Tony, 11
Wood, Robin, 6, 8, 156
Workout culture. *See* Exercise

Xu, Wenying, 89

Zinoman, Jason, 7
Zombie fiction, 12, 14, 139, 141, 146, 171–72, 182, 186, 197
Zombie films, 91, 141, 146–47, 185
Zombies: and the apocalypse, 139, 146, 159, 174, 177; and capitalism, 8, 146–48, 156; and consumer excess, 80, 146, 148, 150–56, 158, 168–70, 177, 179–80, 182, 187–88, 193, 197; and diet, 155, 162, 166, 174, 197; and the environment, 9, 146, 148, 150–51, 160, 162–63, 166, 170–72, 182, 185, 195, 197; and overpopulation, 12, 14, 139, 141, 146–48, 151–53, 157–58, 160, 182–86, 195–97

www.ingramcontent.com/pod-product-compliance
Lightning Source LLC
Chambersburg PA
CBHW030619230426
43661CB00053B/2060